COACH

I dedicate *Coach* to my wife, Maritza, who had to share me with the writing process for more than a year. My first book is also dedicated to Yda Coetsee (1959–2005), in whose Afrikaans class I was taught as a 14-year-old at the Oakdale Agricultural High School to love words and to use them with respect and creativity.

COACH

How South African Sports Leaders Cultivate Excellence

Marco Botha

JONATHAN BALL PUBLISHERS
Johannesburg & Cape Town

All rights reserved.
No part of this publication may be reproduced or transmitted,
in any form or by any means, without prior permission
from the publisher or copyright holder.

© Text Marco Botha 2014

Photos: Supplied by the author, Thys Lombard, FanJam Concepts
and Foto24 (Media24)
© Cover photo: Duif du Toit/Gallo Images

Originally published in South Africa in 2014 by
JONATHAN BALL PUBLISHERS (PTY) LTD
A division of Media24 Limited
PO Box 33977
Jeppestown
2043

Book ISBN 978-1-86842-376-7
ebook ISBN 978-1-86842-374-3

Every effort has been made to trace the copyright holders and to obtain their permission for the use of copyright material. The publishers apologise for any errors or omissions and would be grateful to be notified of any corrections that should be incorporated in future editions of this book.

Cover by Publicide
Design and typesetting by MR Design, Cape Town
Printed and bound by Paarl Media
Set in Bembo and Helvetica

Twitter: http://www.twitter.com/JonathanBallPub
Facebook: http://www.facebook.com/pages/Jonathan-Ball-
    Publishers/298034457992
Blog: http://jonathanball.bookslive.co.za/

CONTENTS

Introduction 7

HEYNEKE MEYER
Prologue: The DNA of blood brothers 11
Chapter 1: Finalists believe; champions know 22
Chapter 2: First sharpen your axe 45
Chapter 3: No man is an island 55

HEYNEKE MEYER AND IAN SCHWARTZ
Chapter 4: The dream merchant 85

HEYNEKE MEYER
Chapter 5: The DNA of success is people 119

BRENDAN VENTER
Chapter 6: Giving more than you take 159

DR SHERYLLE CALDER
Chapter 7: Decision making starts with your eyes 187
Chapter 8: Life-changing science 203

PAUL TREU
Chapter 9: The optimal experience 221
Chapter 10: A creative revolution of the brain 233

GARY KIRSTEN AND PADDY UPTON
Chapter 11: How can we help you? 253
Chapter 12: Old school vs new school 261
Chapter 13: The influence paradox 280

Notes 300

Acknowledgements 303

INTRODUCTION

This introduction is really a postmortem. It is written after the rest of the book has been completed and I have a final opportunity to reflect on it.

This introduction is the start of the book for you, and a way for me to encapsulate in a nutshell the experiences I have had and the insights I have gained over more than a year of writing, and to give you an early impression of what follows.

Imagine if life were like that. Imagine that, at the start of anything you embarked on, you already possessed all the knowledge and all the possible answers. In that case, I know now, I would have liked to understand love better. Not only so that I can be a better husband to my wife, but because after writing this book I now comprehend that love and leadership are really one and the same thing. From that perspective, I would have liked to do certain things differently in my life.

This was not what I initially envisaged with *Coach*, but that is why one writes the introduction at the end, as I know now.

This book started out as a project that Paul Treu and I embarked on together. Our plan was to focus only on sevens rugby, and to compare shared values and principles in professional sport with those in the business world. And vice versa. Both of us enjoy watching the TV programme *Sakegesprek met Theo Vorster*. With that as our point of departure, we went to see Theo in November 2012 at Galileo Capital's offices in Hyde Park, Johannesburg.

It was here that *Coach* first began to assume the form of the end product you now hold in your hands. Theo is an ardent follower of sports and engages with some of South Africa's top business leaders through *Sakegesprek*. His suggestion was that we open the doors to more sports than sevens rugby, precisely because this remarkable and colourful country of ours also has some of the world's foremost sports leaders – people who have done pioneering work. And theirs are stories to be told.

When Ingeborg Pelser of Jonathan Ball Publishers became involved shortly afterwards – again thanks to Theo's good offices – the book evolved further. I started doing my research, asked a number of sports leaders to participate and conducted the first interview on 26 February 2013.

At that stage, most of the people in this book were just famous coaches to me, with well-known successes under their belt. My intention was to explore and recount the background to these accomplishments. Apart

INTRODUCTION

from Paul Treu and Ian Schwartz, I didn't know any of them well, nor did I know what they were like as people.

I had a prior idea of a particular goal I wanted to achieve with each interview, but during each interview, as I got to know the human being better, my approach became completely transformed, and I was personally enriched by ordinary people's inspiring perspectives on sport, life and leadership.

When research and interviews are embarked on with a specific end result in mind, in sport you might expect to hear responses and anecdotes about good strategies, clever techniques and skills, the creation of structures, scientific advances, and leaders who are gifted with almost superhuman insight and virtues.

I know now, however, that none of the people who feature in this book owe their success primarily to any of those things because, for all of them, leadership is like love. You don't have to be a believer to appreciate this description of love from the Bible: 'Love is patient, love is kind. It does not envy, it does not boast, it is not proud. It does not dishonour others, it is not self-seeking, it is not easily angered, it keeps no record of wrongs. Love does not delight in evil but rejoices with the truth.'

There is surprisingly little sport in this book, although, by the end of the book, you will have gained a better understanding of the heart of sport, professional sport and what leadership entails. I know now that if you replace the word 'love' in the above verses from Corinthians with 'leadership', you will arrive at the core of our sports leaders' success stories.

Leadership is about people. It is about sincere relationships and a passionate desire to let those around you grow and develop into even better, more well-rounded and happier people. Leadership is not defined by an order of rank, hierarchy or the number of people 'behind' or 'under' you, but by the ability to enable other people to come into their own.

And it is not an abstract idea. It is the central idea, the primary reason that each of these sports leaders emphasised in our conversations when I asked them about their tangible successes – the cups, the trophies, the championships and the breakthroughs.

This is how and why these ordinary, yet remarkable, people have been able to turn others into champions. This I know now.

Marco Botha

HEYNEKE MEYER

PROLOGUE

The DNA of blood brothers

Heyneke's eyes are red. The tears have turned his eyelashes into tufts that resemble paintbrushes. Broad brush. Pointy brush. Coarse brush. Fine brush, small hairs glued together. He rubs his lucky Blue Bulls handkerchief to and fro beneath his nose with his right forefinger as he inhales deeply to open up the nasal passages again. He is an emotional man. The team talk he has just delivered is still pulsing below the lump in his throat. Today he has surpassed himself, he thinks. That feeling is also shared by every Bulls player, with the whole team salivating at the prospect of thrashing the Aussies after his stirring address.

Loftus Versfeld's large dressing rooms are finished in shades of blue. Photos of successful teams, players and coaches adorn the dark brick walls: framed histories to remind each generation of Bulls of their ancestry. Empty spaces are left for the faces of those who are still to add to that legacy.

There are three minutes left before the team will run onto the field to face the Reds. Each man quickly performs a little last-minute ritual of his choice. Wynie Strydom puts away his own handkerchief and checks that his earpiece is firmly attached: on days like these, a coach has to be able to communicate with and via his team manager next to the field.

The substitutes file past every teammate before they take the containers of Powerade bottles and walk out first. Victor Matfield draws two big handfuls of water through his long, dark hair. Derick Hougaard makes sure that his laces are tied properly.

Gary Botha moves two places to the left, and sits next to the other Botha in the team. 'Bakkies, my tjom,' he says with a moving urgency in his voice, 'check my goosebumps.' He rubs his hand over his left forearm. Bakkies stands up, grabs Gary by the collar and pulls him up onto his toes, and, in a display of brotherly unity, the two butt heads. They don't feel a thing, because the endorphins have been coursing through their veins since that speech. The adrenalin too. Heyneke sure has a way with words.

'Cut!' shouts Clint Eastwood. 'Guys! Guys, that was not convincing at all! Gary, Bakkies – you're heading into battle. Be in that space. Own it.

THE DNA OF BLOOD BROTHERS

Let's do another take. Heyneke, go stand there again. And, Victor, just dry your hair a bit, please. Now, give it to the camera, guys. Let me feel the emotion, the adrenalin …'

The real Bakkies is standing just behind the camera. He and the real Victor have been invited to a film shoot of *Blood Brothers*. About half a decade has now passed since he directed *Invictus*, and Clint Eastwood is once again trying his hand at a 'true' rainbow rugby story.

'Sorry, Mr Eastwoods. Here,' the real Bakkies waves at the director to attract his attention. He is actually 7 cm taller than the actor playing his role, but good camerawork and direction can do wonders for an average guy portraying an above-average *boerseun*. 'Mr Eastwoods, actually we only got chicken flesh, but Gary never hit me with the head. That only happens in the movies,' Bakkies corrects the American. The Dirty Harry in Eastwood starts to emerge, but Bakkies is fearless.

He just doesn't like the fact that 'Mr Eastwoods', as he calls him, is taking liberties with the story of the Bulls' first Super Rugby crown. 'And Coach Heyneke gave that speech a day before the match. It wasn't just before we klapped those Rooies with 91-5.'

'92-3,' the real Victor corrects him with regard to the final score of the Bulls' biggest Super Rugby winning margin, on 5 May 2007 – two games before they won the entire competition.

In principle, though, the analytical Matfield agrees with his emotional former lock partner: when facts are rearranged in retrospect or interpreted uncritically in order to explain a well-known outcome – such as Super Rugby success – one runs the very real risk of overlooking the true reasons for that success. And, at the same time, one may attribute the success to things that had no or very little influence on it – for instance, by presenting a rousing team talk as the catalyst that spurred an adrenalin-driven team on to greater heights.

American writer Michael Mauboussin explores this tendency of seeking to analyse, define and then imitate success in his book *The Success Equation: Untangling Skill and Luck in Business, Sports, and Investing*. The title of the book captures exactly what it is about – a fascinating study of cause and effect, but simultaneously of the undeniable influence that luck has on the success of people and organisations. In the second chapter, Mauboussin identifies a general problem regarding the way in which success is often analysed:

> Our minds have an amazing ability to create a narrative that explains the world around us, an ability that works particularly well when we already know the answer. There are a couple of essential ingredients in this ability: our love of stories and our need to connect cause and effect. The blend of those two ingredients leads us to believe that the past was inevitable and to underestimate what else might have happened.[1]

This is a major pitfall that should be avoided in a book on leadership and success, but one that sports biographies, too, frequently stumble into. Pleasant memories and unrelated successes are arranged into an apparently logical order so as to form a nice narrative, without any light being shed on the real nature of motivation and success in professional sport. This is how misconceptions are created and fostered.

In these first chapters, I discuss Heyneke Meyer's type of leadership and how it made possible the Blue Bulls' decade of sustained success between 2001 and 2010. I do this by means of stories, and I also look for causes that explain the 'answer' – among others, the things that led to three Super Rugby titles and five Currie Cup crowns.

But even with an attempt such as mine to explain that success in a more nuanced manner than in the case of, for example, the fictitious film *Blood Brothers*, Mauboussin cautions one against stumbling into this pitfall.

He advances mainly three reasons. Firstly, success is often not just the product of skill and strategy, but also of luck. Secondly, an individual's ability to make a success of something single-handedly depends on the environment in which he operates. And, thirdly, it also depends on the support an individual receives in that environment from other people, which enables him to give expression to his skill and ingenuity, and to think strategically. In the classic success narrative that Mauboussin warns against, those 'other people' are usually the supporting actors who don't get the credit they actually deserve – the Alfred Pennyworths who make it possible for the Bruce Waynes to be Batman.

People like to read success stories in order to be inspired by them and/or to learn something from them, and then imitate what they have learnt. But, as Mauboussin warns, one should be wary of blind imitation:

The most common method for teaching a manager how to thrive in business is to find successful businesses, identify the common practices of those businesses, and recommend that the manager imitate them.

Perhaps the best-known book about this method is Jim Collins's *Good to Great*. Collins and his team analyzed thousands of companies and isolated eleven whose performance went from good to great. They then identified the concepts that they believed had caused those companies to improve – these include leadership, people, a fact-based approach, focus, discipline, and the use of technology – and suggested that other companies adopt the same concepts to achieve the same sort of results. This formula is intuitive, includes some great narrative, and has sold millions of books for Collins.

No one questions that Collins has good intentions. He really is trying to figure out how to help executives. And if causality were clear, this approach would work. The trouble is that the performance of a company always depends on both skill and luck, which means that a given strategy will succeed only part of the time.[2]

Luck is therefore a factor that has to be taken into account when one analyses the success of a leader or an organisation. But it also depends on how one interprets success.

In Heyneke Meyer's career, there was one particular stroke of luck that stands out a mile – the events that preceded Bryan Habana's winning try for the Bulls in the final of the 2007 Super 14 competition. In brief, Habana scored the winning try in the 82nd minute and Derick Hougaard succeeded with the conversion, helping his team clinch a 20-19 victory.

Frans Steyn played on the right wing for the Sharks that day, and if he had kicked the ball into touch moments before Habana's try, Steyn's team, with the score at 19-13 in their favour, would have become the first South African franchise to win the Super Rugby title. Steyn booted the ball downfield, however, and the Bulls were able to capitalise on that. Therefore, the Sharks made a poor decision and the Bulls were lucky.

When the ball emerged on the Sharks' side of a ruck a few seconds later, the Bulls' Derick Kuün won it back in a questionable fashion. His transgression had not been spotted by the referee, Steve Walsh, or his assistant, Lyndon Bray, and the Bulls were not penalised. At that point, the final whistle should have been blown, and the Sharks would have emerged victorious.

Then, Habana scored a try and Hougaard converted it. So, in the one case, the Sharks made a poor decision and, in the other, they were unlucky, while the Bulls exploited these two windfalls skilfully and thereby recorded the single biggest success in their history.

Since luck can have a proven influence on success, as in this case, one can – if it should suit one's narrative – view that game in isolation and attribute Meyer's success as a coach to luck rather than to skill and good leadership. But that would be a short-sighted way of evaluating success, as the chances are that luck may have a great influence on success only in the short term. The longer success is sustained, however, the greater the chance that luck has less of an influence on it – although it may always be a factor, as when two more or less equally capable teams lock horns in a final.

While the 2007 final was the crowning achievement of Meyer's career as head coach at Loftus Versfeld, his success should also be evaluated in the light of all that he had done in the seven years before that final to prepare the team for precisely such an occasion – without dismissing the influence of luck.

Frans Ludeke took over from Meyer as coach at the end of 2007, and guided the Bulls in 2009 and 2010 to successive Super Rugby titles. When Ludeke and I talked about 2007 and the period that followed, he admitted without hesitation that things beyond the control of a team or of people can have a proven influence on their success.

Said Ludeke: 'If Bryan Habana hadn't scored that try on 19 May 2007, you probably wouldn't have had a story today. We were lucky. Think of that try: possession had been reversed. The Sharks had won the game. Frans Steyn simply had to kick the ball into touch. And that last ruck was actually the worst. The ball had come out on the other side. We had lost. That ball had been knocked on somewhere. But then you speak to Derick Kuün and he tells you he saw the ball lying there when the scrumhalf wanted to take it. Then he took back the ball. Neither the referee nor the touch judge saw it. Steve Walsh said they should play on, and then Bryan scored that brilliant try and we won the competition.

'Things like that do help one to view success in professional sport in perspective. I often sit in the stand and see things happening on the field that I know in my heart of hearts aren't due to our own excellence, but which happen to count in our favour. That is how sport works, and it keeps you humble and grateful.

'Two things must be said about that 2007 final. It was the crowning game of the competition, and people remember titles and cups better than anything else. But just the Bulls' presence in that final match was in itself the result of the visionary leadership Heyneke had by then been providing for over seven years.

'Secondly, that victory led to a belief taking root among the players, management and supporters that undoubtedly helped pave the way for us to win the Super 14 competition in 2009 and 2010 as well. We believed that we could do it. It doesn't mean that we wouldn't have won those titles in any case, but 2007 certainly helped. At the same time, you need to ask yourself what might have happened to the Sharks in the subsequent years if they had won that day.'

When former Springbok captain John Smit was appointed as the Sharks' chief executive in 2013, he was quick to refer to the Blue Bulls' structures. Smit said that the very blueprint that had made the Bulls such a powerhouse in South African rugby in the course of a decade would also be used as a cornerstone of the Sharks' strategy for the future. What exactly that blueprint entails will be discussed in the chapters that follow.

In 2007 Smit was a member of that losing Sharks team and, as Ludeke rightly says, the Sharks' structures could very easily have earned the respect of the rugby world – as was the case for the Bulls – if the home team had been victorious that day. Ludeke also points out in Chapter 5 that the structures alone and the referee's blunder cannot be given the credit for that victory.

Luck, nevertheless, has a huge influence on success and on the perceptions that develop about success. Yet it is seldom mentioned in the success narrative. When a consistently successful coach acknowledges luck as a contributing factor, he is not detracting from what he has achieved, but simply creating a more credible context within which his own contribution can be assessed. In Meyer's case, the pioneering work will be discussed in the chapters that follow.

After luck, the second and third factors that should be taken into account in Mauboussin's view of success are the environment within which a person leads and innovates, and the people that either support or oppose him in that environment.

Exploring the reasons for an individual's success is generally not done merely because it is interesting, but because lessons may perhaps be learnt from it. One would also like to believe that a leader should be able to repeat his success anywhere else. However, as is the case with any universal principle of leadership, it cannot be comprehended or applied elsewhere without an understanding of the unique context within which that principle was singled out as a success factor – for instance, the influence of the organisational culture and the people with whom the leader worked. As in the case of luck, these two factors are not recognised in order to diminish a leader's special contribution, but precisely so that his real contribution can be understood and appreciated within a credible context. Mauboussin writes in this regard:

> Many organizations, including businesses and sports teams, try to improve their performance by hiring a star from another organization. They often pay a high price to do so. The premise is that a star has skill that is readily transferable to the new organization. But the people who do this type of hiring rarely consider the degree to which the star's success was the result of either good luck or the structure and support of the organization where he or she worked before. Attributing success to an individual makes for good narrative, but it fails to take into account how much of the skill is unique to the star and is therefore portable.[3]

The author refers to research done on this topic by Boris Groysberg, a professor in organisational behaviour at Harvard Business School. In one study, Groysberg and his colleagues examined the performance of 20 executives from General Electric (GE) who were appointed as chairmen, CEOs or CEOs designate of other companies between 1989 and 2001. Mauboussin explains that GE is renowned as a source of talented executives, and its 'alumni are disproportionately represented among the CEOs of the Standard & Poor's 500'.

Ten of the companies examined by Groysberg and his colleagues showed strong similarities with GE. The skills of the executives concerned were therefore readily transferable – in other words, their skills were relevant and applicable in both companies – and their new companies thrived with them.

The other ten operated in business sectors that were totally different from that of GE. Mauboussin refers to one manager whose experience lay in selling electrical appliances, but who was then appointed in a company that sold groceries. As might be expected, these ten companies – now with their GE-trained leaders – underperformed.

Mauboussin summarises this phenomenon as follows: 'Again, developing skill is a genuine achievement. And skill, once developed, has a real influence on what we can do and how successful we are. But skill is only one factor that contributes to the end result of our efforts. The organization or environment in which a CEO works also has an influence.'

In a sports context, Groysberg examined the performance of certain American football players who switched from one National Football League team to another between 1993 and 2002. He compared wide receivers with punters. The principal role of a punter is to punt field kicks. A wide receiver, on the other hand, is responsible for receiving and finishing passes. Mauboussin writes:

> Since each team has eleven players on the field at a time, wide receivers rely heavily on the strategy of the team and on interaction with their teammates, factors that can vary widely from team to team. Punters pretty much do the same thing no matter which team they play for, and have more limited interaction with teammates. The contrast in interaction allowed the scientists to separate an individual's skill from the influence of the organization on performance. They found that star wide receivers who switched teams suffered a decline in performance for the subsequent season compared to those who stayed with the team. Their performance then improved as they adjusted to their new team. Whether a punter changed teams or stayed put had no influence on his performance.[4]

Groysberg's conclusion was that those organisations that support a star contribute materially to his success. This, too, applies to Heyneke Meyer. He started coaching residence rugby in his student days at the University of Pretoria and later became involved in club rugby. In 1997, as Phil Pretorius's assistant coach, he moved to George, where they had to help the struggling SWD (South Western Districts) Eagles out of provincial rugby's deepest Slough of Despond.

In 1998 Meyer took over the reins as head coach, and in 1999 the Eagles played in the semifinal of the Currie Cup competition for the first time in their history. In that same year, Meyer was also the Stormers' forwards coach and Nick Mallett's assistant coach at the Springboks. Since these other obligations prevented him from being with the Eagles in a full-time capacity, he appointed two people who were to have an enormous influence on his life and career in the years that followed – Ian Schwartz, chairman of the Bloemfontein police rugby club, as his personal assistant, and Frans Ludeke, at the time still head coach of the then Rand Afrikaans University (RAU), as his assistant coach.

Meyer was appointed as the Northern Bulls' head coach for 2000, but was fired at the end of the season after his team had lost 8 of its 11 matches that year, drawn 2 and won only 1.

However, Barend van Graan, the CEO of the Blue Bulls Company (BBC), had known Meyer since his student days, and asked him to apply for the Blue Bulls' head coach position. Those details will be discussed later, but Meyer had the support of the majority of the Blue Bulls board. He was allowed to appoint his own management team, and Schwartz, as well as his conditioning coach and team doctor at the SWD Eagles, accompanied Meyer to Pretoria.

The Northern Bulls and the Blue Bulls were separate business entities, and SA Rugby fired Meyer again in 2002 after another year in office. But at the Blue Bulls he won his first cup in 2001, and in 2002 the first of three consecutive Currie Cup titles. There was a fundamental clash between Meyer and the Bulls' bosses, while in the Blue Bulls' boardroom harmony mostly prevailed.

When the Blue Bulls eventually became the senior partner in the Bulls franchise, Meyer started coaching the Super Rugby team again from 2005. He used his own management team and after the Bulls had advanced to the semifinals of the Super Rugby competition in 2005 and 2006, they won it for the first time in 2007.

Ludeke took over from Meyer at the end of 2007. It took him a season to find his feet before winning two consecutive Super Rugby titles with the same support and with the core of Meyer's management team. Before his move to the Blue Bulls, Ludeke had been with the Golden Lions, and the Johannesburg team put out feelers to Meyer in 2009 before he was reappointed by the Bulls.

It is impossible to tell, however, whether Meyer would also have reached the same heights with the Lions as he did with the Bulls – for the simple reason that support, a healthy organisational culture and the people around him all contributed to his ability to make a difference. It cannot be assumed with any certainty that Meyer would have had the same experience south of the Jukskei River.

Between his departure from Loftus Versfeld at the end of 2007 and his second arrival in 2009, Meyer coached English Premiership team the Leicester Tigers. He occupied that post from June 2008 and guided the team up to the halfway mark of the 2008/09 Premiership before resigning in January 2009 on account of family circumstances. The English club, too, had given Meyer strong support, and after finishing at the top of the Premiership table, the Tigers beat London Irish 10-9 in the final on 16 May 2009.

The support of the organisations around him, as well as Meyer's strong management teams, undoubtedly contributed to his success as a coach. The initial support he was given in 2000 at the Blue Bulls and the permission to appoint his own people were vitally important to what happened at Loftus Versfeld in the decade that followed.

Meyer is a leader with a very strong entrepreneurial mindset, and at the same time someone who acknowledges his own faults. That is why he openly gives recognition to the people around him – people he appointed precisely because he believes that sustained success cannot be achieved single-handedly.

And yet, as we shall see in the coming chapters, Meyer's standing as coach and leader is not diminished when strokes of luck are acknowledged and a healthy company culture is highlighted as a contributing factor to his success.

He is a trailblazer: he is the first to do things. An unyielding resistance to mediocrity is a part of his nature. He has a respect for the past but is, at the same time, uncomfortable with complacency and being content with the present. He possesses the ability to visualise the future and the ingenuity to carve out a new path towards it together with and for others. He is a pioneer.

What is pivotal in this is not his technical merits as a coach, but rather his empathy towards others, his finely attuned sense of people's needs and of what it takes in a team environment to continuously strive to get the best from individuals. This is what distinguishes Meyer from a multitude of other sports leaders who may even be better than he is from a technical perspective, but whose conception of what structures and strategy involve lacks a true understanding of and sensitivity towards people.

As context for the later chapters, the Bulls' 2007 Super Rugby season will be described in all its nail-biting drama. Thereafter we shall look at the strategy, vision and structures, the groundbreaking work that gave rise to that success and the first real awareness in South Africa of what professional rugby entails.

CHAPTER 1

Finalists believe; champions know

'Look, Coach, I've brought along my umbrella!'
– Jaco van der Westhuyzen

'Guys, this year we can't go down the same road that we did in 2005 and 2006. It won't work.' Heyneke Meyer was addressing his Bulls team on the eve of the Super 14 season of 2007. They had reached the semifinals in both preceding years, and lost twice.

In 2005 the Bulls played in the semifinal in Sydney against the Waratahs. The week before, they had beaten the Stormers 75-14 to qualify for the play-offs. Therefore, there were high expectations among South Africans of a victory in Sydney. But the Bulls suffered a 13-23 defeat.

May 2006 was a similar situation. To qualify for the semifinals, the Bulls needed to beat the Stormers at the latter's home stadium, Newlands, by 33 points. In the run-up to that match, Meyer had gone through all the permutations and possible point variations with his players.

He recalls, 'When Victor walked into the team room, I asked him to write down on the board the points difference by which we had to win. He wrote down 32 and I told him that a victory by 32 points on that Saturday would be nothing more than a draw. So he wrote down 33. And we beat the Stormers 43-10. Our tickets to Christchurch were booked.'

But then they also lost that semifinal against the Crusaders, 15-35.

The chances of winning the Super Rugby competition are extremely slim if you don't at least play a home semifinal. Of the 22 semifinals played from 1996 to 2006, a visiting team had won only five times. And out of the 11 final matches, 8 had been won by the home team. The exception to the rule were the Crusaders, who claimed their title in 1998, 1999 and 2000 as visiting finalists.

Although the Bulls' envisaged final destination for 2007 was the same as it had been for the last two seasons, they needed to approach it via a different route if they were to get there. Meyer explained this to his players as follows: 'There was a man who walked down a specific road every day between his home and his workplace. One day he fell into a hole while going to work and he decided he would simply walk around it on his way home that evening.

'But that hole had grown deeper and wider while he was at work. When he took that same route again after sunset, this time trying to walk around the hole, he fell into it again.

'He kept on falling into the hole until he decided to change his route and walk down another unfamiliar road. And that is what 2007 asks of us – that we have to walk down a different road this year if we want to win this competition. And that road leads to Loftus.'

That 'different road' became one of the Bulls' themes for 2007.

Up to that point, most of the Bulls' opponents had believed that you could run the seemingly excessively physical Pretoria players ragged and then pounce. But Meyer remarked: 'I thought that was nonsense. I looked at the fitness standards of the top sports teams worldwide. I then took those standards and simply raised the bar ten times higher.

I remember how we did a bleep test [an arduous fitness test] one day and the guys stopped just this short of our goal [indicating a distance of about 30cm with his hands].

So I told them: go again. But, again, they didn't finish. When I wanted to send them for a third bleep, the players said I was crazy and Basil Carzis, my fitness guy, said that it was impossible to do three bleeps in succession.

'I then called the players and told them to listen carefully: 'If other teams think they can tire us out with running, that's fine. But not before they themselves are clapped out. This is a different road. And if we're going to walk it, we have to be the fittest sports team in the world. When they think they can run us into the ground with two bleeps' exertion, we'll still have a third one in the tank. Do you get me?

'So we did the third bleep – and we finished it. It was a mental attitude. And I believe in the mind, in the brain. There is much more power in your mind than your body sometimes wants you to believe. I knew that we were going to need that mindset if we wanted to win the Super 14.

'But in South Africa, no team believed that they could do it. You could ask anyone what the Currie Cup looks like and every single player – even little boys – would be able to describe it in detail. But ask them what the Super Rugby trophy looks like and they stare at you blankly. So I made lots of copies of the Super trophy and put the pictures up all over Loftus.

FINALISTS BELIEVE; CHAMPIONS KNOW

'We needed to know what the trophy looked like because we wanted to kiss it later that year. Fitness is important, but it means nothing if you don't condition yourself at a deeper level to do something exceptional with it.'

The Bulls, therefore, had a gruelling pre-season. In 2007 the Super 14 season was at most 15 matches long, unlike at the time of writing this book. In the current 15-team format there may be up to 19 matches plus a break in the middle for three tests. For a top player, perhaps someone who might play in a final, the season was easily seven matches shorter in 2007.

But the short season left one with very little scope for an off day. That is why the pre-season was back-breaking – lack of time meant that one couldn't reach one's ideal fitness and performance levels only later in the season. One had to be in tip-top form right from the word go.

The Bulls' season started off on a dreadful note, however, when the Sharks thrashed them 17-3 in Durban. A week later, the Cheetahs suffered a 20-24 defeat against a hurting Bulls team at Loftus. But a week after that – by about 22:00 on Saturday 16 February – it seemed as if the Bulls had already lost the directions to that 'different road'.

Meyer explained: 'That evening, we were beaten 27-30 at Loftus by the Western Force. Three games; two losses. It didn't look good. The time had just about run out when we got a penalty. We could have gone for the posts, but I don't play for a draw. We kicked for the corner and Victor called a play. But Hilton Lobberts didn't hear it and the whole plan came to grief. We lost the ball and lost by three points.

'We were obviously crushed because we had said at the beginning of the season that we were playing to win – and to win big. Settling for a draw would have been like walking down that old road. But people out there didn't see it that way. Locally, they wanted to hang me. Super Rugby was a short season and we had lost one of our supposedly easier home games.'

After that defeat against the Force, the Bulls had only one game left, against the Chiefs, before they were due to depart for a gruelling overseas tour, which included facing the Brumbies, the Waratahs, the Crusaders, the Highlanders and the Hurricanes.

They had never boarded a plane after having scored a win. And to outside observers it seemed as if that trend would continue after the Chiefs game.

'But, gee whiz, we played! We were motivated because everyone had written us off,' the coach recalled. 'The hooter goes. We're behind. But we retain the ball. We retain the ball. And then Bryan dives over in the corner for a try in the last minute. By grace and with a lot of fighting spirit we won that game 30-27, and we got on the plane with a win under our belts.'

In the two weeks after the victory over the Chiefs, the Bulls defeated both the Brumbies (19-7) and the Waratahs (32-19) overseas for the first time, and then left for New Zealand with their tails up.

'And I could see that the players had become much too clever for their own good. Totally. And the Crusaders are the last team against whom you should have too high an opinion of yourself,' Meyer remarked.

When playing against the Crusaders, the Bulls always stay at the luxurious Peppers Clearwater Resort – a beautiful estate with chalets that overlook water and hundreds of metres of green parkland. But, despite the setting, that week was hell.

The comfort of their accommodation and the excessive complacency in the players' minds worried Meyer. So he 'hit them' with a fitness session early in the week:

'I wanted to bring them back to earth, but the main reason was to test our fitness and know where I had to cut back as far as training was concerned. That pre-season had been extremely gruelling and I thought it would become necessary to take things just a bit slower here and there.

'But the senior players started complaining. Incessantly. Then I lost it and, when I think back now, it was the angriest I have ever been in my life.

'I grabbed the whistle from Basil and told him that I felt like throttling the players. When Bakkies saw this, he started talking to himself: "Come on, old Bakkies, now you have to pull your weight – the coach is angry."'

This particular match against the Crusaders would be a huge one: the Kiwi teams were managing their players far more judiciously than usual because 2007 was a World Cup year and there were still a few unfilled places on the All Black selectors' team list. Games such as this one against the Bulls were just the right occasion to make one's mark.

'If we lost against the Crusaders, our season would be done with.

And I would have rested Victor on the bench for that game in any case. He needed the break and I had promised François van Schouwenburg before the tour that he would get a chance to play.

'So that day I had quite a go at the players and they kept on complaining. I threw the whistle aside and told them, 'You think you're too clever. You think you've made it. Cheers! You're going to lose by 50 points on Saturday. You're too big for your boots and now you can just muddle along on your own for the rest of the week.'

Meyer is a demanding coach but, according to the players who have played under him, he is not someone who shouts at or threatens players, or is unreasonable. But on that day, a monster was released within him.

And when he looked back on it, he believed it was extremely important to shift the responsibility back to the players at that exact time. 'You have to do it. You, as coach, cannot be solely responsible for a team. I put the responsibility back onto the team right there,' he said.

It was raining and icily cold when the Bulls' senior players came knocking at Meyer's door later that day. Victor Matfield, Bakkies Botha, Gary Botha, Wikus van Heerden and Anton Leonard. Said Meyer: 'Pote Human was my assistant coach and he has a fatherliness about him. He came into my room – just in case I was perhaps unaware of the players who were waiting for me outside my chalet.

'I told Pote the players can just carry on on their own. They may have wanted to see me, but I planned to only see them again on the Saturday. And I left the players standing there for probably two hours – in the cold.

'When I finally opened the door, they hadn't moved. Just stood there waiting. I told them that I don't do fitness because I want to punish them. But I *had* to know at that point in the season where we should cut back if we were to walk this road.

'I saw how the message got through to them. And there and then, the season turned. The players accepted responsibility for themselves, for their team and teammates. They were prepared to do anything – even three bleeps.

'I told them that I was still unhappy about their reaction and that we had come too far to throw everything away now before this game.

'The next morning it was sleeting. The conditions were the coldest I had ever experienced on a rugby field. But when I say something, I stick to it. And the same went for the players. So I stood next to the field and watched how they coached themselves.

'If I had facilitated that session, I would have let the guys stop long before they actually did. But there was no way I could stop the players because I had transferred the responsibility to them and they had to decide what they wanted to do with it. And they wanted to make up for what had happened the day before.'

The Crusaders still hit the Bulls hard, securing a 32-10 victory – a score similar to that of their semifinal contest the year before. But it was a lesson that the team had to learn. Matfield was sent on for the last 25 minutes and during that period the Bulls shifted into a higher gear, although not yet into fifth.

The following week, they beat the Highlanders overseas for the first time ever, but the week after that they lost to the Hurricanes by eight points. Meyer explained: 'They were awarded a penalty towards the end of the game and kicked at goal. This was a stroke of luck for them, but I knew that we were close to something special.

'However, for a season of 15 games at most, 5 out of 9 didn't look very good. There were only four matches left before the play-offs: against the Stormers, the Lions, the Blues and the Reds.

'In 2005 and 2006, the place in the play-off rounds came down to an overall points difference on the log. Hence our challenge for 2007 was enormous yet clear-cut – we needed to win all our remaining matches with a massive points difference and score at least four tries in each in order to earn five log points.

'The previous two years, we had shown that we were indeed capable of doing that. Thrashing the Stormers by 75-14 and 43-10 is no easy feat. There has to be something within you that goes further than simply believing that you as a team are capable of achieving something exceptional. You have to *know* it. On our return from the tour, I sat at home one evening doing calculations and I knew that we could go all the way.

'What happened during the next four weeks was simply incredible. For each of those matches, we wrote down a score on the white board in our team room beforehand. And in each case we recorded almost exactly those scores. Exactly!

'We played our first match at Loftus against a very good Stormers team. I told the players that we wanted the same points difference as the previous year at Newlands. We managed to equal that, more or less. We scored five tries and won 49-12.

'Our next game was against the Lions at Ellis Park. In 2002, when most of the players were still juniors, we had beaten the Golden Lions 31-7 in the Currie Cup final, against all expectations.

'So I told the players that we had done this before – at a time when everyone had written us off. "Let's go for that final-match score again. Five log points and a big points difference."

'We beat the Lions with the very same score of 31-7. We had talked about it the entire week. We wrote down that score. We visualised it. Believed. Knew. And did it. Because it wasn't something new to us.

'The second-last match was against the Blues. They were the in-form team at that point and we were competing with them for that last spot in the semifinals.

'I asked the team for 20 points. We needed four tries and there was a points difference to make up. We ended up beating them 40-19: a difference of 21 points. We took it.

'We had only Eddie Jones's Reds left to deal with. And that game merits a movie of its own.'

On the Friday of the Reds weekend, the Crusaders and the Chiefs faced each other in a decisive match. Should the Crusaders win, they would keep the Bulls' chances of a semifinal spot alive. A defeat, on the other hand, would lessen this possibility. The Crusaders lost in the end, but by less than seven points. That bonus point was enough to secure them a place in the play-offs – and probably a semifinal in Christchurch.

The Blues then played against the Western Force directly afterwards. They had the match well in control, but it seemed unlikely that they would score that vital fourth try.

In the 80th minute of that match, however, the Bulls' prospects took a southward turn. The Blues took a quick throw-in, which led to Tony Woodcock scoring their fourth try. The Laws stipulate that a quick throw-in has to be taken with the original ball that went out. But the referee, Jonathan Kaplan, failed to notice that play was resumed with a different ball. And that moment gave the Blues a fifth log point. In addition to this, they won by a wide margin: 33-6. 'I knew then that merely winning the last remaining match was no longer an option. We would have to score four tries and win with a helluva score.

'I was sitting at home that morning, feeling despondent, and our captain's run would take place that afternoon. Then a voice in my head just told me that I had asked the players for 100 per cent and that I should give the same.

'So I phoned Johann van Graan, my technical guy. The Sharks still had to play against the Stormers, and they would probably win and finish at the top of the table, with the Crusaders in second place.

'But this didn't tally with what we had planned for 2007. I asked Johann how many points we needed to score to finish above the Blues – in other words, third. And he said a points difference of 45.

'"And the Crusaders?" I asked. Johann said 72 points. I put down the phone to mull this over. We had trounced the Stormers in a similar situation at Newlands by 33 points before. So 72 points at Loftus should be possible.

'When I phoned Johann back and told him I had decided that we'd go for 72, he said: "Coach, are you off your rocker? One doesn't even win by that far in the Currie Cup and now you want to play cricket against the Reds."

'By that time, I had made up my mind and all I asked of him was to work out all the permutations for us so that I could discuss them with the players that afternoon. It's the kind of thing you can't say to a team right before a game. I firmly believe that the stronger your vision is, the more energy you can draw from it.

'But that vision has to be more than an idea. It must be something tangible. Something you reflect on and get used to. That's why I had to speak to the players on the Friday at least so that they could attune themselves mentally to it.'

Derick Hougaard remembered that day vividly. The captain's run on a Friday generally starts with a technical overview – at that time still held in Loftus's old auditorium.

The oak-panelled room has about a hundred blue theatre seats bolted to the floor, which slopes down towards the front of the room. At the front are a small lectern, a white screen for a projector and a board on which to write.

The captain's run usually starts there. The specialist coaches discuss a few matters with the players for the last time, the head coach concurs and then all responsibility is transferred to the captain. Thus the coach, too, hands over his reins a day before the match.

This was also the case on Friday 4 May. 'We stood outside and did calculations,' Hougaard recalled. 'Everyone – the media, our friends and family, and we ourselves – thought that the most realistic chance would be if we won narrowly against the Reds and finished fourth overall. That would give us a semifinal against the Sharks in Durban and we were reasonably sure that we could win that game. Thereafter, we would have to fly to New Zealand for the final and then anything could happen.'

These thoughts were totally at variance with the Bulls' theme for the year – walking down a different road. And despite how remarkable the past three weeks had been, they were now, towards the end of the season, relapsing into old habits and falling back on the known.

But Meyer still believed in that different road and there was no doubt in his mind that his players would fall into a hole if they had to travel to New Zealand for a final. He related: 'I also heard how they were doing calculations. But I knew that you can't jump clear across a river with two jumps. You either do it in one go, or you leave it. And I decided that we would go for 76 points, not just 72.

'When we had to beat the Stormers by 33 points, the difference at the end was exactly 33. Fourie du Preez told me afterwards that 33 was etched so deeply into their minds that they almost blocked themselves once they had reached that particular points difference.

'Towards the end, the Stormers were awarded a penalty and they could have kicked at goal. And if they had done that, we wouldn't have been in the semis. They tapped the ball, however, and lost it eventually. We couldn't afford a similar scenario against the Reds, so I had added four extra points to the difference beforehand – therefore 72 plus a penalty kick and one point for safety's sake.

'As I walked into the auditorium, I knew what the players were thinking – they, too, had been doing calculations. In their view, a fourth place, a Durban semifinal and an overseas final were what we had worked for. If you have to play a final away from home, however, you simply don't stand a chance. But the media were also saying that we should follow this route.'

HEYNEKE MEYER

On 5 May 2007, the lead story on the back page of the daily newspaper *Beeld* was this realistic, yet still brave, preview:

Victory all that is required
This will secure the Bulls a place in the semis

A victory at Loftus Versfeld tonight is all that stands between the Bulls and a place in the semifinals of the Super 14 rugby competition.

If they pull it off, it would be the third year in succession that the Bulls finish among the four best teams, and Pretoria should seriously consider erecting a monument to the coach, Heyneke Meyer.

Under his guidance, the Bulls and the Blue Bulls have been experiencing an incredible resurgence.

The last hurdle left in the Bulls' path is the Reds.

They are at the bottom of the log and appear to be easy prey – despite their coach, Eddie Jones, having said this week that he and his team know how to knot the horns of the men in blue.

The fact that the Bulls need to secure their fourth successive victory in order to finish at least in fourth place is the only certainty Victor Matfield's team can still count on after yesterday's results in Christchurch and Perth.

The Crusaders' shock defeat against the Chiefs was good news for the Sharks, who have to win against the Stormers without bonus points tomorrow to finish first.

In the unlikely event of the Sharks losing by more than seven points and without any bonus points, the Bulls would theoretically still have the chance to finish first if they beat the Reds by a points difference of 71 – a practically impossible task, even against a pushover such as the Reds.

After gaining their full complement of log points against the Western Force, the Blues are again in a strong position and they will benefit from a Stormers victory. The Blues' more favourable points difference (120-76) may keep the Bulls out of the second spot, notwithstanding a full complement of log points against the Reds.

The advantage that the Bulls enjoy by playing in the very last group match is that they can decide who their preferred opponents would be in the semifinals.

If the Sharks finish first and the Crusaders second, finishing fourth instead of third would be better for the Bulls.

Playing the Sharks in Durban in the semifinal instead of the wounded champion in Christchurch will dramatically boost the Bulls' chances of winning.

The Bulls' pride is one of their great exports, but no one will blame them if they fail to beat the Reds by a difference of at least 45 points.

This is what will be required to keep the Blues out of the third place.

The most important task facing the Bulls is to keep focused and play to their full potential. In that case, they will definitely see off the Reds convincingly and, in the words of Meyer, the rest will take care of itself.

The teams are:

Reds: Clinton Schifcofske, Andrew Walker, Ben Tune, Quade Cooper, Brando Va'aulu, Berrick Barnes, Nic Berry, Tom McVerry, David Croft (c), Mitch Chapman, James Horwill, Ed O'Donoghue, David Te Moana, Stephen Moore, Tama Tuirirangi. SUBSTITUTES: Sean Hardman, Herman Hunt, Cam Treloar, Geoff Abram, AJ Gilbert, Andrew Brown, Peter Hynes.

Bulls: Johan Roets, Akona Ndungane, Wynand Olivier, Wayne Julies, Bryan Habana, Derick Hougaard, Heinie Adams; Pierre Spies, Wikus van Heerden, Pedrie Wannenburg, Victor Matfield (c), Danie Rossouw, Rayno Gerber, Gary Botha, Gurthrö Steenkamp. SUBSTITUTES: Jaco Engels, Danie Thiart, Bakkies Botha, Derick Kuün, Fourie du Preez, Morné Steyn, Jaco van der Westhuyzen. **Referee:** Kelvin Deaker (NZ). **Kickoff:** 19:10.[5]

The same thinking was echoed on *Beeld's* front page, with an introductory paragraph that read as follows: 'South Africa seems set to have two representatives in the Super 14 semifinals again for the first time since 2001 by 21:00 tonight, but the bad news is that the Sharks and the Bulls may face each other in the next match.'[6]

As sports writers, we try to understand the psyche of a sports team as far as possible so that our previews – a compulsory gambling game – are not too far removed from what the team members themselves think and feel.

Although these articles only appeared the morning after Meyer's discussion with the team, the journalist concerned had nonetheless been spot on at the time that he wrote his two stories – because the players were still thinking along exactly the same lines as he was, at more or less the same time.

This did not apply to Meyer, however. 'I walked into the room. Gary Botha, an emotional chap, was sitting right in front of me. I asked the players if they still remembered that game against the Force: when we went for a win, instead of the three points and a draw. Yes, said the guys. Then I told the players that we don't play for low scores. We play to plaster other teams.

'It's against my principles to play without winning by a wide margin. And I believe that we can plaster the Reds. I know it,' Meyer said as he launched into his talk. 'But I can't take that decision on your behalf. I'm now going to walk out of this room, so that you can talk it over and take that decision yourselves. You talk to the man next to you and you decide together whether you want to do the impossible. And I'm not talking about 45 points. We're going for 76.'

According to Hougaard, for a few moments even the most lippy players were dumbstruck: 'We thought Heyneke was high on dagga or something. I mean, he was not coaching an under-9 rugby team – it was Super Rugby. But the longer he was out of the room, the more we started to believe that we might be on the eve of something incredible and we gave serious thought to the possibility of 76 points.'

For Meyer, there was nothing strange about this. In 1997 he had taken on the job of Phil Pretorius's assistant coach at the then decrepit amateur SWD rugby union. It was a side that been subjected to an 8-147 drubbing by the Blue Bulls in 1996.

Meyer took over from Pretorius as head coach in 1998, and in 1999 he was also Nick Mallett's forwards coach with the Springboks. During the times that Meyer couldn't be with the SWD Eagles, he asked the RAU coach at that time, Frans Ludeke, to take care of the team.

The Eagles played in the Currie Cup semifinals in 1999 and they were really very good. But then, on 18 July, SWD lost in an away game to the mediocre Border team – a day after the Springboks had suffered a 6-32 defeat against Australia at the Suncorp Stadium. Meyer was very upset and when he spoke to the Eagles again on the Tuesday after the match, he declared that only 100 points against the Griffons would make up for their disgraceful loss.

The players thought he was joking – but Meyer was deadly serious, and as the recent punchbags of South African rugby started buying into the idea, the Griffons' chance of success diminished more and more. The Eagles ended up thrashing them 102-0 at Outeniqua Park.

'I told the players before that Reds game that I had put 100 points on an opponent before, with weaker sides than themselves,' said Meyer.

When he returned to the auditorium before the Reds game, Meyer found that the atmosphere had changed completely. It was dead quiet. No one was doing sums any more. And the room was perceptibly warmer as a result of those 22 bodies in front of him.

'Gary!' Meyer called on his hooker – a man he could always rely on in moments like these to bring the weightiness of the occasion home to everyone else through the raw huskiness in his voice. 'Gary, are you in?'

'Yes, Coach. I'm in,' he replied with conviction.

'Bakkies, are you in?'

'Coach, I'm in.'

Meyer asked each of the other players in turn whether they bought into the number 76. Everyone said yes. And each player, as he overcame his own dumbfoundedness and gave his 'yes', stood up and put his signature on a sheet of paper that Meyer had affixed to the board in front. It became a contract – a promise. He told the players a story: 'Once upon a time, there was a little bull. A little blue bull. His ancestors and thousands of other animals had been living for centuries on a piece of land that was home to them, but which was fast becoming a barren wasteland. Food was scarce and the water had run out. Their only chance of survival lay in the land of milk and honey – a place they had only heard of – somewhere beyond three mountain ranges, deep rivers full of crocodiles and valleys teeming with leopards, lions and hyenas.

'But everyone (all merely animals who had only heard tales about this Utopia) warned that it was too dangerous to get there and that it would be better to die gradually of starvation than to risk being devoured by a ravenous predator.

'Eventually the survival instinct of a few animals simply became stronger than their resistance to the challenge. With the little energy they had left, they started running in the general direction of the place where salvation was supposed to lie. As they progressed on their journey, however, fears that they would suffer a cruel death caused one animal after another to throw in the towel. But not the little bull. He put down his head and just kept on running. Kept on running without stopping. Three mountain ranges later, he reached the land of milk and honey. And everything that had been said about the place turned out to be true: there was water; there was food in abundance;

there was shade that provided shelter from the sun. And it was safe there.

'When the news reached the other animals and he himself returned after a while to find out what had become of them, everyone wanted to know how he had managed to get there. Where were the lions? How many crocodiles did he encounter? How deep were the deepest waters?

'The little bull didn't answer them. He only smiled. Then the animals realised for the first time that the little bull was deaf. He had been oblivious to the lions, leopards, hyenas, crocodiles and deep waters. All he had seen was that the animals suddenly set off in a certain direction, which could mean only one thing to him – there had to be something better than the circumstances in which they found themselves.

'And, guys, in the same way, from this moment onwards we must turn a deaf ear to every person who tells us that this score is impossible. To every person who wants to tell us what they believe we are capable of. And it's not only possible; to us it can also be easy.'

Meyer's conviction that the size of a vision also determines how much energy a team will derive from it depends on the fact that it must be easy to explain that vision on paper. Therefore, although he knew that his players now believed in the 76, it was necessary to quantify the unthinkable for them: 'I told them that to win by 76 points, we had to score 13 tries. To score 13 tries, our back three had to score seven: three for Bryan, two for Roetsie and two for Akona. I asked each of the players if he could do it, and each one agreed. Johann wrote this down.

'I was still looking for six guys for the other tries. Pierre Spies put up his hand for two. And a bunch of other players nominated themselves. Johann wrote down these undertakings.

'I told them that we had to steal 30 per cent of the Reds' lineouts and the locks said they were in. I told Derick he had to succeed with more than 80 per cent of his place kicks and he said he had no problem with that.

'We also can't afford to concede more than seven penalties, I told them. Wikus is allowed to concede two, but then I need ten other guys in the team who aren't going to concede a penalty. The guys nominated themselves and Johann wrote it down.

'In that way, we went through every single thing we could think of and we constructed that 76 like a jigsaw puzzle until everyone could see the picture. It actually turned out to be terribly easy to win by such a wide margin if each guy in the team just did what he had undertaken to do.

'When the players walked out of the auditorium, I knew that they believed every word that had been spoken and every promise that had been made. That vision gave us energy, and it was necessary for us to spend time on it so that the players could internalise it and would run onto the pitch with the right mindset the next day.'

The following day was Meyer's father-in-law's birthday. When Meyer arrived home that Friday evening, his wife observed that it would be difficult to make something special of the birthday celebration because, on returning home after the game, he would have to pack his bags for his flight to New Zealand early the next morning: 'But I told her that she didn't understand – we wouldn't be going to New Zealand. We would be staying right here in Pretoria.

'I was in a cheerful mood that evening and asked Johann to compile a video for us, with clips of all the best tries we had scored in the course of the year. That, as well as each player's promise. We would show some of our best moments and, for example, Pierre's face with the words "two tries" below it. The number 76 would be flashed on the screen in between clips. The cassette bore the title in bold letters: "The Biggest Victory Ever".

'Johann showed it to the players the next day about an hour and a half before the start of the match. I knew that doubt would have crept in here and there since our talk that Friday afternoon. I strongly believe in positive reinforcement and visualisation – it's basic psychology, yet so powerful.'

Early the next morning, Meyer went to see the referee, Kelvin Deaker, at his hotel.

'I just went to tell him that we were going to win by at least 76 points and asked him to allow us to get quick ball and to ensure that the Reds didn't play negatively. He looked askance at me and repeated what everyone had been saying to us before the game, "It is impossible, mate!"'

When Meyer showed the players the video before the game, it was the last motivational message of the day. In the 90 minutes before a match, the players are as relaxed as it is possible for tense people to be: they are focused, they warm up and the captain talks to the team. When the Bulls ran out onto Loftus on Saturday 5 May at 19:08 in front of a 44 870-strong crowd, not one of the players doubted that they were going to win the game by as large a margin as they had envisaged. By that time, the Sharks had already beaten the Stormers 36-10 at Newlands and scored five tries, thereby moving to the top of the Super Rugby log. The Crusaders were still in second place. But that spot on the log was the absolute minimum on which the Bulls had decided at the start of the season.

The Reds' Clinton Schifcofske recorded the first points of the match in the third minute with a successful penalty kick. There were 77 minutes left. By then, the Bulls had already forfeited the points buffer of three through a penalty. There was simply no time for hesitation.

Bryan Habana scored two tries in the five minutes after the Reds' penalty. Then Pedrie Wannenburg bagged a try. So did Gary Botha. Wikus van Heerden, too, went over for a try shortly before half-time, while Hougaard succeeded with all his conversions.

Two tries went awry before the break – one was Habana's, who lost the ball over the try line. The first half ended with the score at 38-3.

'I gave the players a tongue-lashing when they arrived in the dressing room at half-time. We were leading by 38-3, and I scolded them! But on that day, 38-3 was not an acceptable score. Especially because we had thrown away two tries.

'So far, Derick had lived up to his promises of 80 per cent and Bryan could already have had his third try before half-time. We decided to score at least 50 points after half-time.'

Wynand Olivier scored a try four minutes into the second half. And Spies followed shortly afterwards with the two tries he had pledged. The Bulls won 19 out of 19 lineouts and seven out of seven scrums, in addition to winning a tighthead on three of the Reds' four scrums.

Wikus van Heerden hit 29 rucks, reversed possession three times and was responsible for 12 completed tackles out of a team total of 113.

Spies carried the ball 13 times and broke through the first line of defenders four times. He, too, stole three balls at a ruck. And Hougaard slotted 12 of his 13 kicks at goal for a success rate of 92.3 per cent.

In the brief 35 minutes and 51 seconds (in an 80-minute match) during which the ball was in play, the Bulls had only 60.7 per cent of the possession. This means, firstly, that the Reds also adopted a positive approach to the match because they clearly did not kick away the little possession they had. But, more importantly, the Bulls amassed almost 100 points in just 21 minutes and 46 seconds of active play, with the final score a 92-3 victory. Hence 54 points in the second half. And a points difference of 89.

Hougaard related how he and the All Black centre, Aaron Mauger, reminisced about that game a few years later. Mauger had played for the Crusaders at the time and – because of the massive and almost unthinkable points difference the Bulls had to wipe out to finish above them – the Kiwis didn't even watch the match or book flights.

'But their team manager woke them one by one that night with a phone call, telling them to get ready to leave for the airport, as they had to play the Bulls at Loftus,' the flyhalf recalled. Hougaard and Mauger were teammates at the English club Leicester when Meyer started coaching that side in 2008.

The semifinal match turned out to be a mere formality. The Bulls defeated the Crusaders 27-12, with Hougaard contributing all the points through eight penalties and a drop goal.

In a similar fashion, the Sharks gave the Blues a drubbing in Durban and scored a 34-18 victory.

So, for the first time ever, South Africa had two teams in a Super Rugby final.

The Bulls faced the prospect of playing against a particularly strong Sharks side in Durban on 19 May, and the Crusaders' Super 12 victory over the Brumbies in Canberra (20-19) in 2000 had been the last time a visiting team had lifted the trophy after a final. That served partly as motivation, but there were greater factors that inspired the Bulls.

Even before the World Cup tournament of that year, it was being said that Jake White would be sacked as the Bok coach. Meyer was the logical choice to replace him and although White was retained in his post, he would not remain at the helm of Springbok rugby after the tournament.

Because there was a realistic chance that Meyer would take over from White, that final match in Durban would be his last one with the Bulls since he had started coaching the Northern Bulls (as they were known) in 2000.

The final also gave the Bulls the best chance yet to reap the fruits of a journey that most of the players and their coach had been on since 2001 – alternating between the Bulls' and the Blue Bulls' Vodacom Cup and Currie Cup teams. Meyer recounted: 'It was an incredibly emotional week for all of us. But because a team is faced with so much pressure and expectation before a final, you take a step back in that week. The hard work has been done. The guys know what is expected of them. But if you expose a team to all those external factors, you run the risk of totally missing out on the joy of rugby. Ultimately, one should enjoy a final – and this was the biggest final of our lives.

'There was an American college basketball coach, Jim Valvano. I had read a lot about him and he talked about the custom in basketball of cutting down the net after winning a big competition.

'With that as the metaphor, in the week of the final we didn't practise playing better rugby, but rather how we were going to cut down that symbolic net in Durban and bring it home to Pretoria. I had been on a journey with most of those players since they were 19 years old. And now they were men – guys that, as far back as 2001, had bought into our dream of making Bulls rugby not just the best in Super Rugby, but the best team in the world. I was firmly convinced that we could play and win test rugby with that Bulls squad.'

The last team talk took place 90 minutes before the final at Kings Park. In the case of away matches, the talking is done at the hotel before the players travel to the stadium by bus.

Johann van Graan had come up with something similar to the Reds video. He had edited a photo of Matfield to produce a new one where he was standing with the Super Rugby trophy, photos of which had been pasted up at Loftus for the past season. Van Graan printed the photo onto a fake front page of the *Rapport* Sunday paper, with the headline: 'Bulls first SA team to win Super Rugby'.

In our first interview for this book, Meyer became tearful as he recalled that last team talk: 'I was extremely emotional. The players too. Seven years of our lives had come down to that day – D-Day in Durban. We were all tense. Bakkies was sitting right in front of me, sweating profusely. I was crying because it was possibly my last game with the Bulls. The players were crying. I knew we were ready for this. It was the Super Rugby final. That which we had dreamed of.'

A Meyer team talk always included a story or three. These anecdotes often took place in a 'little Free State town'. Once again on this occasion there was a story: 'There was this little Free State town that was in the grip of a drought. There was not a single cloud in the sky. The farmers were suffering; their animals were dying; and prayer meetings were held on a weekly, later daily, basis.

'So, the people of the town decided to hold a big day of prayer for rain in the town square. Hundreds of men gathered in the square, and the air was filled with the droning sound of their prayers. After about an hour, another man arrived, who had brought along his young son. "Daddy, what are the men doing?" the little boy enquired. And his dad answered that they were praying for rain. "But do they really believe it's going to rain?" he asked.

'"Yes," his dad replied. "These men are believers."

'His dad bowed his head again and began to pray. But the questions kept lingering in the boy's eyes as he gazed at the hundreds of kneeling men. Hands in the air. All of them praying. Pleading.

'"But, Daddy, there's one thing I don't understand," the boy said. His dad told him that prayers required perseverance.

'The boy replied: "That's not what I'm wondering about, Daddy. I just don't understand how all these men can believe it's going to rain and yet none of them have brought along an umbrella …"'

Meyer told his players that it wasn't enough to merely believe that they were going to win this final. They had to know it: 'I guarantee you that the Sharks, too, believe that they can win the match: they're playing at home, they're at the top of the log. You can rest assured that those guys also believe.

'But believing isn't going to be enough today. You have to know. Even if we're still behind in the last minute of this match, you have to know that we're going to win it. Because *that* is the difference between a finalist and a champion side.

'Let's say I give each of you a parachute and tell you to jump out of a plane. But you want to know whether the parachute will open. If I just say I believe that it will open, I promise you that none of you would jump.

'But if I say I *know* that it will open — I know it, because I've been packing parachutes all my life — I'm asking you again: Bakkies, will you jump? Gary, will you jump?

'"Yes, Coach, I'll jump," said both Bothas.'

Then Van Graan produced his *Rapport* front page. Visualisation. Positive reinforcement. As the players rose to go to the bus, Habana walked past Meyer. 'Bryan,' he told him, 'I just know that you're going to do something special today.'

The final was played in front of 52 000 people and it started off at a tremendous pace. Percy Montgomery put the first points on the board for the Sharks in the eighth minute when he converted a penalty. Spies scored a try five minutes later, with JP Pietersen of the Sharks responding with a try after another six minutes. Montgomery and Hougaard also exchanged penalty kicks. At half-time, the Sharks led 14-10.

'But in the 78th minute, it felt as if my heart was being ripped from my body and seven years of my life were lying in ruins.' Meyer watched from the coaches' box as lock Albert van den Berg scored the Sharks' second try: 'I had given my all. And all of a sudden, it was just gone. It was over. Pote Human was sitting next to me: his hands were in his hair. I saw Wynie sitting next to the pitch, removing his earpiece from his ear and waiting dejectedly for Frans Steyn to kick the conversion.

'But then something happened and people still laugh at me today about it. I heard a voice. I literally heard it. In Afrikaans. And the voice said to me: "Listen, Heyneke. You tell the guys they shouldn't believe. They should know — right into the last minute. But you're not even prepared to believe."

'When I heard that voice, I grabbed the walkie-talkie and called Wynie. I told him the conversion attempt would fail [Frans Steyn indeed missed the conversion] and that we had to regain the ball from the kickoff and just hang on to it.

'Wynie stuffed that earpiece back into his ear and said, "Coachie, I know you're a positive guy, but …"

'I told him, "Wynie, just get the flipping message out."'

'Then I saw that Pote's spirits were rising. "This thing isn't over yet," he said. I remember how in those last two minutes we did just about everything we had practised over seven years. Props scissored. Gary Botha kicked a grubber. I thought I would soil my pants! I hate grubbers.

The Sharks won the kickoff, put together several phases and, with only 25 seconds left, Butch James kicked the ball downfield. Jaco van der Westhuyzen caught it, sped to the midfield and gave the ball to Akona Ndungane, who ran back to the supporting players.

Another few phases followed and Gary Botha got the ball. He hit a gap in the midfield and, with 79 minutes and 57 seconds on the clock, he kicked a grubber, which landed directly in Frans Steyn's hands. Steyn was under no pressure and could simply have kicked the ball out to seal the Sharks' victory. But he didn't.

He kicked the ball into the hands of Victor Matfield, who started yet another counteroffensive. They were on the opposite sides of the field. The ball was flung back and Spies slipped through a gap in front of the main stand. He threw a one-handed pass to Habana, who sprinted along the right touchline and cut a few steps infield. A ruck formed, with the referee, Steve Walsh, on the one side and the touch judge, Lyndon Bray, on the touchline.

The ball popped out on the Sharks' side, but Derick Kuün won it back. The Bulls tossed it quickly towards the opposite touchline, where the receiver was the prop Jaco Engels. He stepped towards the touchline and in a switch move gave a backhand pass to Ndungane, who progressed to seven metres from the Sharks' try line.

Again, the ball was sent to the main stand. This time via Heini Adams, who threw a long skip pass to Habana. The Bok wing cut infield and, with the clock on 81 minutes and 35 seconds, made a dash for the try line. He dived over just to the right of the right-hand goalpost, with JP Pietersen trying in vain to stop him. The score was 19-18 in favour of the Sharks. Hougaard still had to kick.

Looking back on that day, Meyer said, 'It was like watching the Red Sea parting for Bryan.'

Hougaard placed the ball and the Sharks charged too early. The Laws stipulate that the opposing team are only allowed to charge at a kicker once he has started with his run-up and Hougaard had not yet done so.

But it was as if he hadn't even noticed the players rushing towards him, and as the Sharks were ordered to return to their positions on the instruction of the referee, Hougaard started his run-up and executed the kick. 20-19.

The Bulls were the first South African Super Rugby champions. Meyer related: 'Some people say that Derick Kuün won back the ball illegally. I also reckon that there had been a few fishy things that made Albert van den Berg's try possible. Be that as it may, I still think it's incredible that we managed to retain the ball for so long after the hooter, in a final, to score the try and for Derick to get the conversion – even though it was close to the posts.

'We had practised that stuff and called it situational training. Derick, Morné Steyn and Jaco van der Westhuyzen would each take three kicks at goal from the touchline. And if they missed two, the entire team would have to work hard for ten minutes. They weren't allowed to lose the ball. You kept it for ten minutes. Those sessions were called Blue Blood sessions. And if Derick and the others constantly missed kicks, they would soon have incurred Bakkies's wrath. So, you get your kicks over – no matter how exhausted you are.

'*That* was my message to Wynie – tell the players I want Blue Blood. When those players rushed at Derick, he had been conditioned in such a way that in Blue Blood situations he was able to shut out everything around him and kick the ball through the posts. He was in the zone. And we won the game.'

A further touch of colour was added to the dramatic final-match victory shortly after the game when Jaco van der Westhuyzen climbed up the left goalpost and lifted his jersey. Underneath it he wore a T-shirt on which he had written the words 'Jesus is Koning' (Jesus is King). That gesture sparked off a massive reaction – both criticism and praise – in the weeks after the final, more so than the Bulls themselves, who had just captured South Africa's first Super Rugby title.

Van der Westhuyzen is a religious man. Although his showcasing of his faith elicited divergent responses, it had value in the Bulls' team environment for another reason.

Meyer recounts that Van der Westhuyzen ran up to him directly after the match, lifted his jersey and said, 'Look, Coach, I've brought along my umbrella.'

'People said that Jaco was crazy. And maybe he was a little bit, but not in the ugly way in which he was portrayed in the media. He didn't make that T-shirt in the hope that he would give his faith the credit for the team's success on a huge public platform. He *knew* he was going to do that. And it was incredibly precious to me to see that the players knew – and not only believed. So Jaco's T-shirt was like that net we were going to cut down in Durban.'

Since that thrashing in Christchurch against the Crusaders, the Bulls had shifted into a higher gear and had a greater awareness of the team, the individuals and their goals. For about two minutes they had the optimal experience of 'flow' – a concept that is discussed in the chapters on Paul Treu. It represented the crown of their labours on a seven-year journey. Meyer said in retrospect: 'When I look back on that season, the last four regular matches in particular were something special. In each case, we reached almost exactly the score we were aiming for – against the Lions it was 100 per cent. In each match, we scored at least four tries. We eliminated the points difference as a factor that could sink our dream.

'But it had been a long road to get to where we were. Because in that season we were basically out of the race after only three matches. Then we fought back. Every game was a fight. I told the guys that if Bryan hadn't scored that try against the Chiefs in the last minute, we would have been out. And when the senior players took responsibility for the team in Christchurch – even though we lost – it was the turning point in the season. That match had to turn out the way it did.'

When I asked Hougaard about that season, he recalled all the memorable highlights – the Hollywood moments. The turning points, climaxes, friendships, joys and sorrows of team sport are the things of lasting value, which live on long after a player has hung up his boots.

Hougaard said, 'But people will be wrong if they attribute the success of 2007 only to inspiring team talks and the hype in the media. What we achieved in that season was simply the result of visionary leadership and a dream Heyneke had already started working on seven years before. And most of that work was done behind the scenes.'

CHAPTER 2

First sharpen your axe

'The problems of the world cannot possibly be solved by skeptics or cynics whose horizons are limited by the obvious realities. We need men who can dream of things that never were.'
– John F Kennedy

Andrew Grove talks about a 'strategic inflection point'. According to this former CEO of Intel Corporation, at some or other time, all individuals, institutions and organisations are faced with an inflection point. It may be new technology, a new way of thinking, some form of paradigm shift that draws a clear dividing line between what has been thought and done in the past, and what the future holds.

In his book *Only the Paranoid Survive*, Grove describes changes of this kind as '10× forces' – in other words, changes or forces that have become ten times what they were just recently.

The first reaction to such an inflection point is usually to see it as a crisis. The manner in which the individual or institution responds to it determines their destiny. If you do the right thing, the inflection point becomes the platform for survival and an upward curve. Should you act wrongly, however, you are doomed to certain ruin.

FW de Klerk was at such an inflection point in 1990 when he decided, fairly unilaterally, to make his speech of 2 February, announcing the release of Nelson Mandela and the unbanning of the ANC and other political organisations. So, too, was Nelson Mandela when he started talking to the National Party in secret in 1985 without the knowledge of the other ANC prisoners and exiles.

I discussed these ideas with Tim du Plessis, who at the time of writing was the executive editor of Afrikaans News at Media24. To illustrate further the impact of making the right decision at an inflection point, we also talked about the 16th United States president, Abraham Lincoln. He was president during the American Civil War, which was fought between a majority of northern states and 11 in the south. The major contention was the abolition of slavery. The industrialised north was in favour of doing away with slavery, while the more rural southern states regarded slaves as essential to their agricultural activities and therefore to their economy. The southern states wanted to secede from the United States of America and formed the Confederate States of America – a rebel entity.

Although Lincoln knew that the abolition of slavery would be extremely contentious, he stood by his convictions because he believed that slavery flew in the face of the founding principles of the USA – that all citizens were entitled to freedom and equal treatment.

'When his decision started a civil war, he looked deep into the future and realised that the preservation of the Union was of paramount importance,' Du Plessis remarked. 'If Lincoln had been a laissez-faire leader, he would simply have avoided taking a stand when it came to both decisions – the abolition of slavery and the secession of the south. My guess: had Lincoln done that (backed away from the challenge and done nothing), it is quite possible that North America could have looked like Latin America today: fragmented, prone to instability, with a superficial commitment to democratic freedom.'

The crux of the matter is this: when confronted by a 10× force, an organisation or an individual has only two choices – either take the bull by the horns, or think that you have no chance of survival.

On 26 August 1995, rugby union was hit by a 10× force when the International Rugby Board (IRB) declared this sporting code 'open' – in other words, without regulations that prohibited the payment of players. The 10× force was the advent of professionalism for a code that had hitherto been run by amateurs.

Professional sport was not a novelty in 1995. In the US, baseball had acquired professional status as far back as 1869, when the Cincinnati Baseball Club (the Red Stockings) became the first professional team. And 12 November 1892 has been recorded as the day on which American football acquired professional status when the Allegheny Athletic Club offered a certain William 'Pudge' Heffelfinger a match fee of $500 to play against the Pittsburgh Athletic Club.

There was no such history, however, in South African sport from which it could draw lessons that could be applied to rugby.

According to Grove, the absence of a road map for the future is one of the characteristics of a strategic inflection point. As in the case of Lincoln and the Civil War, it requires the person or organisation to look far into the future to weigh up the consequences of doing nothing, or maintaining the status quo (certain ruin), against those of a fundamentally new way of doing things. This is mostly pioneering work.

When a hurricane of change such as a 10× force starts blowing, it does not necessarily mean that all ships would know immediately what to do with their sails – or whether they would even still need sails.

This also applied in the case of rugby. The IRB made that decision in 1995 because there were simply too many external factors that threatened the future of rugby union. One was rugby league, which was practised as a professional sport in several traditional rugby-union countries. It had become increasingly attractive for players to switch from union to league to earn a salary.

This was a particular source of concern in England, New Zealand and Australia. In South Africa, however, rugby league was not as popular as it was in those countries. Locally, there was greater concern about a breakaway faction in Australia, the World Rugby Corporation, who wanted to create an international professional competition for union players funded by media tycoon Kerry Packer – similar to the Indian Premier League T20 cricket competition of today, but without the support of the sport's international governing body.

Players were warned that they would no longer be eligible to play for their national team if they participated in the Packer rebel competition. As a further countermeasure, the then South African Rugby Football Union paid the World Cup Boks a bonus not to do so.

In the event, the Packer competition never got off the ground because players from South Africa and New Zealand – and, later, from Australia – entered into contracts with their local national rugby unions.

The overarching governing body for rugby in South Africa, New Zealand and Australia, SANZAR, was established in 1995 – largely in reaction to the Super League in Australia. On the eve of the 1995 Rugby World Cup final, it was announced that SANZAR had concluded a deal worth £370 million with Rupert Murdoch's News Corporation,

FIRST SHARPEN YOUR AXE

which secured him the exclusive broadcasting rights for all provincial and international matches from those three countries for the next ten years. In 1996 the Super 12 and Tri-Nations competitions were presented under the banner of SANZAR for the first time.

That deal with News Corp was later renewed until 2015, which is why it is so difficult to make changes to the format of the Super Rugby competition at present – such as entering a sixth South African team before 2015, or participating in SANZAR competitions at all.

Nevertheless, in 1995 two things happened: first, rugby union went professional and, second, it was consequently permissible to remunerate players, which made money part of the picture.

Forking out big sums of money to players falls far short of an adequate definition of professionalism in sport, in the same way that democracy cannot be fully defined as merely the right to vote in an election. For five years after the IRB's decision, however, this was how rugby was defined in South Africa. The Golden Lions was then still a proud union, and buying in and buying big was its way of doing business. It was also the 'big lion', Louis Luyt, who came up with the plan of combining the Free State and the Lions as the Golden Cats in the Super 12 competition from 1998. The Western Stormers, the Northern Bulls and the Coastal Sharks were also born as regional teams at that time.

The Northern Bulls, however, were a fiasco from the outset. The franchise consisted of the Blue Bulls, the Falcons, the Leopards and the Pumas. None of these sides did well in the Currie Cup competition, and there was a spitefulness among the players when they had to play together as the Northern Bulls.

Each union received R20 000 for each of its players in the Super 12 group. Coaches were frequently exchanged, and when the Falcons had the opportunity to hold the reins, more Falcons players were included in the Northern Bulls side than Blue Bulls – probably the kind of politics Dr Danie Craven had anticipated when he said that rugby should never turn professional.

Because the Blue Bulls failed to distinguish themselves in the Currie Cup competition, barring 1998, they could not assert themselves as a senior partner. The Bulls and the Northern Bulls were in the doldrums.

Very few players were still keen to play for the Blue Bulls. Barend van Graan, the CEO, recalled that dismal period: 'We were seen as a graveyard because our player budget was so small. Nobody else wanted the players who played for us. By then, the Sharks were poaching only senior players from other unions, and Western Province had their own guys. The Lions were already going downhill at that stage. The guys who couldn't get into the Sharks or Western Province went to play for the Lions. But no one wanted to come to Loftus.'

While the Currie Cup competition continued to generate great excitement in South Africa, the country's Super Rugby teams failed to make the grade. In 1996 Natal reached the final and was defeated 21–45 by the Blues. The Sharks lost to the Brumbies by 6–36 in the 2001 final. For the rest, however, Super Rugby was an Australasian affair.

In addition to the financial and racial politics that bedevilled sports matters in South Africa, there was no comprehensive understanding of what professional sport involved. Players were bought and sold year in, year out without anyone having a model for sustainable success – namely, to remain competitive and win tournaments. And because the process of buying and selling was regarded as the full definition, the situation favoured only those unions that had money at their disposal.

The Bulls did not fall into that category. After winning the Currie Cup in 1998 for the first time since 1991, the Bulls ended fifth in 1999, and in 2000 they were relegated to the B division after the first half of the competition.

In one of their home games in 1999, a penalty kick taken by Casper Steyn was all that enabled the Blue Bulls to ward off a ferocious assault by the SWD Eagles. The coach of that SWD side was Heyneke Meyer. Frans Ludeke was the assistant coach, Ian Schwartz Meyer's personal assistant, Hennie Kriel the fitness expert and Tommy Smook the team doctor – all of them people who were to play important roles in Bulls rugby.

Van Graan had known Meyer since his student days when the latter was chairman of the University of Pretoria's student rugby association, and from 2000 their paths would again cross daily when SA Rugby appointed Meyer as the Northern Bulls' new head coach. Van Graan visited Meyer on 4 September 1999 in his hotel in Sandton to discuss the new challenge that awaited Meyer in Pretoria. This was just before the Eagles were due to play in a Currie Cup semifinal for the first time in their history later that afternoon, at Ellis Park.

By that stage, the 31-year-old Meyer was already the Stormers' and the Springboks' forwards coach. The young man knew his rugby, and he had the blessing of the then Springbok coach, Nick Mallett, to coach his own Super Rugby team.

In his capacity as the national coach, Mallett was a member of the panel that had to make the appointment. He was responsible for the technical questions. SA Rugby then offered Meyer a six-month contract to take over the Northern Bulls from Eugene van Wyk – the man he would replace as head coach of the Blue Bulls a year later.

But there was never a chance of success with the Northern Bulls. Meyer had to select a team from the Bulls (5th in the 1999 Currie Cup competition), the Pumas (9th), the Falcons (10th) and the old North West (14th and last).

When the Northern Bulls, with Meyer at the helm, won only 1 out of 11 matches and finished second last – just above the Sharks – he was sacked as coach, and Phil Pretorius, then the Falcons coach, was appointed for 2001.

'I told the guys from the beginning that we couldn't win with that team,' Meyer related. 'But I thought I was going there for three years, though. At that time, SA Rugby still appointed the Super 12 coaches, and I had nothing in writing that promised me a three-year term. So I found myself unemployed at 32.'

But Van Graan still believed in Meyer. And Meyer believed that the only way in which the Bulls could eventually become a successful franchise was for the Blue Bulls to start winning again and thus become the senior partner.

Meyer and Van Graan sat next to each other on a flight to Sydney in 2000. During the flight, Meyer told the big boss of Blue Bulls rugby about his vision of turning the Bulls into the best rugby team in the world – a ludicrous idea in that particular year.

'I knew Meyertjie well by then,' Van Graan recalled. 'And during that entire flight he spoke about nothing else but rugby. Not cars. Nothing.

Nowadays he at least talks occasionally about buffaloes too. But he lives for rugby, and as smart as his plan was that day, at a point I asked him to please just stop. I couldn't take it any more. The entire flight, from the time we took off until we landed! But it was a good plan.'

In 2000 the BBC became the first provincial professional entity in South Africa to announce halfway through the season that it was going to advertise its head-coach position. Eugene van Wyk's days were numbered. The Currie Cup success of 1998 had been just a flash in the pan at a time when the Bulls had lost their potency.

On 9 August 2000, almost five years after rugby had become a professional sport, Meyer was summoned to Loftus Versfeld for a job interview. He had a second chance.

'I never agreed with Doc Craven that rugby shouldn't become professional,' Meyer said. 'I knew that day would come. My strength and my weakness are that I look only into the future. But I knew the only way we would be able to run rugby professionally and sustainably some day was if we constantly tried to look at least ten years into the future.'

———

According to Andrew Grove, a strategic inflection point is often not something that arrives with a bang or is heralded by an announcement, but rather something that unfolds gradually. And, in most cases, an inflection point can only be defined as such when a series of events or processes is examined with hindsight.

That is why the Bulls' Super Rugby success of 2007 – the first of three Super Rugby titles in four years – provides the important context for seeing both Meyer's job interview of August 2000 and the buy-in he secured for his proposals as a strategic inflection point. Because, in 1995, rugby had been hit by a 10× force – professionalism. In the subsequent five years, big salaries and star players defined the sporting code without any South African team achieving sustained success.

But then, on 9 August 2000, Heyneke Meyer sold the BBC a vision in which he looked so far into the future that both the old guard and the so-called early leaders in professional rugby laughed at him when he started implementing those strategic plans with strategic actions – one of the signs that what one is doing is revolutionary, according to Grove.

FIRST SHARPEN YOUR AXE

Grove also says that only the first mover, the one who responds to the challenge of that 10× force, has the real advantage over his competitors. He emphasises that no blueprint exists for that new order, and that it has to be visualised and created from nothing. In retrospect, Meyer's presentation to the BBC was the strategic inflection point that not only made the Bulls' success in the following decade possible, but undoubtedly also that of Springbok rugby.

Meyer began his presentation with the anonymous saying that it takes many years of hard work to achieve overnight success. He described the work that needed to be done to eventually make the Bulls successful in the form of five pillars:

'Our vision is to bring into being, build and lead the most successful rugby team in the world and thus be a world leader in all areas. This will be achieved by:

- Putting together the best available management team and developing them further.
- Recruiting, retaining and developing the most talented players.
- Creating a professional environment within which the players can develop into world-class players and individuals.
- Establishing a science-based programme that will allow these players to develop to their full potential.
- Playing a brand of rugby that is marketable, fills stadiums and attracts sponsors.

The board later proposed a sixth pillar: a sustainable financial model.

The first four pillars made the fifth possible. And the fifth would ultimately make the sixth possible, to the point where the sixth could sustain the first five pillars. For those who have ever wondered what is meant by the 'structures' of a rugby team, these six pillars provide a neat summary of all the things they entail.

Such structures make sustainable success possible, and this means that no team ever has to start rebuilding from scratch in the event of changes in terms of, say, the leadership of management or players. That is why Frans Ludeke was able to slot into the Bulls at the end of 2007 and needed only one season to find his feet before guiding the team in 2009 to the most successful year in their existence. The structures were already strong enough to function under a new leader who subscribed to the Bulls' vision and strategy.

This is what Lincoln meant when he said that if he had six hours to chop down a tree, he would spend the first four sharpening his axe. He knew what he was talking about – Abe was a skilled woodcutter who had cut up logs to make rail fences in his youth. To prepare properly for success, first get your structures in place.

This is not to say that sharpening the axe is easy or pleasant, especially if you have no model of how to go about it. In Grove's view, when an organisation experiences such a strategic inflection point without a model that represents what the future will look like, it finds itself in the 'valley of death'. This is a perilous part of the transition from the old way of doing things to what the future holds. One has to persevere while traversing the valley of death. I will discuss this later in more detail, but in 2002 the BBC came very close to firing Meyer.

In order to quell impulses such as the one exhibited by the BBC, it is important to visualise what the organisation, in this case the Bulls, should look like when it finally moves out of that valley of death. Therefore, one has to look into the future – as Meyer and Lincoln did. And that vision – in Meyer's case, to be the most successful rugby team in the world – has to be so tangible that it can easily be explained and made intelligible to the people who have to go on this journey with you. Because all of them – those who persevere – have to pull in the same direction if the dream is to be realised and sustained.

To achieve this vision, the Bulls could not continue with their old way of doing things. In part, it also meant that they couldn't simply be content with the situation that players had started preferring Loftus to Ellis Park when they were no longer good enough for the Sharks or Western Province.

If they wanted to be the best in the world, they had to think differently about rugby and employ their resources differently from what had been the norm up to that point. For the unions with money, the 'old way' was to buy star players from elsewhere without doing development of their own. This approach, however, clearly didn't yield benefits for the big buyer, the Sharks.

It was in any case not a possibility that was available to Meyer when he landed the job as the Blue Bulls' new head coach from 2001. John Plumtree, Laurie Mains and Eugene van Wyk were among the other candidates who had competed for the Bulls' coaching position at the end of 2000. Mr Price was then still the Blue Bulls' major sponsor, but the company suddenly withdrew its support shortly after Meyer was appointed. The Bulls' player budget was cut from R13 million to R8 million – almost half of what the Sharks and Western Province had at their disposal at that stage.

Hence buying top players was not an option. The Bulls' management budget for coaches amounted to R1.5 million at the time. Instead of asking for more money for players, Meyer asked the CEO to approach the board with a request for R3 million for a management team – not for salary increases, but so that he could appoint more people.

'To me, it was straightforward. If we couldn't buy Boks, we would give our young players the best chance to become Boks,' Meyer explained.

That is why a world-class management team is the Bulls' first pillar.

CHAPTER 3

No man is an island

The management team

'You can take my factories, burn my buildings, but give me my people and I will build the business right back again.'
– Henry Ford

Meyer's interview for the Blue Bulls position in August 2000 was conducted by an appointment committee who mostly knew nothing about him. Barend van Graan was the exception. Fortunately, the 65-year-old chairman, Boet Fick, was receptive to whichever candidate had the best plan.

The Blue Bulls had had a tough year both on and off the field. The Bulls players in the Northern Bulls team were not happy to play in a light-blue jersey. This Super Rugby franchise was a regional team, after all, and, because it was so weak, the Blue Bulls did not want the Northern Bulls team to be regarded as an extension of Loftus and, therefore, of the former Northern Transvaal.

But the Currie Cup team of 2000 was so weak that it was relegated to the B division of the competition a few weeks after the interviews for a new head coach were held. There was enormous pressure from both administrators and players that the former mayor of Pretoria and then president of the Blue Bulls Rugby Union, the late Piet Olivier, should vacate his position. The Blue Bulls team was regarded as a ship that had run aground, and at the end of 2000 two executive committee members, Vic Kleynhans and Dave Bergman, resigned.

When an organisation finds itself in such stormy waters, it often happens that long-serving administrators put their faith in what has worked in the past. It may be the appointment of someone with whose methods they are familiar, or even just the preservation of the status quo in the hope that the storm will eventually die down and that, in time, the organisation will be able to function again as it did in better times.

Van Graan, Fick and Olivier did not allow themselves that luxury and, to this day, Meyer gives them credit for having supported his appointment in that very trying period.

'I wasn't the kind of guy that would just be accepted at Loftus without further ado,' Meyer recalled. 'I wasn't a general in the defence force or a big shot at Tukkies. I was an ordinary guy with an objective plan for how we could make the Bulls the best rugby team in the world.'

This tallies with Andrew Grove's assumption about what a strategic inflection point may require – the so-called 'Cassandras' in an organisation.

Although one may find these people everywhere in the hierarchy, the Cassandras are usually people who aren't in top management. Because they operate outside of that immediate sphere of influence, they experience the ebb and flow of an industry at first hand. They can generally sense the winds of change at an earlier stage and thus respond to them more quickly.

In 2000, therefore, Meyer could have been viewed as a windsock and the appointment committee as a weather tower, which allowed itself to be guided at a critical juncture by the movement in the sock.

'You don't easily say no to Meyertjie. His vision was unconventional and new. His presentation was ahead of its time – he had looked at things that worked elsewhere in professional sport and applied those principles to rugby,' Van Graan related.

There were, however, a number of obvious obstacles on the road towards realising that vision. The first was money, as Meyer explained when recalling that period: 'It was customary at the big unions to contract the senior players from year to year. So there was no continuity in any of the squads, but teams would sporadically win trophies with those senior players without guarantees that success could be sustained. The Bulls didn't even have that luxury.

'The problem was exacerbated by the fact that no Super Rugby coach in South Africa, except Gert Smal at the Stormers (2002–2005) and, later, myself had lasted for three years. Domestically, there was no stability in the way professional rugby was managed. If you had money, you could at least buy yourself short-term success, but when I arrived at the Bulls, everything was cut and I was given R8 million with which to make these strategic plans a reality, as opposed to the R15 million or R16 million the other big unions could spend on players.'

That financial inequality would not change immediately either. By 2003 a senior player in Pretoria earned almost three times less than one who played for the country's highest-paying rugby union (see Figure 1).

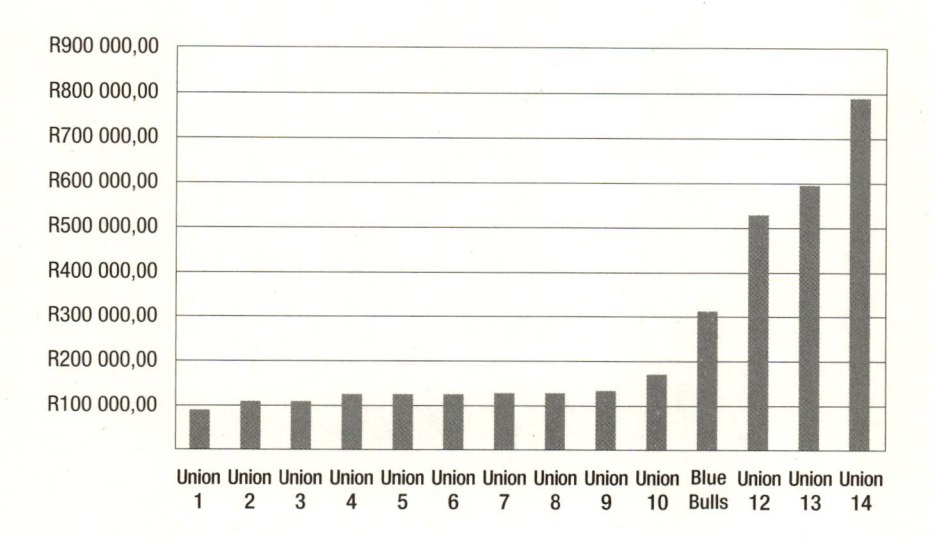

Figure 1: Average salary of a senior player (2003)

Despite the financial constraints, the Blue Bulls lifted the Currie Cup on 1 November 2003 for the second year in succession when they gave the Sharks a 40-19 thrashing at Loftus – and this was one of the early results of a strategy that did not initially focus primarily on players.

Meyer had seen in the SWD what could be achieved with a group of young, zealous players when he and Frans Ludeke took the Eagles as far as the Currie Cup semifinals in 1999. His total player budget was nearly R2 million and with third- and fourth-choice players he finished among the top four in the Currie Cup competition, at a time when all 14 teams still played against each other.

Therefore, if he could manage to end in third and fourth place with third- and fourth-choice players, he would surely be able to finish in the top spot if he had the very best players at his disposal.

'In contrast to other unions, who signed senior players on annual contracts, I decided that with the Bulls' small budget we would bring the best young players in the country to Pretoria on long-term contracts,' said Meyer.

'We couldn't offer them a lot of money, but we had a dream of becoming the best rugby team in the world and I was firmly convinced that we would achieve it in time with those players. The country's top young players simply had to be brought around to our vision and we would be able to make them Boks if they were to stay with us and pursue that dream.'

When Meyer won the Vodacom Cup competition in 2001, his squad of 36 players included 26 youngsters who had played for the Bulls for the first time that year. This transitional competition between junior rugby and the Currie Cup competition was established in 1998. In the first season, the Blue Bulls' win rate was 33.3 per cent; in 1999 it was 50 per cent; and in 2000 it improved to 62 per cent. When Meyer took charge of the team in 2001 and involved the new players, their win percentage shot up to 91.7 per cent. There is an interesting story about their sole defeat, against the Pumas, which will be discussed in Chapter 5.

But talented players alone were not a guarantee for sustained success. Those exceptional players would ultimately become nothing more than an average team unless they were developed, both in terms of their individual sporting talent and as human beings, to meet the demands of professional sport in all its facets. However, at the time in South Africa, all the facets of professional sport were not yet understood.

'To explain it to the appointment committee, I told them a story about a village that needed water to be supplied from a river on its outskirts to a well in the village centre. Two men were awarded tenders for the job.

'The first guy bought five buckets, involved his three eldest sons and ran a line of buckets from the river to the well. He took all the business and everyone made use of his services. Of the second man, however, there was no sign for six months.

'But one day he arrived in the village accompanied by a team of people: an engineer, an architect, a town planner and an accountant. They started laying a pipeline between the river and the well. But that would take another six months. In the meantime, the first man and his sons continued with their business and made all the money. But, then, after a year's work, the second man opened a stopcock for the first time and the water roared as a steady supply was pumped from the river into the well.

'When the first guy saw this, he realised that it spelled trouble. So he bought more buckets and got his wife and youngest child to help them draw water. They had to run more and more to keep up, and worked harder and harder. After a while, the residents began to complain about the quality of the water because the man's buckets were rusting. Six months later, his business collapsed.

'I told the committee that the same principle applied to rugby in the professional era. It is no use trying every single year to buy top players within the budget. The time will come when that will simply no longer be good enough. We need a pipeline within which we can develop junior players to come up through our structures to prevent occasions when we suddenly lose a senior player and have no one to fill his shoes.

'Because we couldn't afford expensive players, we not only needed to recruit the best young players, but also had to create an environment that made it so good to be a Bull that a player wouldn't want to leave if another big union tried to buy him some day. And part of the joy of this environment must be that there are people who really invest in the players' development and well-being – so that they can fulfil their potential and become Springboks.

'So our strategy for the future did not start with players, but with a world-class management team that could assist me to build that pipeline. And when we open that stopcock for the first time – even if it takes us three years to get to that point – no one will be able to catch us.'

For this reason, Meyer asked the board, in the absence of a large budget for players, to at least increase the budget for a management team from R1.5 million to R3 million.

Thereby he partly overcame the financial obstacle. The biggest problem, however, was cultural.

'When I arrived at the Bulls, the under-19 coach hoped that the under-21 coach would mess up so that he could get his job. And the under-21 coach hoped that the Currie Cup coach would fail so that he could get that position. The Currie Cup coach, in turn, had set his sights on the Super

Rugby position. The same culture existed among the players: everyone begrudged anyone else any success – and you could see it in their results.

'That culture would never work in the new structure. One practical reason for this was that we intended playing exactly the same rugby in all of the teams. We would use the same attack, the same defence structures and the same lineout calls. Everything! Hence there needed to be much closer cooperation and synergy between the different teams. In the beginning, I personally picked and signed off those junior sides to ensure that the pipeline was functioning as it should.

'Because we signed young players, I wanted to know that when I brought an 18-year-old guy to Pretoria, I could fast-track him from a junior side to the Vodacom Cup or the Currie Cup at any point, and he would know exactly what was expected of him. It also saves a vast amount of coaching time.

'The other reason concerned a culture in which everyone shares in everyone else's success, and every person and every team are essential parts of the same engine rather than competing entities. Credit is due to everyone. Whenever I appointed a junior coach over the years, I told him that he wouldn't be coaching the Currie Cup side, he wouldn't be coaching the Super Rugby side – he would be our junior coach and he would be incredibly important to us in the capacity in which he had been appointed. He had to teach the new players our culture. He had to teach them how we play at the Bulls. And if the Super Rugby team should win, he would have a part in it and would be just as excited as all of us.

'This was a vital cultural shift at management level that people bought into. The ones who did so were never fired and some of them have now been on the journey with me for more than ten years. They thought long term and understood that they were not appointed to move up, but they knew that they were just as important as the senior coaches. The structures' and top teams' dependence on a sound junior section was emphasised, and this was embraced as such by everyone. Ashley Evert [currently the Springbok sevens side team manager], the late Peter Maimane [technical adviser to the Springboks between 2007 and 2011] and George Bezuidenhout were our first junior coaches. Nico Serfontein [currently national manager of rugby development at schools, clubs and universities] was a later addition. All of them top people. A family culture was created in which even the guy who mowed Loftus's grass was important.'

The principle applicable here was that all pursued a higher goal together – greater than the task that each individual focused on in his immediate environment. Nothing happened in isolation, however. But the vision – to become the most successful rugby team in the world – could only be realised and sustained if every individual gave their undivided dedication to their task. To Meyer, 'buying into' the vision was the crux of the new culture. Therefore all he demanded was dedication, not for people to relinquish long-term personal aspirations for the sake of a greater goal.

This culture was a way of thinking about success and teamwork rather than guidelines aimed at maintaining a rigid hierarchy. As will be discussed, Meyer appointed many people in junior positions who were so good at their job that, in time, they moved up spontaneously to more senior teams and positions.

So, in his presentation to the appointment committee, he offered solutions to two of the Bulls' problems – money and the culture at management level.

His understanding of what management should look like, however, differed fundamentally from the norm at the time: namely, a head coach with only an assistant for forwards and backs.

'In 1995, as a schools' coach, I had wondered what rugby would look like in ten years' time,' he said. 'I read voraciously. I wanted to become the best coach in the world and there's hardly a book on coaching that I haven't read. There weren't any books of that kind in South Africa at the time, but Vince Lombardi of the Green Bay Packers was my role model. By hook or by crook I made sure that I got hold of everything that had been written about him.

'I read about how no one wanted to play for Green Bay and how Lombardi turned it into a successful team. I read about Bill Walsh of the San Francisco 49ers and how seven of the coaches under him eventually also became head coaches. It told me two things: first, that he must have had an incredible management team; and, second, that under Walsh as head coach, they must have grown and developed into people who could become head coaches themselves.

'When I wondered about the future of rugby, I knew that we couldn't carry on in the same way we had up to then – it had been solely about the players. But, in my business model, the management team is the most important element and the players second. Not in terms of their importance as people, but in terms of how the structures and pipeline work. Our second pillar was to recruit and develop the best players in the world, with – number one – a management team that is established on precisely the same principles.

'Before I did my presentation, I had already started applying some of these aspects in 2000 during my first term with the Northern Bulls. And one of the things I saw in American sport was that their management team, in addition to the general coaches, also included specialists. I told Barend that this pipeline was only going to work if we gave specialised and dedicated coaching for things like kicking, defence and attack – something that didn't exist at all in South Africa.'

Meyer then broke away completely from the traditional small management team and represented the way he saw the future by means of an organogram (Figure 2 below).

This model completely changed the role of head coach, who, in the past, would have selected, conditioned and coached a team.

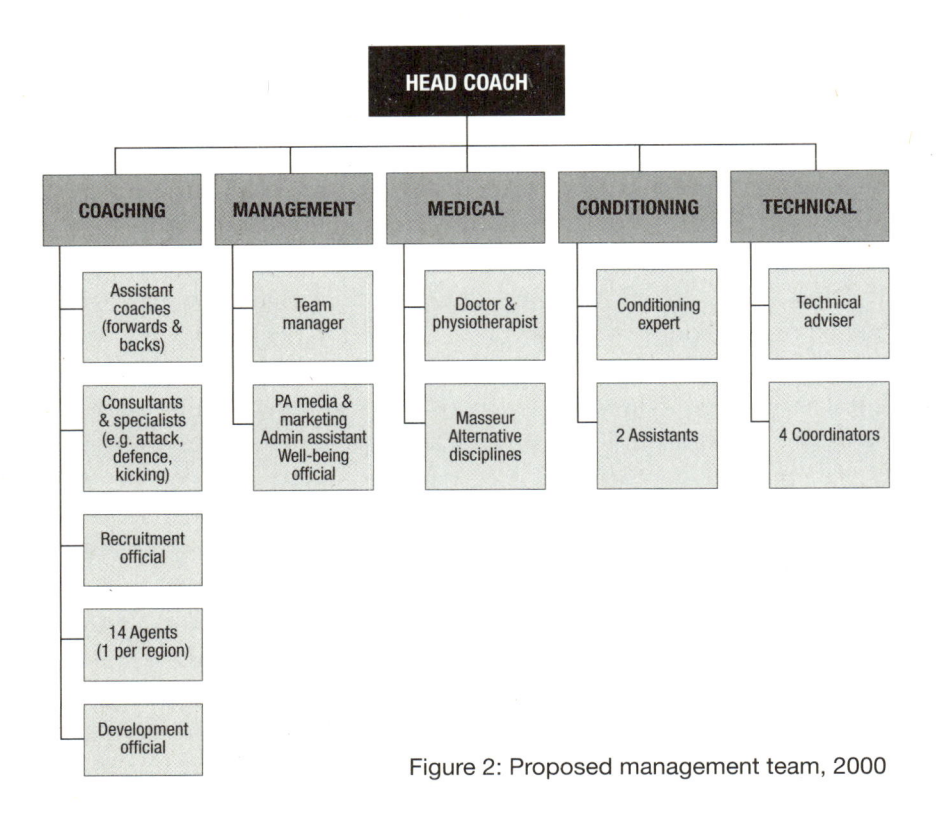

Figure 2: Proposed management team, 2000

'For this structure to work and become successful, the head coach needs people who can complement him and help create and sustain the structure. No one can bring about sustained success in professional sport single-handedly,' Meyer emphasised.

In the new structure, the head coach would function like a chief executive, who exercises overall control over every department, the vision statement, strategic planning, the development of people, time management, and effective internal and external communication. In each of the departments, people would be appointed who were, in Meyer's words, 'absolute experts' in their field.

Van Graan recalled the initial reaction to Meyer's proposal: 'The committee members nearly fell off their chairs when they saw this organogram. They wondered what the hell Heyneke himself would be doing if he wanted to appoint so many other people. I laughed too when he told me that he wanted to get the best available management team in the world. But, in retrospect, that was indeed what he managed to do.'

This plan would never have paid off, however, if Meyer had not succeeded in persuading the Bulls bosses to buy into his vision. Van Graan also made it clear from the outset that he was no technical rugby expert and that he would, therefore, never interfere in Meyer's work.

'My and the board's function in the company is to create the space within which the coach can function and to try to make the resources for that available. You can't be in this position because you think you know more than the coach, or because you want to tell people that you drink beer with the likes of Victor Matfield. It's a business and every guy must know exactly what his role is and see to it that he executes it with absolute dedication,' Van Graan said.

Therefore, at his request, Meyer was allowed to appoint his own management team. Still, effective utilisation of a small player budget and a bigger management team would only mean something if there was harmony among management and the players. Once again, it comes down to culture: 'Game plans, and good coaches and players mean nothing if your culture isn't right,' Meyer explained. 'If you don't fit into my culture, you're out. Everyone's arrows should point in the same direction, otherwise chaos reigns.

'It's like a magnifying glass. If you keep moving it around, you can't focus the energy. But if you keep it still and focus all that energy on one spot, you can set an entire field alight. That's how my culture works.

When I appoint people, the very first thing I try to determine is whether they will fit into that culture and whether they will also pursue the big vision from which we draw our energy. It has happened occasionally that people initially bought into that culture and vision, but in time started moving outside it. Thus I have let a few management members go in my life – even people who had become my friends. Culture is everything – and you're either in or you're out.'

Compared with the Bulls' present-day organogram, the one drawn up in 2000 was a primitive version. The structures have since developed to such an extent that it is impossible to discuss every person and their function.

There are certain individuals who need to be mentioned because they either helped to build the pipeline or serve as proof of how members of a management team, just like Bill Walsh's, thrive in a culture that fosters development, growth and excellence.

Coaching and technical

In 1999 Meyer was appointed as assistant coach of the Springboks under Nick Mallett, an association that had a great influence on Meyer's selection of some of the management staff at the Blue Bulls.

Former Western Province centre Mike Bayly had succeeded Mallett at the end of 1997 as head coach of Boland; thereafter, he coached for a brief spell at Italian club Rovigo. Mallett thought highly of him and, with that reference, Meyer appointed Bayly in 2001 as his backline coach.

Meyer's deputy at the SWD Eagles, Frans Ludeke, was appointed as the Northern Bulls' forwards coach in 2000. He had been due to start working at the Blue Bulls in the same capacity from 2001, but the BBC released him from his contract when the Golden Lions offered him the position as their head coach.

John Williams, later Namibia's national coach, was one of the Bulls' loose forwards at the time and Meyer was of the view that an intelligent person with leadership qualities would be able to coach at professional level. So he appointed Williams as his forwards coach.

Likewise, in 2007 Meyer persuaded former Bok Ricardo Loubscher to coach the Bulls' under-19 backline instead of becoming a player agent, which he was considering because of a lack of career prospects. At the time of writing, Loubscher is the Springboks' backline coach.

In 2000 there was nothing novel about having a forwards and a backline coach. In Meyer's new structure, his two assistant coaches would help him to develop and implement a particular style of play. These two worked not only with the senior sides, but also with all contracted players in order to ensure continuity in the pipeline.

Something that distinguished Meyer, however, from other coaches in that period was his decision to involve specialists. At first he did this only on an occasional basis. He brought in Jonny Wilkinson's kicking coach, Dave Alred, a few times to work with the Bulls' kickers – including, for example, with a young Derick Hougaard.

Chris Anderson, the respected Australian rugby-league coach of, among others, the Melbourne Storm, had already been called upon in 2000 to assist the Northern Bulls with defence. He was the first world-class league specialist to work in South Africa.

'I experimented with a vast number of things at the time,' recounted Meyer. 'I used American football to help us with our planning and technical approach to professional rugby. There were vision specialists that worked with the players. Karate guys. I involved the Special Forces. We broke rugby down into much smaller pieces and skills than had been done up to that point, and studied it in that way.

'But the Americans didn't just bring in these specialists every now and then. The gridiron teams have a guy who focuses solely on attack, and there is a guy who only does defence. This is general practice in professional rugby today, but it was not the case in 2000.'

Unlike the cases of Bayly, Williams and visiting specialists who came and went, Meyer's association with Mallett led to one of the most significant appointments during his tenure at the Bulls and, currently, the Springboks …

John McFarland

'Nick asked me in 1999 to do our technical analysis during the World Cup tournament. This had just started in rugby and technical was not one of my strong suits, but I told Nick that I would get someone to assist us,' Meyer recalled.

NO MAN IS AN ISLAND

'Brendan Venter played for London Irish and he told me about this English guy who coached for them – John McFarland, a former Saracens hooker. So I asked John to help us during the World Cup tournament. He played a huge part in our 44-21 victory against England in the quarterfinal.

'In those days, there was no stats computer software or agencies. I told John I wanted to give each player a document about his direct opponent. He had videos of every single game that those English players had played in the previous 12 months: the Heineken Cup, the Premiership, tests, the works.

'So he recorded a cassette for each guy with all the video clips of his opponent, and we gave each player a cassette that he could study before the game. It was incredibly hard work.

'John assisted me in 2000 with the Northern Bulls and when I was appointed at the Blue Bulls, I brought him in as our very first full-time technical analyst.'

Meyer sent McFarland on various rugby-league courses so that the Bulls no longer needed consultants such as Anderson. For a while, McFarland took charge of their technical work and their defence. Meyer later made other appointments to allow McFarland to focus exclusively on defence.

In the early 2000s, most of the top teams scored the majority of their tries from turnovers. The Bulls' style of play was adapted accordingly. Firstly, like the present day, they played a tactical game with a flyhalf that could get the team into their opponents' half by kicking. With that, possession was usually conceded. However, since most tries resulted from turnovers, it became increasingly important to have defensive structures to force your opponents to make mistakes. Therefore, McFarland transformed from a technical analyst into the very first specialist defence coach in South Africa.

'John then did defence for all our teams – not only the seniors. It would have been useless to us if the under-19 side made use of defence, but the senior teams did something else. I wanted to see from the under-19 level whether a guy was good enough to play at a higher level, and defence is a good yardstick. Even if he first played under-19, under-21 and only then senior rugby, the guy would already have two years' defence in him.

From the outset, therefore, we would have an advantage over teams who needed to teach a player how to defend from scratch every time he started playing at the next level,' Meyer explained.

Uniformity is the norm nowadays, but that wasn't always the case back then. When Rassie Erasmus moved from Free State to Western Province in 2008, he immediately introduced a uniform style of rugby within all of Western Province's professional teams.

The physiotherapist, Jacques Nienaber, went with him to the Stormers, where, like McFarland, he became a defence guru. Since 2010 the Stormers have conceded by far the least amount of tries annually of all Super Rugby teams.

The problem, however, was that the Stormers defended excellently but at the same time, and despite a good deal of overturned possession, scored very few tries. When Meyer was appointed as Springbok coach in 2012, he first approached Allister Coetzee for the position of his assistant coach, but did not hesitate to choose McFarland over Nienaber as his defence specialist.

According to Meyer, good defence should not only be measured in isolation by the number of tries it prevents, but also by the team's ability to score tries thanks to good tackling. In the 2012 Super Rugby competition, the Bulls had conceded the fifth-least number of tries (15 more than the Stormers) by the end of the regular season, but at the conclusion of the competition they were the only team to have scored more than 50 tries.

Taking into consideration the way Meyer wanted to play rugby at the time (and still does today) thrifty defence makes sense only if it is complemented by an effective attack. In the past, the attack was almost fully defined as what the backline does with the ball after the forwards have won it in the set pieces or at the breakdowns.

Although today this is widely regarded as an archaic view, that was not the case in 2000. The man who would define the role of specialist attack coordinator first became involved with the Blue Bulls as a 21-year-old, for a fee of R100 per Sunday.

Johann van Graan

The ball boys at Loftus Versfeld are like a select band of brothers. They are not merely a hastily assembled group of boys in oversized rugby jerseys.

It's not just any knobbly-kneed youngster in white socks: membership is subject to the approval of the stadium manager.

When a ball boy receives his uniform, it is expected of him not only to be fit and to ensure that the hookers always have a ball to feed their lineout, but a Bulls ball boy also decides if and when an opposing hooker may get the ball. Johann van Graan became a member of this club at the age of four.

'At first I was a ball boy at Loftus's B, C and D fields, but at the age of seven I was promoted to the A field. In 1988 I did duty as a ball boy in my first Currie Cup final and in 1994 in my first test. It was South Africa against England, and it was also the day on which I personally met Mr Nelson Mandela. Another highlight for me from those days was when France played against Scotland during the 1995 World Cup tournament. I'll never forget Émile Ntamack's try or the intense look in Philippe Sella's eyes,' Van Graan recalled almost 20 years later.

At the request of the then stadium manager, Johan Kruger, the young Van Graan took over the management of Loftus's ball boys and performed this task until 1998. But when he enrolled in his grandfather's old school, the Afrikaanse Hoër Seunskool (Afrikaans Boys' High School), or Affies, in Pretoria as a 13-year-old, his dreams and focus shifted increasingly to what he really wanted to do.

'My dream was to play for the Blue Bulls and the Springboks some day, and later to coach both those teams,' Van Graan said. However, his teenage years were still a bridge to be crossed between this dream and its envisaged realisation, and, as is the case with most teenagers, his dad had house rules for him. Only two: 'If you sleep over elsewhere, you must make sure that you're home before 06:00 the next morning, otherwise I want to know before 06:00 if you're going to be late. And if you have a girlfriend, you do your smooching here under my roof.'

The young Van Graan had no problem conducting his relationships according to these guidelines. After all, his main relationship was with rugby. He had two video players in his room and he spent hours watching and analysing rugby matches. He would record clips from one cassette onto another so that he could study the game in even finer detail. He was gradually adding substance to his childhood dream for the future.

'I didn't know Johann well,' said Meyer. 'He was always just the guy you bumped into at the rugby. In 2000 and 2001, John and I would sit through weekends and nights analysing matches. But then I simply couldn't get around to everything any longer and so we appointed Johann in 2001 at R100 a day to help John on Sundays with the technical coding. I was requesting more and more statistics from John and I knew that Johann was interested in that. In 2001 he was still a member of the Blue Bulls' under-21 team.'

Van Graan swiftly proved to be a valuable asset and his acumen as an analyst was widely recognised. The Pumas appointed him in 2003; later, he became involved with the Leopards, the SWD Eagles and Affies, in turn, until 2004.

McFarland's focus on defence made it hard for him to do justice to the growing need for even finer technical analysis and statistics at the Bulls. Because Meyer wanted to use him exclusively as his defence specialist, he decided to appoint a technical specialist: in other words, no longer a person who could only capture video clips and code statistics, but someone who was able to interpret those statistics and make strategic and technical recommendations based on their analyses. The Bulls' coach appointed Van Graan as his first technical specialist.

Purely from a rugby perspective, Van Graan gradually became Meyer's right-hand man. When John Williams left at the end of 2004, Pote Human took over his duties as forwards coach, and when Human said farewell to the Bulls at the end of 2007, Van Graan took over those duties.

His most important function, though, was that of specialist attack coordinator. This is a wide-ranging position because – in contrast to the general assumption that a backline coach, by implication, has to be in charge of the attack – it entails the overall coordination of forward and backline play, as is customary in American football.

When Van Graan was in charge of the attack and forwards coaching, Victor Matfield, while he was still a player, was asked to coordinate the lineouts as a building block of the greater attacking strategy. When Matfield first hung up his boots at the end of 2011, he was brought in as a lineout specialist on a part-time basis. He always wanted to coach, but first worked at SuperSport because there were no domestic coaching jobs available.

When Meyer was appointed as the Springbok coach, he approached Van Graan to perform the same duties as he had done for the Bulls up to that point. Matfield was subsequently employed in a permanent capacity as both forwards coach and defence coordinator at the Bulls – a move that perplexed the average Bulls supporter at first.

This indicates that, more than a decade after Meyer had expressed the need for such a specialist during that interview, there were still misconceptions about what attacking play involved.

And yet in 2001 Meyer had brought a 21-year-old student into his structures in the form of Van Graan. He moulded him in the same way as he would a junior player to the point where he earned a Springbok blazer – incidentally, at the same age at which Meyer had first started coaching at national level under Mallett.

Vlok Cilliers

'Vlokkie, if you can drop-kick the ball over the crossbar from here, I'll appoint you permanently,' Heyneke Meyer challenged his part-time kicking coach at the time, Vlok Cilliers.

Meyer and the former Western Province flyhalf were standing at the left-hand corner flag on Loftus Versfeld's B field. Meyer was actually pulling Cilliers's leg, but five years had passed since he first said he was looking for a specialist kicking coach. In the early days, Dave Alred had travelled to Pretoria for a few sessions to coach kicking. In 2004 Cilliers commuted from Bloemfontein three days a week to lend a helping foot.

Place kicks, field kicks, kicks into touch, drop kicks, up-and-unders – all kinds of kicks were becoming more and more important – not only for the flyhalves, but for all backs. For the sake of the pipeline, the Bulls needed a permanent kicking coach to bring young players through the system. By 2004 Derick Hougaard was already dubbed the darling of Loftus, but yet another young flyhalf was coming up through the ranks – Morné Steyn.

Meyer wanted his kicking coach to help with the team's warm-up on match days as well and it was during a conversation about this one day in 2005 that he asked Cilliers to put a drop kick through the posts from the corner flag.

At Loftus B Cilliers did just that. He struck the ball so that it arced from the right foot and turned inwards until it went over the crossbar.

'Vlokkie, I mean it. If you can do that with your left foot too, I'm appointing you on the spot,' said Meyer.

Cilliers positioned himself and repeated with the left foot what he had done moments before with the right. He struck the ball and this time he curved it from left to right until it crossed the bar. He was indeed appointed afterwards, and his partnership with Steyn in particular is noteworthy.

Meyer reckons one should distinguish between Steyn and Hougaard in order to accentuate the value of a specialist kicking coach like Cilliers.

'Derick was a natural kicker, hence he could put any kick through the posts under pressure. It came naturally to him. But Morné didn't do goal kicking for his school, or for the Free State's Craven Week team, or for the Bulls' under-19 or under-21 side. He couldn't kick, but he was one of our flyhalves. One year we had a tour to George and we took a few young guys along. The flyhalves took aim at the posts and if Morné had 12 place kicks that day, he missed probably 10 of them right in front of the posts. But Morné has the most unbelievable work ethic and when he and Vlok started working together, he just persevered and persevered until he became one of the best kickers in the world,' Meyer said about the player who became a Bok in 2009 and clinched the series against the British and Irish Lions with a monumental penalty kick.

Cilliers believes that it took a lot of work to transform Steyn into a kicker: 'Morné was very good at getting a backline going. He was a running flyhalf but a hopeless kicker. Heyneke liked the dimension Morné gave to the Bulls' attack but he often picked Louis Strydom as fullback in the Vodacom Cup so that he could take the place kicks. And when the Bulls were in their own 22-metre area, Louis also moved to flyhalf to take the field kicks. Morné couldn't do it.

'His kicking gradually improved, but Heyneke said it was of no use if Morné only did well in practice sessions. He wanted to see what the guy could do under pressure. And the turning point came on 16 July 2004, when Morné substituted for Derick in a Currie Cup match against the Pumas. That day he slotted in three conversions and a penalty goal, and we won by 33-32. This convinced Heyneke that Morné could become a well-rounded flyhalf who would be able to play under pressure.'

Hougaard left the Bulls in mid-2008 to accompany Meyer to the Leicester Tigers. Steyn took over the kicking baton from him and the Bulls subsequently won two more Super Rugby titles and their fifth Currie Cup of the decade.

'To me, that distinguishes the Bulls from other teams,' Hougaard said. 'There are really a multitude of excellent rugby players in South Africa, but not all of them are capable of winning trophies. When I left the Bulls, Morné took over and they still kept winning trophies.'

However, it required a full-time kicking coach to help Steyn acquire a totally new skill set. Players like Naas Botha and Derick Hougaard have created the impression that kicking is a natural talent. According to Cilliers, though, there are very few truly natural kickers. Said the country's first full-time kicking guru: 'Fortunately, Morné is someone who works incredibly hard and usually performs under pressure. These are the most important qualities of a kicker because, without them, you can't win trophies and you won't be able to acquire a skill in the way that he did.'

'I remember very well how people told us that we overanalyse rugby at the Bulls and that kicks are not that important. But people don't understand what a big part kicking plays in an entire match. They think we only help the players to kick at goal, but kicking is actually about a real understanding of rugby and how a game is put together. That understanding and the ability to make the right decisions under pressure are part of what a kicking coach teaches the players, and Heyneke was the first guy who recognised the value of a permanent kicking specialist and incorporated one in his structures.'

Hougaard was appointed as the Bulls' second specialist kicking coach at the beginning of 2013. He works mainly with the junior players and, in his role as kicking coach, he forms part of the management structure replicated across every Bulls team – whether it is the Super Rugby team, Currie Cup, Vodacom Cup, under-21 or under-19 – each team has exactly the same management structure, with some overlap. Therefore, each has a head coach, a forwards coach, a backline coach, a technical analyst and a specialist for kicking, defence, first phases and attacking play.

Meyer's organogram of 2000 was eventually used as a structural blueprint for all the teams. Although the members of the management team differ, the same 'curriculum' is followed at all the levels.

Medical and conditioning

Flight QF064 to Sydney took off from OR Tambo International Airport at 17:50 on Tuesday 5 March 2013. The Bulls were on their way to Australasia for the overseas leg of their Super Rugby campaign.

Shortly before the players had boarded the red Avis team bus at Loftus Versfeld at 14:00 that afternoon, Wynie Strydom had handed each of the 40 members of the touring party a pocketbook. The initial success of the tour would mostly depend on the players' willingness to take heed of page 38: 'Tips for the long flight'.

Jet lag is a problem that tends to become more severe with each time zone one crosses while travelling in an easterly direction. One's biological clock will be out of sync with the time at the destination, because it will be experiencing daylight and darkness contrary to the daily rhythms to which it has grown accustomed. For South African rugby teams, the travel has always been a much greater factor than for New Zealand and Australian teams, who fly west to come and play here.

To help players avoid the debilitating effects of jet lag, page 38 of the team manager's travel guide read as follows:

NB: THE SECRET IS TO ADJUST AS QUICKLY AS POSSIBLE TO THE TIME DIFFERENCE AND GET BACK INTO YOUR NORMAL RHYTHMS.

- Take along a set of comfortable clothes to wear during the flight.
- Eat supper after take-off in Johannesburg and go to sleep as soon as possible afterwards.
- The doctor will give you a bag with melatonin pills and a sleeping pill. Take melatonin before sleeping during the flight and before you go to bed for the first two nights on the tour.
- The sleeping pill is optional.
- Wear compression stockings during the entire flight.
- Use Locabiotal spray in your nose and throat before take-off and landing, and in the morning and evening for the first week on tour.
- Ask the doctor for a nausea pill (or any other medication) if it should be necessary.
- Stay awake at all costs on the second flight from Sydney to Auckland.
- Until the match on Sunday 10 March, go to bed late (at least after midnight) and try to sleep until at least 13:00 in the afternoon. Our arrangements have been adjusted so as to allow for this sleeping pattern. Therefore we try to keep more or less to South African time during the first week.
- NB to stay awake for the rest of the day during the first two days.

- Take supplements, such as Fear Factor and Vita-thion and/or other multivitamins and minerals, on tour to keep yourself healthy.
- Take long recovery skins to wear on the plane.
- Drink lots of water during the flights.

On that Sunday, the Bulls won their first match of the tour, beating the Auckland Blues 28-21. It was their best game yet that season, against a side that had beaten the Hurricanes and the Crusaders in the previous two weeks 34-20 and 34-15, respectively.

The team doctor, Org Strauss, was responsible for the guidelines. Such small, yet vital, details had come about because Meyer had recommended in 2000 that the Bulls appoint a permanent doctor – which no other union in South Africa had.

Up to that point, teams had a part-time doctor on match days, who took care of injuries on the pitch. 'But Meyertjie was thinking far beyond that when he said he wanted a doctor,' recalled Barend van Graan.

'It's actually frightening when I think of it now, but when a player sustained a serious injury in those days, the coach would ask him after a while how he felt. If the guy replied, "All right, Coach", he started playing again immediately.

'But Heyneke said it was irresponsible to look after people that way. He wanted a permanent team doctor who looked after all players. And if the doctor and the full-time physiotherapist told the coach a player would be out for, say, two weeks or six months, the coach didn't question it. The medical team's word became law when it came to the diagnosis and treatment of injuries.'

Meyer wanted the doctor to do weekly medical examinations and prescribe vaccinations, vitamins and supplements to players and management. The doctor was the one to decide what protective gear and shields players were allowed to use. Meyer had argued in support of this step in his presentation 'because shields will reduce the budget for plasters considerably'.

The team doctor was also responsible for identifying symptoms of overtraining in players on a daily basis by monitoring 'pulse rate, suppleness, the hours and quality of their sleep, appetite, muscle soreness and training drive'.

The doctor would also prescribe a balanced diet in conjunction with the full-time dietician and keep an eye on players' fat percentages together with the fitness expert. Massages, Pilates exercises, swimming, rehabilitation and the management of jet lag were also among the team medic's responsibilities.

Dr Tommy Smook was subsequently appointed as the first full-time rugby doctor in South Africa. He had been Meyer's doctor at the SWD Eagles. As a former Maties flyhalf, Smook had a good understanding of rugby and its demands. In 1999, under him and Meyer, the Eagles became the first professional team in South Africa whose players had medical aid.

When Smook joined the Bulls in a permanent capacity, he performed groundbreaking work as far as the medical care of professional rugby players was concerned. Other unions did not follow the Bulls' example until later. In 2013 the BBC was still the only union in South Africa with two full-time doctors in its employ: Org Strauss for senior teams and Herman Rossouw for juniors.

In addition to a doctor, Meyer also wanted a specialised conditioning team. When he and Phil Pretorius had first joined the SWD in 1997, the players trained only once a day. Under Pretorius, a group of full-time professional players were contracted, who trained three times a day.

Hennie Kriel, who had been involved at the Pretoria rugby club NKP with Pretorius and Meyer, went with the team to George to take charge of the conditioning of the players. As he did with Smook, Meyer subsequently appointed Kriel at the Blue Bulls.

'Hennie and I had come a long way,' Meyer recalled. 'At the SWD, we did *everything*. While I was watering the pitch at night, Hennie would be sewing numbers onto the jerseys for the players. We did everything. And he was incredibly important in what we eventually achieved with the Bulls too.'

Kriel coached South African 400-metre athlete Myrtle Bothma when she ran a world-record time. According to Meyer, his background in speed and gymnasium work was something that the Bulls needed at that stage.

'Hennie had been to the Olympic Games and understood what it took to be successful at the highest level. I appointed him at a time when there were no full-time conditioning coaches in rugby. He became my right-hand man and was instrumental in the creation of the structures and infrastructure that the Bulls have today,' Meyer said.

Barend van Graan points out that from a conditioning viewpoint, their greatest contribution was perhaps not infrastructure but the professional mindset they instilled in the Bulls players. He remarked, 'We had a serious shortcoming at the time: there was a problem with the players' work ethic. Sometimes the senior players would just say that they didn't feel like a captain's run and then they didn't train.

'But I remember a Friday in 2001 when Meyertjie sent the team to the gym after a hard training session, and how Hennie put them through a workout. Well, you have to imagine what went through the bosses' minds – they got the fright of their lives and wanted to fire Heyneke. Because how in hell do you do gym work the Friday afternoon before a match?

'Some of today's players do a gym session on their own the Saturday morning before a match – they've become so used to it that they can't do without it.'

But in 2001 this came as such a shock to some of the officials and senior players that Piet Uys led a delegation to get Van Graan and Meyer sacked.

Meyer attributes the Bulls' successful 2002 Currie Cup season largely to the fact that he and Kriel made the players train 'until they saw purple spots in front of their eyes'. Ditto for 2007 in the Super Rugby competition.

However, by that time Kriel was no longer with the Bulls. Instead, they had a young fitness expert from Tukkies called Basil Carzis – at the time of writing, the Springboks' conditioning coach.

'My plan had always been that the person in Hennie's shoes should have two assistants,' said Meyer. 'And after a while I told Hennie that I wanted to appoint someone for him at the juniors. We approached Tukkies and asked who their best sports-science student was. Everyone immediately said Basil Carzis.'

So Meyer offered him the junior position. Just like Van Graan had under the Englishman McFarland, Carzis (of Afrikaans and Greek heritage) established himself as such an asset that he later became head of the conditioning department.

When Carzis went to the Springboks in 2012 with Meyer, Van Graan, Loubscher and McFarland (among others), André Volsteedt took over from him. Another conditioning coach, Stephen Plummer, now works under Volsteedt and focuses exclusively on the rehabilitation of players. He works closely with Strauss, Rossouw, two full-time physiotherapists and a masseuse.

Not a single member of Meyer's original management team still works for the BBC. The structure, however, was always supposed to be stronger than the individuals, provided that the individuals – whoever they may be – comply with the 'first-pillar' principle that has been pursued from 2000: 'Putting together the best possible management team and developing them further.'

Although Meyer has always been excellent at recruiting and developing capable management members, and letting them come into their own, for the most important appointment of all, luck was on his side when a stranger from nowhere crossed his path.

For both Meyer and the Bulls, that piece of luck – a factor of success that is not often acknowledged frankly as such – was called Ian Schwartz.

Team management

Schwartz's involvement with the Bulls contributed a good deal to Meyer's proposed structure being viewed today as a strategic inflection point. Once again, Abraham Lincoln's decision to persevere with the abolition of slavery is a good example of a strategic inflection point in American history. However, strategic plans require strategic actions if they are to bring about strategic change. And a visionary leader is never single-handedly responsible on a large scale for these actions and the resultant new order.

Lincoln was an outstanding politician and a visionary leader, but the Civil War in his first presidential term was an enormously expensive struggle to wage for the principle of freedom and the preservation of the unity of the United States. The northern states (the Union) funded the war through the imposition of additional taxes. However, these efforts were insufficient because the state was unable to repay its debts and this destroyed the value of the dollar.

When Lincoln stood for re-election in 1864, there was widespread division about the war and his presidency. Too many soldiers had died, the war was too costly, and there was no real reason to believe that the Union would ultimately be its old self again or that the war was a thing of the past.

A turning point came when Lincoln appointed the controversial, yet highly effective, General Ulysses S Grant as commander of the Union forces. Several generals had failed in their attempts to gain the upper hand over the Confederate forces. But Grant won one battle after another, and although he was by no means a well-rounded character, he was a real soldier, a brilliant strategist and someone who got the job done.

In response to the criticism that Grant was far too reckless, Lincoln replied: 'I can't spare this man. He fights.'

The Civil War began in 1861 and Grant was appointed as the commanding general of the Union forces in March 1864. Under him, the war soon gained direction. He fought a bloody campaign, with high casualty rates among his own soldiers. With him at the helm, the Union finally forced the Confederates to surrender on 9 April 1865 and the Civil War came to an end.

Lincoln died just five days later, but his decision to appoint Grant had undoubtedly led to the conclusion of a very expensive and bloody war. Therefore, if a strategic inflection point can be referred to as such when one looks in retrospect at a number of events, Grant had a huge hand in Lincoln's legacy.

Likewise, Ian Schwartz can be referred to as Heyneke Meyer's Ulysses S Grant. At the time of writing, he is the Springboks' team manager, but until the beginning of 2012 he was the BBC's high-performance manager. In short, he was the man who was in charge of the maintenance and development of the five pillars.

A former policeman, Schwartz was chairman of the Bloemfontein police rugby club, the Secretary of the Year of the Free State Rugby Union from 1993 to 1996 and, at the age of 31, the vice president of the Free State Rugby Union from 1997 until his resignation in 1999. When the CEO of the SWD Eagles, Wium Albertyn, retired in early 1999, Schwartz applied for his job. He, Freek Burger and Cupido Cupido were the last three candidates on the shortlist.

'I met Heyneke for the first time during the interviews – in fact, I didn't know who he was when he was part of the panel that interviewed me,' Schwartz said. Meyer was head coach of the Eagles at the time.

'I did the interview, it went well and I returned to my hotel. Later that evening, Heyneke phoned me. He congratulated me on the interview and asked whether we could meet somewhere.

'Heyneke, Hennie Kriel and I then met in town, and he said that the appointment committee wanted me as chief executive. With that assurance, I went home to Bloemfontein.'

In the days after Schwartz's interview, however, an awkwardness arose. His answers had been so spot on that some of the local bosses accused Meyer of having provided Schwartz with the answers beforehand – even though the two had never met before. After a discussion with his wife, Elma, and with Meyer, Schwartz decided not to make himself available for the position any longer and withdrew from the process.

'But Heyneke told me we would still work together some day. When he performed well in 1999 as the Stormers' assistant coach, he was asked to assist Nick Mallett at the Boks. Heyneke then looked for people who could take care of his team in his absence. He asked his players for their views on a good coach and a number of them came up with Frans Ludeke's name. He asked Ludeke to help him out by coaching the Eagles and he asked me to act as team manager for those six months.

'I took unpaid leave and went to George for the Currie Cup campaign. At the same time, I was asked by the president of Free State rugby, Harold Verster, to consider the position of team manager for the Cheetahs. But by then I had already decided to stick with Heyneke. After the Eagles' semifinal match at Ellis Park, I returned to Bloemfontein and for a while I didn't hear anything further from Heyneke.'

When Meyer was appointed as the Blue Bulls' new head coach in August 2000, Wynie Strydom was already a seasoned team manager at Loftus. Because the development of junior players would play such a pivotal role in future, Meyer wanted a manager of junior rugby as well. On 2 November 2000, Schwartz was appointed in that capacity on a two-year contract. He was responsible for the recruitment of young players and served as team manager for the under-19, under-21 and Vodacom Cup sides. In 2004 he was appointed as the BBC's business manager and all contractual matters regarding players and management became his responsibility. The position of high-performance manager was created in 2008, and in that capacity Schwartz managed about 60 per cent of the BBC's total budget of approximately R90 million.

NO MAN IS AN ISLAND

Barend van Graan recalled that unusual decision to appoint a manager for junior rugby, 'Ian had to prove himself – it was a new position. But, boy, did that policeman entrench himself here!'

Two things in particular stand out above the rest of his virtues. Firstly, Schwartz was the man who noticed the details in Meyer's big plans and helped to realise them. Their relationship can be compared to that between an entrepreneur and his business manager. Schwartz had an exceptional understanding of Meyer's strengths and weaknesses, and he could complement them better than anyone else.

It was interesting to hear in the interviews for this book that they did not frequent each other's houses. Yet a brotherly understanding and incredible mutual respect existed between these two colleagues, which allowed Meyer to dream big because he knew that Schwartz would help him turn that dream into reality.

Schwartz's second great virtue was his ability to identify players and sell the Bulls' vision of world domination to players and their parents without dangling large sums of money before them.

'Ian is a masterly negotiator. Masterly. I don't know anyone else who can do a deal with integrity in the way that he can,' Van Graan stated.

His skill as a negotiator was a vital component of the Bulls' ability to realise the second pillar: 'To recruit, retain and develop the most talented players.' In 2003, for example, he contracted Pierre Spies at just R3 500 per month when he was not selected for either the South African Schools team or the under-18 Academy team. Spies was also not included in the then national Green Squad for the 100 most promising under-18 players in the country. A decade later, he was the Bulls' most highly paid player.

Schwartz's presence underlines the reason why a world-class management team was the first pillar. And that, according to Van Graan, represents Meyer's biggest legacy: 'When Frans was appointed in Heyneke's place at the end of 2007, his very first meeting with our players took place at our training camp in George. While he was driving there, people phoned him and told him he was off his rocker to coach this team after they had just won the Super 14. He was putting himself under too much pressure.

'But Frans came in from outside and he was warmly received by a management team that looked after him. People like Ian Schwartz, Pote Human, Wynie Strydom, Basil Carzis, John McFarland and Johann.

'For three, four months afterwards, Frans stayed up till three in the morning and studied the Bulls' rugby, structures and culture, while that world-class management team helped coach the guys. Heyneke's principle was always that you should appoint better guys than yourself and that those specialists would make life easier for you. And they were the people who received Frans.

'Initially I was frightened out of my wits when we lost seven of our first nine Super Rugby matches in 2008. I wondered what we were going to do without Heyneke. But then the players, Frans and the management team rallied and made 2009 the most successful year in our history. We became the only South African team yet that managed to win both the Currie Cup and Super Rugby trophies in one year.

'We wouldn't have been able to do it without Frans. He gives his own dynamic to the Bulls. But we also wouldn't have been able to do it without that management team who gave him time to find his feet before he guided the Bulls to greater heights.

'And to me, that is the crux of what Meyertjie had foreseen as far back as 2000. It was visionary to shift the focus from players to management. With that, he completely changed the playing field with regard to player management. It was groundbreaking work in rugby – not only at the Blue Bulls, but also elsewhere in South Africa and across the world. Nowadays, our core business is the development of human capital, and Heyneke succeeded in doing that by getting the best from his management team and the players. It led to success on the pitch and rekindled enthusiasm and passion for Blue Bulls rugby among supporters. And the irony is that people laughed at us at first when Meyertjie arrived at other stadiums with that big management team. Today everyone has management teams like that.'

HEYNEKE MEYER
AND IAN SCHWARTZ

CHAPTER 4

The dream merchant

'There is no end point to excellence and no final destination for those who crave sustainable success in sport. Winning means much more than just doing it once.'
– Wayne Goldsmith

It was touch-and-go, but in 2002 Heyneke Meyer was nearly fired from his head-coach positions at both the Bulls and the Blue Bulls. In 2001, when Meyer worked with the Blue Bulls only, Phil Pretorius had had a poor Super Rugby season with the Bulls. So Meyer was persuaded, against his better judgement, to coach the team again in 2002, although he would have preferred to devote his full attention to a group of young Blue Bulls. The dilemma was that a new way of thinking about professional rugby was taking root at the Blue Bulls, but the Bulls were still the decrepit and chaotic regional side of the past. It was a mountain to climb for any coach. Meyer's Bulls ended up losing all of their 11 matches in 2002. And on 24 May 2002, the day before the Super Rugby final between the Crusaders and the Brumbies, he was 'chased away' for the second time.

The Bulls franchise and the Blue Bulls are different business entities (albeit a distinction that is made only on paper nowadays), but after that disastrous Super Rugby season some of the then administrators at the Blue Bulls wanted to fire Meyer immediately, halfway through his three-year contract with the BBC. Meyer recalled: 'I remember that day as if it happened yesterday. I stood at my wife's hospital bed. She had cancer. My father-in-law was in the ward next door after he had undergone major heart surgery. I had just been fired from a job I didn't want in the first place and, on top of that, some board members and some of the senior players no longer wanted me at the Blue Bulls either. I knew that we were on the right track. And I remember telling Wynie Strydom that while I didn't care about myself, I had no idea what would become of my wife if I were to be fired from the Blue Bulls as well. I wouldn't have been able to pay for her treatment, and if something had to happen to her, I would be unable to continue coaching. We had three small children, and the youngest was then only six months old. It was a very difficult time.'

What saved him, among other things, was one of his own creations – a big management team. If the Blue Bulls were to have fired Meyer, they would probably have had to compensate not only him, but also his 12 management members for the remaining year and a half of their contracts, and they did not have a budget that would have allowed for those payouts.

He was still on thin ice, however, and on 7 September of that year it seemed as if the ice would crack on the very field where Meyer had made a name for himself – Outeniqua Park, in George.

'That Currie Cup match just had to finish, because we weren't going to win it. We were pathetic and the SWD were good,' said Meyer. 'Derick Hougaard was on the bench. He was 19 years old, and I thought I might as well send him on now. We were awarded a penalty in the final minutes. But instead of going for the posts or the touchline, Derick tapped the ball, scored a try in the corner and converted it. We won by 18 points to 13.

'Shortly after I met him for the first time, I told Derick I believed in what the German philosopher Arthur Schopenhauer had said: "Talent hits a target no one else can hit; genius hits a target no one else can see." I was convinced that Derick fell in the latter category, and he also proved it in the games after that one in George, when he was the man of the match in, among others, the semifinal and the final. We won that Currie Cup final at Ellis Park 31-7, with Derick contributing 26 points. While he certainly cannot get all the credit for that cup, I believe that tap and go at Outeniqua Park was a critical moment that made the success in the subsequent months and years possible.'

That Currie Cup was the first of five won by the Blue Bulls between 2002 and 2009. It would be a safe guess that the Blue Bulls – and, later, the Bulls – would not have achieved their subsequent success had Meyer been shown the door at Loftus in 2002. If he had been fired, however, it would have been a common phenomenon in what Australian sport performance and coaching guru Wayne Goldsmith calls the 'performance cycle'. According to Goldsmith, the fortunes of a professional team or organisation can be explained in five stages:

- **Stage 1:** Non-competitive – The organisation is failing to perform and struggling to survive.

- **Stage 2:** Striving for success – A passionate person and/or motivated team ignites the desire to succeed and inspires the organisation to strive for success. The acceleration of progress comes from embracing change and learning, and through the commitment to turn learning into action.
- **Stage 3:** The right culture – The right people and the right environment are in place, and the opportunity has been created for the club to be successful.
- **Stage 4:** Success – The organisation gets to the top but then loses momentum by ceasing to change and learn at the same rate. They adopt a 'secret formula' mentality, i.e. 'We know what it takes to win, therefore all we have to do is repeat what we did last year and we will keep winning.' In the meantime, the competition is accelerating their learning and enhancing their performance, determined to become the next number one.
- **Stage 5:** The fall – Things start to fail. Management and staff get sacked, reviews, reviews and more reviews are commissioned, finally the board is overthrown, there is public brawling and the organisation is at the brink of collapsing altogether ... And we are back at stage one again.[7]

If Meyer and company had been sacked, the Blue Bulls would have found themselves back at stage 1. According to Goldsmith, this cycle is shockingly common in professional sport – one that keeps repeating itself. The mind-boggling thing is that success is generally defined by that short-term triumph in stage 4: one trophy, one good season, one crackerjack competition.

Goldsmith says that true success cannot be defined in that way because there is a good chance that luck may be a material factor in once-off success – as Michael Mauboussin has also pointed out. In Goldsmith's view, sustained success – that ability to stay competitive year after year – comes from good planning, good management, a good vision and hard work, and he reckons *that* is the real goal that should be pursued.

Goldsmith calls this ability to sustain success 'high-performance sport'. And it was in his capacity as high-performance manager, among others, that Ian Schwartz played a significant part in the Blue Bulls' decade of sustained success from 2001 onwards.

In the partnership between Schwartz and Meyer, the latter had the vision of what the Bulls could become – the most successful rugby team in the world. With that vision, Meyer put together a management team that helped him build the structures and the player pipeline that could ultimately make that dream a reality – in other words, the first pillar (putting together the best available management team and developing them further).

Schwartz, an administrator in the true sense of the word, used Meyer's vision as a blueprint for the day-to-day maintenance of those structures and that pipeline. The player pipeline is mentioned separately from the rest of the structures because Schwartz was at first only responsible for the identification, recruitment and contracting of junior players. Then, from 2004, his responsibility increased considerably, and he was put in charge of about 60 per cent of the BBC's budget. This involved the day-to-day management of high-performance sport, as Goldsmith defines it.

Schwartz's contribution should therefore be discussed in two parts: firstly, as high-performance manager and, secondly, as talent spotter without equal. He was the man who made the player pipeline work with his own distinctive touch.

The high-performance manager

'Sustainable success is the reward for successful structures. Successful structures mean that the right people are appointed in the right positions and that everyone strives for a common goal,' explains Schwartz, thereby giving an insight into the many different reins that the high-performance manager has to hold together.

'Winning trophies year after year is not only about coaching: it's about the leader, it's about the culture, it's about the player pipeline, conditioning, rehabilitation, medical care, specialist training – and then obviously the right players, who have to be improved and be exposed to the different levels of rugby at the best and right time for them as players.

'Furthermore, sustainable success means that the decision makers have to trust those appointments and that they have to understand that both teams want to win when there is a scoreboard involved. They have to understand that you will lose too, and that continuity is absolutely vital to future success. They have to understand that someone was appointed for a specific reason and hasn't suddenly become a weaker, or a bad, coach. But without your structures, the right people and the right culture, you cannot be sustainably successful. It is of paramount importance to make absolutely sure before any appointment or contract is made that everyone buys into the structures and culture. Everyone must face in the same direction, otherwise sustainable success is not possible.'

Like Goldsmith, Schwartz believes that sport works in cycles and that it is normal for a team to excel at times and sometimes to fare less well. Even a consistently successful team goes through performance cycles that vary in standard.

'But that doesn't mean it's necessary to start from scratch over again. Not when your management team changes and, with the Bulls' pipeline model, not when senior players leave. The secret is to maintain your vision and structures with good planning. You have to anticipate what the future will hold and plan accordingly,' reckons Schwartz.

In this regard, players pose different kinds of challenges from those one encounters in a management team. One of the reasons is that the turnover of playing staff is much higher than that of management. In a healthy working environment, you don't regularly have new management staff. Managing players, however, is a considerably more intensive task because factors such as age, injuries, financial considerations, career prospects and the relatively short period that a player can play professional rugby all have a daily and significant influence on how a player pipeline needs to be maintained. Furthermore, the value of the euro, the pound and the yen has an increasing impact on South African players' career choices every year, with players transferring to overseas clubs. All of these factors inevitably influence the way in which players are developed, recruited and managed.

Therefore, short- and long-term planning are needed – planning that requires an in-depth understanding of performance cycles. Without that understanding, you don't know what you need to plan for and when to do so. Take the example of Victor Matfield. As soon as he informed the Bulls of his intention to retire at the end of 2011, Schwartz brought back lock Juandré Kruger at the end of 2010 for a second stint at Loftus. He was in England at the time, playing for the Northampton Saints. Hence he was able to play under Matfield for a whole year and learn from him before Matfield retired. Although Kruger was not expected to have acquired the same experience as Matfield by the time he had to replace him as the Bulls' top No 5 lock, he was brought in early into an environment where he could learn and develop his skills so that

Matfield's eventual departure would have less of an impact on the team's ability to keep performing.

The principle exemplified here is that a promising player becomes the best by learning from the best, and that that player learns the most by being in the same structure as his 'teacher' or predecessor.

In their first years at the Bulls, however, Meyer and his management team did not allow themselves the luxury of letting new players learn from seasoned stalwarts. There were financial and cultural reasons for this. (The latter will be discussed in the next chapter.) Meyer decided to let a number of the Blue Bulls' Springboks go, along with some other players. He wanted to create leeway in his budget to sign young players with whom he could venture into the future together, as he had done earlier at the SWD.

He and Schwartz had already adopted a cyclical planning model with which they tried to gauge a team's development, achievements and possible obstacles. The model, which had been part of Meyer's original interview presentation in 2000, consisted of the four quadrants of the matrix shown in Figure 3.

'Over time, supply and demand determine what your needs are in specific positions, and this requires planning. It is just as important, however, to be constantly aware of where the entire team is on this matrix,' explained Schwartz.

'We had heard that some of the players in the past would simply inform the coach that they couldn't be present at a training session because they had to attend, for example, a golf day hosted by one of their sponsors. This attitude represents the fourth quadrant. With good planning, you can make sure your team and players never end up there.

'Players like that were let go when Heyneke was appointed head coach of the Blue Bulls. This did not apply in all cases, however. Financial considerations also played a huge part, and when it comes to contracting it is vital to do it without emotion.

'Heyneke removed all emotion from his decisions and let all the senior players go except Joost van der Westhuizen, Piet Boer, Hannes Venter, Schutte Bekker, Jannie Brooks, Pierre Ribbens and Danie van Schalkwyk. We didn't give contracts to Ruben Kruger, Os du Randt, Naka Drotské, Derick Grobbelaar, Casper Steyn, Marius Goosen or

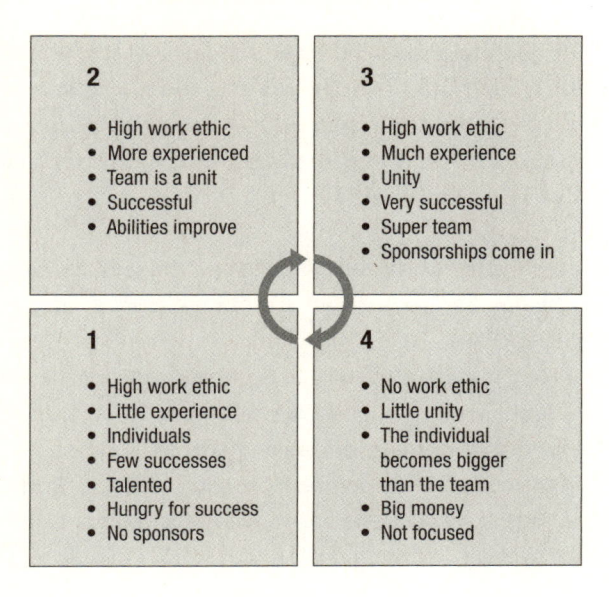

2 • High work ethic • More experienced • Team is a unit • Successful • Abilities improve	**3** • High work ethic • Much experience • Unity • Very successful • Super team • Sponsorships come in
1 • High work ethic • Little experience • Individuals • Few successes • Talented • Hungry for success • No sponsors	**4** • No work ethic • Little unity • The individual becomes bigger than the team • Big money • Not focused

Figure 3: Cyclical planning model with four quadrants

Franco Smith. Heyneke didn't even sign Jacques Olivier, despite Jacques's mother being his secretary. He couldn't afford them, and with the budget we had at our disposal, we had to make a fresh start,' Schwartz recalled.

They then took control of the structures and the cycle, which enabled them to work in the direction of the third quadrant and, when necessary, to let players go before they could become problem areas in a healthy team. Meyer wielded those pruning shears at the end of 2000 and again at the end of 2010 and 2011.

Schwartz used this matrix for a long time and then later started subscribing to yet another of Goldsmith's high-performance models, which corresponds to a large extent with the performance cycle: the performance clock. This is a very instructive model for analysing the Bulls' decade of success from a high-performance viewpoint.

The performance cycle, as discussed earlier, applies to teams that plan poorly, perform well sporadically and struggle for periods that are longer than their successful periods. The performance clock is more detailed than the cycle model, and for Schwartz this timepiece was a useful tool for monitoring both the Bulls' success and its attendant risks, so that the less successful periods could become considerably shorter than the good ones. This clock starts at 10:00.

- **10:00** The team is hungry for success and changing rapidly. It is accelerating its rate of change by learning fast and by being innovative, creative and committed to success.
- **11:00** The team is close to its best. It is playing consistently well; it reaches finals and is continuing to strive for success. Most importantly, it has established a culture that encourages and enables success.
- **12:00** The team wins a top competition, such as Super Rugby or a World Cup tournament. It reaches the top of the ladder and is at the peak of its performance cycle.

It often happens – but not always – that by 12:00, when a team is at its very best, it stops doing many of the things it was doing to make it successful.

- **13:00** The team stops being creative and open-minded. It starts believing that its is the only way and that it has the infallible secret formula for success. This is the beginning of disaster.

Goldsmith says about this phase: 'The teams who have to make the greatest commitment to change and improvement are the ones who are successful. Why? Because your resistance to change is greatest when you believe you have all the answers and that's why most teams fail to repeat success. So, what happens? The team starts losing.'[8]

- **14:00–15:00** The coach gets sacked. The club starts spending money on new players, new equipment and new coaches in a frantic attempt to stop the decline in performance. But the team keeps losing. It finds itself in a promotion-or-relegation situation and gets relegated to the next league.
- **16:00–17:00** The chief executive and management get sacked. The organisation is in disarray.
- **18:00** The team cannot win a single game. The fans and the sponsors have deserted it. It appears that the team may never experience success again.

BUT THEN ...
- **19:00** Someone decides things have to change. They put together a plan, and find some people and money to make it happen.
- **20:00–21:00** People start believing that things can change. There are new players, new coaches, new staff, new ideas. There is a spirit of enthusiasm, energy and passion in the club.
- **22:00–23:00** The cycle is complete and the team can look forward to a short period of success as their performance cycle is at its peak once more.

'The reality for most sporting teams is that they spend one or two seasons at most between 10:00 and 12:00 and then often spend many years between 13:00 and 18:00,' says Goldsmith. 'And for no reason! There is no reason for sporting organisations to spend years at the bottom of competitions.'[9]

According to Schwartz, in 2008 the Bulls' clock came close to 12:30, but in the end they managed to avert a 13:00 collapse. A few months before, in 2007, they had become the first South African franchise to win the Super Rugby competition. Yet the Bulls finished the 2008 season in the tenth spot – in the eyes of external and also some internal observers, not a good testimonial for sustainable success. It was Frans Ludeke's first season as head coach of the Bulls, and many observers attributed their success up to that point to Meyer and foresaw a deep decline at Loftus.

'But I was part of the leadership team with Frans at the time, and I can tell you exactly what happened. There were changes in leadership. Frans was appointed only at a very late stage, and Pieter Rossouw joined the team as backline coach a week before the start of the 2008 Super Rugby season. That's all that happened,' said Schwartz.

'Any company goes through a minor slump when the leadership changes, and in 2008 the old head coach and two of his assistant coaches were no longer there – Heyneke, Pote Human and Todd Louden.

'Besides, our leadership group among the players had changed. Victor Matfield went to France for six months. Gary Botha joined Harlequins. Johan Roets retired, and it had also been Derick Hougaard's last season with team. Anton Leonard – a former captain and a brilliant and successful leader – was also still part of the team in 2007. In 2008 Fourie du Preez took over the captaincy. Those things change the dynamics of a team and time is required for them to adjust.

'Suddenly, the core of our leadership group was gone. This was a normal event, but the structures were still in place. They had to keep serving as our compass, our guidelines. And we simply had to maintain and keep improving them. A few other things happened off the field that might have had an influence on the team's performance, but 99 per cent of all defeats and setbacks are explained by providing excuses – something we were not prepared to resort to. It is well known that anything off the field can influence performance. That influence can be either positive or negative. I prefer to see only the positive,' Schwartz explained.

The negative influences included issues such as John Mametsa expressing his view in an interview with the *Pretoria News* that senior white players had received preferential treatment at the Bulls' training camp in George. And Bakkies Botha was involved in a court case against the BBC about a contract he had signed with Toulon.

Matfield writes in his autobiography, *Victor: My Journey*, that Ludeke put his foot down about this kind of thing shortly after his arrival at the Bulls:

> But by then, Frans had had enough. He called us all together and made it clear that he would no longer tolerate any distractions. 'This team has certain principles and values according to which we must behave and act,' he said. 'You must decide as individuals whether you want to be part of the team. If you don't want to be part of the team, take your things and leave. We can't afford to make a big deal about every little issue that comes up.' It was the first time Frans had given us such a serious and straight talk. The players quickly realised that they couldn't just do what suited them.[10]

The danger existed that these matters would put the Bulls off their stroke. But that did not happen. In 2009 they won both the Currie Cup and the Super Rugby trophy, and in 2010 they defended the Super Rugby title successfully.

Schwartz attributed this to a number of things: 'Although we, understandably, went through a small dip, our structures were established. We were also still in that cycle of success, and there was no reason for the team to suddenly experience a lengthy downward curve in terms of performance. The new leadership bought into the structures and the continuation of our vision. And, most importantly, a culture of success existed. I never got a sense that the ship was sinking. In fact, I knew that success was just around the corner.'

So, good planning is what ultimately enables success. But the preservation and awareness of a healthy culture are essential for sustaining the pursuit of a vision and of success on a day-to-day basis.

Goldsmith encapsulates this by saying that there are only three things that can hold a team back from sustained success: a lack of leadership, a lack of creativity and an abundance of arrogance. Thanks to the presence of good leadership at the Bulls, that abundance of arrogance was nipped in the bud before it could cause the BBC to slide into those dark hours on the performance clock.

Among his other duties, the high-performance boss of the Bulls manages the day-to-day rugby business activities that provide for that sustained success. Hence the position necessitates a good deal of planning. What this meant predominantly in Schwartz's case was that he made plans, recruited players, performed all contracting work and handled all 'rugby-related issues outside of the four chalk lines'. He also maintained the relationship between the amateur wing (the Blue Bulls Rugby Union) and the BBC with regard to certain services made available to the union by the company. As a substructure of the player pipeline, the BBC under Schwartz, for instance, took over the management and development of the provincial school teams from the amateur wing, unlike other rugby unions.

But high-performance sport à la Goldsmith involves much more than merely a structured business approach to sport. Sustained success demands a team effort (as opposed to chaos) that rests on pillars, which, in turn, are anchored by a healthy culture.

The Bulls' culture centres on five core tenets: trust, family, willingness to learn, work ethic and respect.

The willingness to learn is the creativity that Goldsmith refers to as one of the three elements that have to be present if you are to sidestep volatility. To avoid that volatility – the dark hours between 13:00 and 18:00 – the Bulls adopted the *kaizen* philosophy as an integral part of their culture. *Kaizen* is a Japanese philosophy based on the assumption or mindset of a commitment to ongoing, continuous improvement and changing for the better.

The *kaizen* principle cannot be applied in an environment where arrogance and big egos dominate or even just taint the culture. That is why the culture needs to be emphasised regularly, as Ludeke did in 2008 when he lambasted the team for all their 'sideshows'.

'My focus for that first year was to get a real grasp of what made the Bulls successful,' Ludeke said. 'And by then I had known Heyneke since 1999 and knew how important culture is to him. He's like a brother to me, and I understood that that culture was one of innovative thinking. Therefore we had to keep to the principles that had made the Bulls successful, and to me as a coach and a leader it also meant that I would continuously have to make small changes that would enable the Bulls to remain a world-class sports brand.'

To improve continuously, you therefore have to be flexible and receptive to change. In rugby terms, this requires a profound awareness of your strengths, your weaknesses and your environment, as well as knowledge of the market (players) in which you find yourself. *Kaizen* also demands regular and honest self-examination. A clear distinction is made between sustainability and merely maintaining the status quo.

According to Goldsmith, too, sustainable success is built on a *kaizen* culture. This is what Schwartz, besides his day-to-day tasks, also 'managed' at the Bulls in his unobtrusive way – continuous development, renewal and improvement of the five pillars. So, if high-performance sport is measured by continuous success, Schwartz, albeit as part of a greater management team, discharged his high-performance duties outside of the chalk lines extremely well.

At the time of writing, the Blue Bulls and the Bulls combined have participated in 63 competitions since 2001 (see Table 1). These include the Super Rugby teams of Phil Pretorius (2001) and Rudy Joubert (2003, 2004). After 2002, Meyer coached the Bulls again from 2005 to 2007. These Bulls teams played in the finals of 37 of those 63 competitions. Of these matches, they won 20 and drew 2. They were also involved in 13 semifinals and one quarterfinal, which they lost. Therefore, over 13 years and in 63 competitions, the Bulls failed

	Super Rugby		Currie Cup		Vodacom		U21/U20*		U19	
	Advance	Result	Advance	Result	Advance	Result	Advance	Result	Advance	Result
2001	12th	12th	6th	6th	Final	WIN	½	Lose	½	Lose
2002	12th	12th	Final	WIN	Final	Lose	Final	Draw	2nd	2nd
2003	6th	6th	Final	WIN	Final	Lose	Final*	WIN	*	*
2004	6th	6th	Final	WIN	Final	Lose	Final*	WIN	*	*
2005	½	Lose	Final	Lose	½	Lose	Final	WIN	Final	WIN
2006	½	Lose	Final	Draw	3rd	3rd	Final	WIN	Final	WIN
2007	Final	WIN	½	Lose	Final	Lose	Final	Lose	Final	Lose
2008	10th	10th	Final	Lose	Final	WIN	Final	WIN	5th	5th
2009	Final	WIN	Final	WIN	Final	Lose	½	Lose	½	Lose
2010	Final	WIN	½	Lose	Final	WIN	Final	Lose	Final	Lose
2011	7th	7th	5th	5th	Final	Lose	Final	WIN	Final	Lose
2012	¼	Lose	½	Lose	½	Lose	Final	WIN	Final	Lose
2013	½	Lose	5th	5th	½	Lose	Final	Lose	Final	WIN

Note: * indicates when an under-20 side played

Table 1: Bulls' domination since 2001

to reach the play-off rounds only 11 times. In 2002 the under-19 championship was decided on competition points, hence without a play-off match or a final.

Figure 4 clearly shows how the Blue Bulls and the Bulls have dominated domestic senior rugby since 2002.

THE DREAM MERCHANT

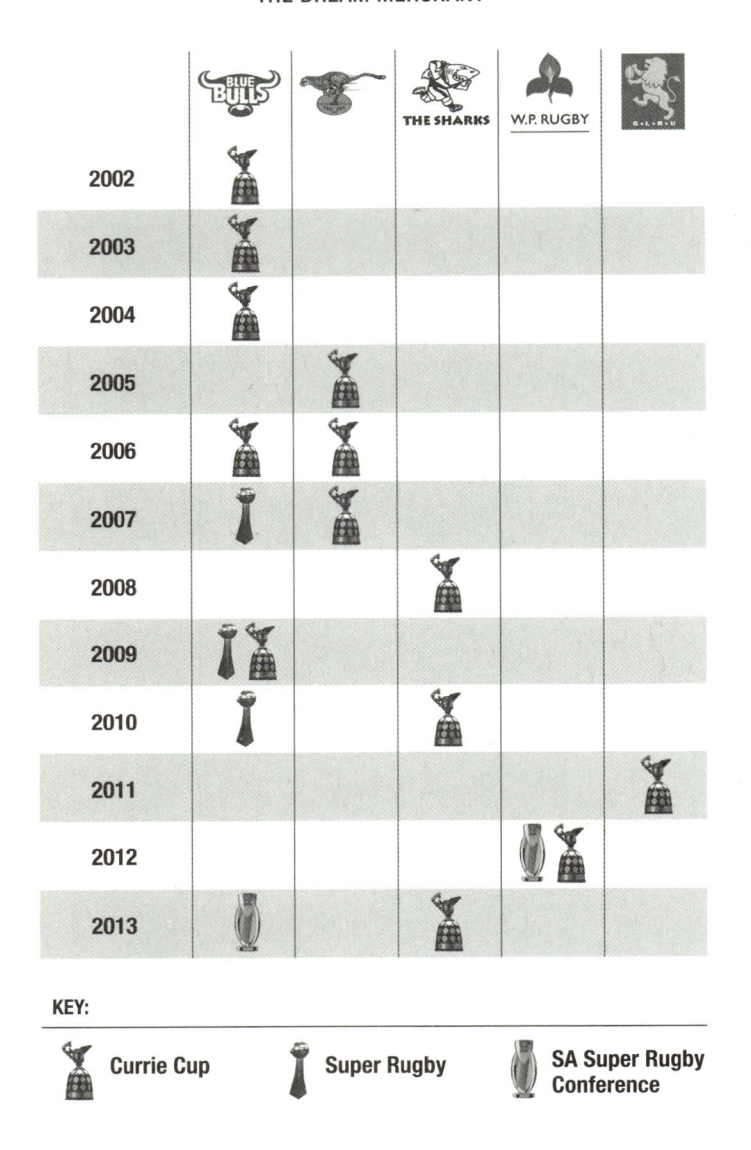

Figure 4: Blue Bulls' and Bulls' domination of domestic senior rugby since 2002 (Design: Jaco Grobbelaar, Grafika24)

In various capacities, Schwartz had been directly involved in 53 of those 63 competition sides and in 32 of the 37 finals. He left the employ of the BBC after the 2012 Super Rugby season. During his 12 years with the Bulls, the under-19 team was always particularly close to his heart because those players were the rough diamonds he had persuaded as schoolboys to start their rugby career at the Bulls.

Since 2001, however, the under-19 team has won only three of its seven finals. Schwartz reckons that this should be understood within the context of the Bulls' player pipeline: 'I believe the under-19 coach has the toughest job of all because he gets a group of boys who were still playing unstructured schoolboy rugby a few months previously. The Bulls play in a highly structured way, and it is the responsibility of that coach to familiarise the newcomers with the Bulls' style of rugby. That's why Heyneke always wanted an incredibly good coach *and* mentor at the under-19 level. By the time those juniors play in a final in their first year as professional players, they're still learning how the Bulls play.

'Once they reach the under-21 level, however, no one has equalled the Blue Bulls over the years. The under-21s (two years as an under-20 team) played in 11 finals, of which they won 7 and drew 1. This illustrates the interplay between a world-class management team and talented players who are developed in a pipeline model,' said Schwartz.

Of all his merits, Schwartz's ability to maintain that pipeline with exactly the right players was probably his greatest contribution to the Bulls' success.

The dream merchant

'A person must be able to commit himself to something greater than what he is achieving at that moment. He must have a dream,' said Schwartz, describing his first job at the Blue Bulls. 'The Bulls' pipeline would only work if the players who had to come up from the bottom could aspire to reach the top. And what Heyneke wanted was that those players should not only aspire to reach the top, but also be good enough to get to the pinnacle of the player pyramid – to become Boks and to realise that great dream of becoming the best rugby team in the world. It was my job to ensure that we got those players into our structures. My way was always based on integrity. I never bought a player with a suitcase of money. What I did instead was to sell him a dream.'

But players like that do not just appear out of the blue, and they certainly were not flocking to Loftus of their own accord when Schwartz started this job of recruiting players. Western Province won the Currie Cup in 2000 and 2001, and, to make matters worse, after Mr Price pulled out, the Bulls had no sponsor. This was painfully obvious when they won the Vodacom Cup competition in 2001. The daisy was still displayed on the left on the players' jerseys, but at the front, where a sponsor's name would customarily appear in the middle, there was now a Blue Bulls emblem to cosmetically conceal the absence of a financial partner.

In this department too – the second pillar of Meyer's structure (recruiting, retaining and developing the most talented players) – the principle applied that you first have to sharpen your axe before you cut down a tree. The Bulls laid the groundwork by firstly creating a recruitment structure with which they wanted to cream off the most talented South African rugby players.

Schwartz set up a countrywide informal network of 'informants', which he described as follows:

'My scouting network consisted of teachers or rugby people from across the country whom I had come to know over the years as guys who could spot talent. There is no difference between good selectors and good talent scouts, because both have to know the game, they have to understand the person and they need to have the ability to identify a talented player before anyone else does. These people became my team. You can seldom pride yourself on having recruited a player on your own: it's a team effort, and I trusted my network like family to notify me of the best young players in South Africa. For instance, there were players like Jan Serfontein, who was so good as a 15-year-old that by 2008 his talent was already obvious to all. In such a case, my job was to negotiate better than anyone else. Jan was in grade 9 at Grey High School, Port Elizabeth, when we entered into an agreement with him and his parents to sign a contract with him for the Bulls in a few years' time.

'Jan was spotted for the first time as a grade-9 learner playing in a grade-10 team at the under-16 Grant Khomo Week in 2008. On the other hand, I never saw Wynand Olivier, for example, playing at school level. He was injured in his matric year and was therefore not included in the Blue Bulls' Craven Week team. He was spotted in the informant network and we signed him up. Before Wynand left the Bulls in 2013, he had played in 37 tests, won a World Cup and was the inside centre in all three of the Bulls' teams that won Super Rugby titles.

'I mention these two players in particular because Wynand is ten years older than Jan, but Jan eventually made Wynand's No 12 jersey his own. Jan played his first Super Rugby season during Wynand's last. I never had any influence on whether or not a coach picked a player and, in any case, I had already left the Bulls when Jan was in his second year. My network and I just had to ensure that there were quality players from among whom the coaches could make their selections. The moment the Bulls lost Wynand, Jan was able to fill his shoes, and he also became a Springbok in that same year. This is what you want to see happening with the player pipeline – you identify the best young players early and sign them up, and, with good coaching and management, they can come up through the system as soon as possible and reach the pinnacle of the player pyramid. This necessitates good planning and the ability to complement that planning with the best young players.'

Besides his own network, Schwartz also developed a very good relationship with rugby agents – the people who represent players and negotiate on their behalf, and are supposed to have the players' best interests at heart.

'A rugby union needs agents. And there has to be a relationship of trust. Nowadays, most of the talented young players already have agents before the unions have had the chance to talk to them. To me, it was always vital to win the trust of those agents, because you would like them to regard you as their players' first option for a professional contract. That is why honesty and integrity are the two most important ingredients in this job – whether you're dealing with agents, parents, teachers, schools, your network, or the players. If there has been just one instance of dishonesty between two parties, the trust is lost for good. I'm firmly convinced that integrity is an indispensable ingredient for sustained success,' Schwartz stated.

Relationships of that kind have always been important to Schwartz and Meyer. Absolute trust and honesty are hallmarks of their relationship, and the Bulls also benefited from that when Meyer concluded his short-lived career as coach in the English Premiership.

THE DREAM MERCHANT

After his departure from the Bulls at the end of 2007, Meyer spent some time in the business world and then did a brief stint as head coach of the Leicester Tigers before being appointed as the Bulls' executive for rugby in 2010. He had already been involved with them since 2009 to look after the Bulls' junior rugby, before his appointment to the executive position. His return to Loftus was the result of Barend van Graan's handiwork.

Van Graan explained: 'The Golden Lions were considering Heyneke as director of rugby at the time, but I knew that you would rather have him in your structures than against you, and he wasn't involved with a rugby team at that stage. So I told the people we couldn't let Meyertjie slip through our fingers, and said jokingly that we had to get him back, even if he did nothing but read newspapers until we had a function for him. So he started working with our juniors again, and Dick Muir was appointed as the Lions' director of coaching.'

In those first months of his contract, he could look anew at the Bulls' junior structures together with Schwartz, just like he had in 2001.

In 2009 Schwartz saw young eighth man Arno Botha play in a practice match for Limpopo's under-18 team. During Craven Week, Botha only played for five minutes before sustaining an injury. Schwartz was nonetheless so impressed by the player that he contracted him for 2010. However, Schwartz is quick to point out that players don't make it purely because they were spotted and contracted by him: their success is due to the staff who work with them afterwards. For that reason, he, like Meyer, considered that good ongoing mentorship rather than technical expertise was the paramount virtue of anyone coaching at Loftus.

After all, Meyer's second pillar is not built solely on the recruitment of the most talented players, but also on developing and moulding them. An excellent illustration of this (one that also illustrates the interaction and understanding between Schwartz and Meyer) is provided by the trajectory that Arno Botha's career has taken since 2010.

Rugby writer Pieter Jordaan described it as follows in the Sunday paper *Rapport*, a day after Botha had played in his second test for the Springboks:

> He remembers the day well enough to recall the date smilingly without a moment's hesitation: 13 January 2010.

That was the day on which Arno Botha, then a bashful youngster who had just matriculated from Nylstroom High School, was called aside by Heyneke Meyer after a training session with the Blue Bulls' U19 team.

'Heyneke was still there at the time [as the Bulls' executive for rugby coaching]. He came to me and told me that there was one thing that would hold me back from becoming a great rugby player.

'And I myself knew what it was. He said that I allow people to walk over me,' Botha, the Bulls' and the Boks' new golden flanker, told *Rapport* earlier this week.

The cheerful young Bushvelder with the bucketfuls of natural talent of which even established Springboks can be envious was well aware of the fact that his self-confidence needed a boost.

'I was self-conscious and shy. Felt comfortable among my friends and the people close to me. In primary school I was in a private Christian school with only about 30 kids. When I started attending the public school in Nylstroom, there were 30 in my class. It gave me quite a fright,' he said.

So when Botha joined the Bulls after school, he found himself in even more intimidating company. His new peers hailed from renowned rugby factories: Grey College, Affies, Waterkloof, Monument ...

'When Heyneke spoke to me that day, something told me that I had to start standing up for myself there and then. If this guy, who *knows* rugby, could say it to me, I had to listen. I suddenly learnt how to become a man. I was no longer scared of going against the current.'

A year after his 'Heyneke talk', Botha was the captain of the Baby Boks: 'It took me out of my comfort zone, because before the time I had thought: there are players here with better leadership qualities than I have.'

Yesterday Botha, still only 21 years old, played in his second rugby test for South Africa.[11]

Limpopo, where Botha hails from, is a sub-union of the Blue Bulls Rugby Union. However, there were very few players like Botha who came from the Bulls' own catchment area and eventually made their mark in the professional side. Therefore, the union was frequently criticised for poaching and buying other unions' players, instead of employing their own.

A big rugby union can offer contracts to, at most, 25 junior players per year. To expect a player in the professional era to kick off his rugby career in the same area where he was born or grew up is as unfeasible as telling a schoolboy from Pretoria that he is not allowed to study at Stellenbosch.

THE DREAM MERCHANT

In 2009 Meyer and Schwartz were turning their attention to the value of a strong rugby culture in the local schools. By that time, there had emerged a countrywide emphasis on strong junior structures, and early contracting and development. This was no longer something that distinguished the Bulls from other unions.

In line with the *kaizen* culture of continuous progress and improvement, Meyer and Schwartz then shifted their focus to schools rugby. In contrast to the practice where the amateur wing was in charge of provincial-schools rugby, the Blue Bulls Rugby Union seconded all high-performance responsibilities to the BBC, the professional wing.

'Thereby it was ensured that, from the lowest level, the player pipeline was managed with the same vision and structures as in the case of our junior teams,' Van Graan explained. 'The crucial thing was that we didn't select schools, but joined forces with the schools that truly wanted to be part of this bigger picture. The company's services and structures were at their disposal.'

The strategy made sense: the development of players was something that happened at school and not in the course of three matches during the Grant Khomo, Academy or Craven weeks. These occasions only gave players exposure. Meyer and Schwartz were keen to start drawing players into the Bulls' structures and culture earlier and more regularly. There was a problem, however. Only about 5 per cent of the schools in the Bulls' catchment area played rugby as an official sporting code – the northern parts of Gauteng, and Limpopo. Moreover, those schools were predominantly white. And of the Pretoria schools, only Affies featured consistently among the country's top 20 under-19 teams. Compare this with the proportion of nearly 95 per cent of schools in the Western and the Eastern Cape that offer rugby, with six to eight of these provinces' teams regularly counting among the foremost school sides in South Africa.

So the Bulls would not have been able to supplement their player pipeline solely from their own ranks, although it would have been desirable for them do so. In 2010, therefore, Meyer created the Top Schools project and incorporated it with Schwartz's high-performance department. They identified a number of schools from their own area, as well as Gauteng, Limpopo and Mpumalanga, which, in their view, had a 'culture of excellence in rugby and academic achievement'. The BBC became very closely involved with the development of players and coaches in these schools, and in 2012 they reached the point where they signed up 18 of the Blue Bulls' 22 Craven Week players.

According to Schwartz, the Top Schools project, the permanent recruitment staff who were later appointed and his network enabled the BBC to always know three years in advance which players they wanted to contract – both from their own ranks and from elsewhere in South Africa.

'Every year there are stories in the media about rugby unions that apparently walk around with a chequebook during Craven Week,' said Schwartz. 'But, by that time, 90 per cent of the Bulls' contracting work has already been done. All that you're supposed to do during Craven Week is identify players who aren't yet on your database. Then, you invite that boy's parents for coffee, you try to gain their trust and you exchange contact details. Still, the chances that the Bulls are not aware of a promising player are very slim.

'Besides, I believe that it's extremely insensitive to sign up players during Craven Week. For many kids, that is the highlight of their school career, and if a boy knows that you may make him an offer there, he and his parents will invade the Bulls' box instead of focusing on those three matches for his province. You do a kid an enormous disservice by negotiating during Craven Week. Allow him to enjoy it, and, once the event is over, you can follow up on your conversation with the parents.'

Since recruitment is such an intensive job, Schwartz considers it is preferable that a head coach does not concern himself with the process at all. 'Your head coach is not supposed to know who all the country's best young players are,' he said. 'He must be able to trust you to take care of that, though. His attention should be focused on senior players, teams and competitions. This means, of course, that your recruitment team has to be excellent and that there must be a very good rapport and regular communication between the head coach and the guy who signs up players.

'Because Heyneke is someone who thinks in terms of a bigger picture and the future, he has always been interested in schools rugby and the dynamics of the player market. Frans Ludeke is a much more focused guy, and he likes to concern himself with the finest detail – only those things that happen between the four chalk lines. When he arrived at the Bulls at the end of 2007, he was taken aback by the extent of the structures, how every guy was a specialist and that there was a team of people driving this thing. That is precisely the reaction you want from a head coach. I always say every guy should carry only his own briefcase – keep to his own function in the organisation. So Frans trusted me completely to get him the best players, to understand the market and to ensure that the pipeline worked. He wanted to focus his energy exclusively on looking after the top of the player pyramid.

'At the same time, it means that you need to know exactly what your head coach is looking for and, with guidelines, you and your team then recruit with a mandate from the head coach.'

The Bulls use both a set of general and position-specific guidelines to assess players. In the general category, a player has to tick at least four out of five boxes. For a scrumhalf, for example, the criteria would be as shown in Table 2, where the right-hand column can be regarded as a good summary of Fourie du Preez's merits and consequently as the Bulls' blueprint.

For Schwartz, guidelines like these are just that – guidelines: 'I prefer to trust my hunch about a player rather than follow a checklist. Sometimes you just see that something special in a player, even if he doesn't have a very good game, and that's the player you'd like to have. You could draw up another list that says: "The bigger, faster, stronger and cleverer, the better."

'But talent and work ethic are two of the most important things you look for in a player. A guy with both will definitely make it. A player who has talent but no work ethic won't make the grade; a player with little talent who has a good work ethic will always rise above a player who only has talent,' believes Schwartz.

This corresponds with Meyer's own philosophy on recruitment. 'As much as I love rugby,' he said, 'anyone has to admit that it's just a small part of life. And that's why I always first want to find the human being and then the rugby player. You can teach a guy rugby, but you can't teach him decency, humility and empathy. And those things were part of our culture at the Bulls.

'Therefore, character is paramount to me. I look for and choose guys with character, because it's like carbon: it means nothing until you've put it under pressure. Because under enormous pressure, you get diamonds that shine. In some cases, Ian and I persuaded players when they were only 16 years old to play for the Bulls because they had character. I only need to talk to someone for an hour to know whether or not he will make it. Talent is important, but I don't recruit for talent. There are thousands of

General criteria		Criteria for scrumhalves	
Mental toughness	✓	Tactical understanding of the game	✓
		Good general awareness	✓
Speed	✓	Excellent visual skills	✓
		Good communication and organisational skills	✓
Strength	?	Must be able to take control	✓
		Must be able to make decisions	✓
Skills	✓	Accurate passing and ability to kick from/with both hands/feet	✓
		Good acceleration to break through first-line defence	✓
Coachability	✓	Must be able to draw defenders and thereby threaten defence	✓
		High work rate in supporting play and as cover defender	✓
		Must be able to organise defence	✓
		Must be able to absorb pressure	✓

Table 2: Recruitment criteria for scrumhalves

talented youngsters in South Africa and thousands of talented alcoholics in the world. What I look for is character. Once all teams have good structures, character becomes the biggest differentiator at the top level.

'Because it's hard to win finals, a guy must be mentally tough enough to absorb that pressure. I always told the players: "Easy training makes hard-core matches, but hard-core training makes easy matches." Although we created an environment at the Bulls where players were happy and they wanted to stay, it didn't mean that it was an easy environment to work in. And, for that reason, we wanted to ensure that we brought in new players who would come into their own in that environment, rather than simply talented players, who might go to pieces as soon as more pressure was put on them.'

Preserving the integrity of that second pillar (recruiting top players) therefore rested on a good recruitment structure, a solid first pillar (Schwartz and his team), and, once again, the premium that the Bulls place on culture and the quality of the people in their structures.

At the centre of this is the player pipeline – not only because it has practical benefits, but also because of the ideal it represents to the players: the opportunity to dream and aspire to something greater, such as striving to become Springboks and the most successful rugby team in the world.

Schwartz believes that this model and player structure are the best for achieving sustained success and keeping players happy. There are other models – for instance the one whereby the head coach does the recruitment and signing of players. According to Schwartz, though, this is often a hidden reason for escaping from a financial predicament and causes those teams to get stuck between 14:00 and 15:00 on Goldsmith's performance clock: 'The coach gets sacked. The club starts spending money on new players, new equipment, new coaches in a frantic attempt to stop the decline in performance.'

In Schwartz's view, this model places an enormous strain on the budget. 'If you're with a team where the coach does the contracting, but also gets fired regularly,' he said, 'after four years you can easily sit with the 20 players signed up by the first coach, the second guy's 20, and the present coach's 20 as well. At a rugby union like that, there are seldom good structures. As a result, every coach can do and play as he likes. By the time that the third coach has been appointed and has brought in his players, the company find itself with 60 players on its books, with the present coach only interested in 25 or 30 of them at most. The rest get salaries, but they don't play. Their careers stagnate, they aren't motivated and the team collapses as soon as a few guys are injured because there is no structure or financial model that can help them through tough times.'

In another popular model, players are contracted according to categories. A category A player is someone who can become a Springbok, a category B player a good Super Rugby player, and a category C player someone who can at most plug holes in the Currie Cup competition when the 'A's and possibly some of the 'B's are playing test rugby.

Inevitably, there are cases where it is not to a rugby union's advantage to sign up a player who may eventually become a Super Rugby player, even more so if their larder is already fully stocked in that position. However, although it is important to some provinces not only to be competitive at under-19 and under-21 levels but also to win trophies, the supply and demand in the player market should also be taken into account. It is also an ethical issue, because it is wrong to sign up all the country's top juniors for a certain position when not everyone will get an opportunity to play or to realise their full potential at senior level because the union already has enough players in that position.

There will be occasions when it is not the right thing to contract a potential test player from the school field. To Schwartz, however, the principle of labelling a schoolboy as an A, B or C player is disturbing:

'By doing this, you openly place a ceiling above a young person's dreams. Regardless of whether or not he will ultimately become one, the vast majority of provincial schoolboy players dream of becoming Springboks one day. There's something cold and inhuman about passing judgment on another person's dreams. You may have the best structures and they may make sense to you on financial statements, but if you put a person's right to be allowed to dream at the mercy of someone else's subjectivity, you don't understand people at all. Sustained success is not achievable if the human being and an appreciation of his needs are not central to everything you do,' said the man who was the Bulls' 'dream merchant' for many years.

While the Bulls' financial situation has improved considerably over the years, in 2001 Schwartz and Meyer didn't have much more than dreams that they could sell. And, for Schwartz, Derick Hougaard's story is a personal highlight of his 12 years at the BBC.

In 2001 Hougaard was in matric at the Hoër Landbouskool Boland (Boland Agricultural High School), near Paarl. In 2000 he had played at flyhalf for Western Province in Craven Week, and when the rugby boundaries were changed just for 2001, he turned out for Boland that year. He was the top points scorer in the country in his matric year. Everyone wanted to get their hands on him, but this youngster from Piketberg had set his heart on playing for Western Province – after all, Province were the Currie Cup champions in 2000 and 2001.

By contrast, the state of affairs in Pretoria looked grim from a distance and the first time Schwartz talked to Hougaard, the youngster's reaction was: 'But you don't even have a sponsor, Oom!'

Schwartz recalled that time as follows: 'Back in 2001, there weren't so many cellphones. So I called the school's telephone booth to speak to Derick. The boy on telephone duty had to go and look for Derick in the hostel before we could talk. We got along well, and from the beginning I felt a special affinity for Derick. He was 18 years old, but he had the head of a 40-year-old on his shoulders – that was my earliest experience of him.

'I still remember when Boland Landbou went to play against Oakdale in Riversdale in 2001. Oakdale had a much stronger team, but Boland won that match 15-0 after Derick scored all the points. Callie Wannenburg felled him with a massive tackle that day, and no one thought Derick would get up again. But he did, and he won that game with drop goals and penalty goals, as he did a year later in the Currie Cup final.

'That afternoon, I had a meeting with Callie and Derick at the Wimpy in Riversdale. Callie's dad told me about his elder brother, Pedrie, who sat on the bench for the Sharks' under-21 side. So I signed up both Callie and Pedrie, and Pedrie became a Springbok that year.

'I believe Derick is indeed the Bulls' biggest success story. Everyone in the country wanted him. They hunted him. He was absolutely phenomenal. When all the Paarl schools played for Boland in the 2001 Craven Week, there was inevitably a great deal of interest because Derick was in the team. I found it frustrating to see how agents and rugby unions chased after him there. The Bulls eventually became trendsetters with regard to the way in which we contracted players, and our way was to do it the right way at all times. You would perhaps contract a guy in January or at the end of Craven Week in his standard-9 year. But never at the Craven Week itself.

'I kept track of Derick's school matches after Craven Week. I went to meet his parents so that we could build a relationship. My golden rule with contracting was to treat the player as if he were my own child. Therefore, it was very important to me to meet his parents so that they could feel assured that we really did have their child's best interests at heart. So I made a point of phoning Derick before every match to wish him luck.

'That kind of interest must be sincere. People can sense it if you talk to them or are nice to them for your own selfish reasons, but when that interest is sincere, you can build a relationship and really develop an understanding of the other person's dreams and needs.

'Derick wanted to go to Western Province, however. He was a Province supporter. He had played for Western Province in standard 9. All these things made it difficult to persuade him to come to Pretoria.

However, I wasn't prepared to open a suitcase full of money in front of him and his parents. We didn't have that kind of money in the first place, and I also wouldn't have liked to see someone offering bags of money to my 18-year-old son. I had a ceiling of R100 000 per year, and in my 12 years at the Bulls, only two players reached that amount – Derick and Chiliboy Ralepelle. Nevertheless, it was still a relatively small amount of money to earn.'

Hougaard had told Schwartz from the outset that he didn't really want to play for the Blue Bulls and that it was a move he would be reluctant to consider: 'But one thing about him that impressed me right from the beginning was his honesty and his interest in how I was doing,' Hougaard recalled. 'I wanted to play for Province, however. My parents were there, my friends were there, and if you told me in standard 9 or early in my matric year that I would end up playing for the Bulls, I would have said you were smoking dagga or something stronger.'

Meyer didn't see Hougaard play until Boland's under-19 team took on the Bulls at Loftus. Schwartz, though, undertook frequent trips to the Western Cape, and Meyer and Hougaard had one or two telephone conversations after Schwartz had convinced the coach that this schoolboy could become *the* player he would need at the Bulls.

'I'll never forget the day that Hennie Bekker and Rob Wagner from Western Province came to visit me at the hostel at Boland Landbou. It was the visit I had been waiting for my entire school career,' said Hougaard.

'I told them that if I was good enough, I wanted to play senior rugby as soon as possible. Their response was a sarcastic little laugh, which is probably how you react when a schoolboy says such things to you. Rob and Hennie said if I was really good, I would play for the under-21 team immediately. Otherwise, I would start at the under-19 level and work my way up through the age teams over the years. I was upset by this, and I realised then that I had to move.

'I said the same thing to Heyneke, and he told me later he had also wondered who this cocky laaitie was, because up to then, only Ian had attended my matches. He said that if I was good enough, I would play and that it would then be up to me to determine how quickly I advance.'

Hougaard's need to play senior provincial and international rugby as soon as possible was not only due to the high opinion he might have had of himself: 'In standard 9, I had problems with my back and went to see a doctor about it. I can't remember his name, but I'll never forget his face. He told me I could have a normal life without being troubled by backache, but then he laughed and said I'd never be able to play for the Springboks. That was my childhood dream, and after I walked out of that doctor's consulting room I sat crying in the toilets for half an hour. This was the main reason why I wanted to play provincially and for the Boks as soon as possible – I didn't know how long I would be able to play rugby for,' he said.

When Schwartz and Meyer appeared on the scene, Hougaard's dream started looking like something that might become a reality. And, according to Meyer, team goals can only be achieved if they can be intertwined with individual goals: 'The first thing I do when I meet someone is to ask what his goals are. Derick was 18 when I asked him that question, and he told me he wanted to become a Springbok before the age of 23. He had very good reasons for this. I then told him that I could make him a Bok if he would buy into the Bulls' vision. And if he was good enough, he would play.

'You have to intertwine an individual's goals with those of the team. This is simply how human nature operates. For example, when you go through a drawer and find an old class photo, you look at yourself first and only then do you look at your friends and the class as a whole. People look at themselves first, so you need to look at what an individual's dreams are and how you can incorporate them into a bigger dream. This is where people lose the plot. They scold players, swear at them and chase them away when, actually, you should be able to tell even the most difficult guy: "Okay, look – this is what you want to achieve and I'll help you to get there, but then you'll have to work hard for me."

'That was how we worked with the youngsters in particular. When a kid was signed up by Ian, he didn't yet have much money, a posh car, fans and his own family. He only had that dream of playing for the Springboks. If you are worth your salt, you contract people who can enter into a partnership with you to realise a greater vision by linking their dreams to that vision. This, and the way in which Ian works with people, is why Derick decided to play for the Blue Bulls – a year before winning his first Currie Cup at the age of 19 and two years before he became a Springbok.'

For Schwartz and his wife, Hougaard eventually became like one of the family, which is why he cherishes special memories of the player and what it took to persuade him to come to Pretoria. Schwartz's skill as a negotiator and his ability to identify talented players extended far beyond just one player, though, and much of this is illustrated in Table 3. Of the 126 Springboks who had played for the Bulls by June 2013, Schwartz had contracted 36 of the last 39. Only four of that 39 were already Boks when they were contracted – Bryan Habana, Wikus van Heerden, Gurthrö Steenkamp and Wayne Julies. Three players – Norman Jordaan, Danie Rossouw and Gary Botha – were already with the Bulls when Meyer took over the reins, but they only became Boks later.

Not all of these players had necessarily come through the pipeline. In 2002 Derick Hougaard was one of the first schoolboy players Schwartz signed up on a long-term contract, and he immediately played senior rugby. But the 'young' players with whom Meyer had started working in 2001 in the Vodacom Cup and Currie Cup competitions were mostly 20 and 21 years old. Thereafter, the focus shifted increasingly to the recruitment of the country's foremost schoolboy players.

Schwartz points out, however, that the top team should in the first place have more experienced and senior players, and then young players, rather than young and inexperienced players with some seniors: 'The balance has to be perfect, and the pipeline should also be seen in that context. The pipeline is there to bring your players through at the earliest possible time and then to ensure that the very best of them reach the top of the pyramid. It involves identification, conditioning and coaching.

'But it happens at times that you lose the core of your players in one go – like in 2011. The players in the pipeline are certainly good enough to play top rugby, but they still need time to get to the top of the pyramid. Then you look for someone more experienced and senior from outside to maintain that vital balance between junior and experienced players.

'You can play with young players and be successful, but you can't play finals with only young players and expect to win. Not every junior is a Jan Serfontein: some take longer to get to the top, and then you need to bring in players that are at the middle of the pyramid or higher to get depth, seniority and experience in certain positions. Author John C Maxwell said that great teams have great depth, and I believe that. To get that depth and experience, you sometimes have to search outside of your own structures.

THE DREAM MERCHANT

Bull Bok #	Player	Notes
88	Jaco van der Westhuyzen	Played for the Pumas in 2000 and for the Bulls' Vodacom Cup team in 2001.
89	Victor Matfield	Played for Griquas and Cats in 2000. At the Bulls from 2001.
90	Danie Coetzee	Played for Free State in the Vodacom Cup in 2000. Became a Bull in 2001 and a Bok in 2002.
91	Bakkies Botha	Played flanker for Falcons in 2000. Meyer moved him to lock in 2001. Became a Bok in 2002.
92	Wessel Roux	Played junior rugby for the Bulls from 1996, from 1999 for Falcons. Bulls brought him back in 2001.
93	Pedrie Wannenburg	Failed to make Sharks under-21 starting team. Became both a Bull and a Springbok in 2002.
94	Norman Jordaan	Already at the Bulls from 2000.
95	Richard Bands	Played in 1999 for Free State President's Shield team. Became a Bull in 2001 and a Bok in 2003.
96	Geo Cronjé	Played for Griquas in 2001, for Bulls in 2002 and for Boks in 2003.
97	Derick Hougaard	In 2001, top points scorer in SA schools rugby. Wanted to play for Western Province; Schwartz persuaded him, 'without a sponsor', to join the Bulls.
98	Danie Rossouw	At the Bulls from 1999, but under Meyer he became a Bok with 64 tests.
99	Fourie du Preez	Signed up by Golden Lions while at school, but after a request from Meyer, Loffie Eloff released him from his contract. He then became a Bull.
100	Jacques Cronjé	A Blue Bull from the outset.
101	Bryan Habana	Became a Bok at the Lions, but Bulls signed him up before he played his first test in November 2004.
102	Gurthrö Steenkamp	Became a Bok at Free State in 2004. A Bull from 2005.
103	Gary Botha	At the Bulls from 1999, but Meyer moved him from flanker to hooker and he became a Bok in that position.
104	Wynand Olivier	Schwartz contracted him on recommendation without ever having seen him play. Was injured in matric and not present at Craven Week.
105	Akona Ndungane	Lured from Border to the Bulls in 2005 after his twin, Odwa, had exchanged the Bulls for the Sharks. Became a Bok in 2006.
106	Pierre Spies	Wasn't classed as one of top 100 under-18 players in SA in 2003. Schwartz contracted him at R3 500 per month. Became a regular player in the Springbok team at 21.
107	Chiliboy Ralepelle	Was put on an agreement as 15-year-old player at Pretoria Boys' High and became a Bok while still a junior.

Table 3: Blue Bull Boks since 2001

HEYNEKE MEYER AND IAN SCHWARTZ

Bull Bok #	Player	Notes
108	Hilton Lobberts	Schwartz contracted him as a grade-9 player from New Orleans Secondary, in Paarl. Became a Bok at 20.
109	Wikus van Heerden	Became a Bok under Rudy Joubert. From 2007 a Blue Bull and a member of the team that won the World Cup.
110	Wayne Julies	Played for Boland Cavaliers when he became a Bok in 1999. From 2002 a Blue Bull.
111	Morné Steyn	Schwartz had known Steyn since his primary-school days in Bloemfontein. Substitute for Free State Craven Week team in 2001 and 2002.
112	Zane Kirchner	Signed up at the end of 2007 to replace Johan Roets. André Markgraaff granted him an early release from Griquas at Schwartz's request.
113	Francois Hougaard	Didn't have a contract with Western Province when Schwartz signed him up from 2008. Became a Bok at 21.
114	Dewald Potgieter	Led Eastern Province and SA Schools team in 2005, and Emerging Springboks against British and Irish Lions in 2009. Schwartz contracted him in grade 11.
115	Bandise Maku	Was contracted as schoolboy player at Dale College, Eastern Cape.
116	Flip van der Merwe	Didn't make the team at Free State. Became a Bull in 2009 and a Bok in 2010.
117	Deon Stegmann	Schwartz contracted him in his matric year.
118	Werner Kruger	Played for Falcons' under-21s while still at school. Joined the Bulls after school.
119	Dean Greyling	Contracted as schoolboy player from Afrikaanse Hoër Seunskool (Affies).
120	Bjorn Basson	Scored a record number of 21 Currie Cup tries for Griquas in 2010. Became a Bull in 2011.
121	Juandré Kruger	Didn't play in Craven Week, but Schwartz identified him at school. Tried unsuccessfully to contract him. Recruited as Maties lock in 2008. Left Bulls in 2009 to gain European experience; returned in 2011 to replace Victor Matfield. Became a Bok in 2012.
122	Jacques Potgieter	Played for Eastern Province Kings and before that for Sharks. Became a Bull in 2011 and a Bok in 2012.
123	JJ Engelbrecht	Didn't regularly make the team at Western Province, and it took him a season to find his feet at the Bulls in 2012. Became a Bok in 2012.
124	Arno Botha	Schwartz identified him in 2009 in warm-up match for Limpopo Craven Week. Injured after just five minutes at Craven Week. Became a Bull in 2010, Junior Bok captain in 2011, and in 2013 a Springbok at 21.
125	Jano Vermaak	Brought from Lions to Bulls in 2011 to fill Fourie du Preez's shoes together with Francois Hougaard. Became a Bok in 2013.
126	Jan Serfontein	Was spotted in 2008 at the age of 15 in Eastern Province's Grant Khomo team. Schwartz entered into an agreement with him at that stage. In 2009 Serfontein moved from Grey, Port Elizabeth, to Grey, Bloemfontein. Was International Rugby Board Junior Player of the Year in 2012. Became a Springbok in 2013 at 20.

'In the case of our core group that left in 2011, it should be taken into account that most of those players had been with the Bulls for ten years. It was a unique situation, and you can plan for certain positions – as we did with Juandré Kruger and Victor Matfield. But it also means that your next line of players, like in 2011, are predominantly young men.

'The same often applies when you suddenly have a spate of injuries. Then you need to look outside the pipeline. The principle is to maintain the integrity of the second pillar, and what it boils down to is that you contract players to make yourself stronger. If you can fill gaps from within the structures, that's the first prize. But it's not the only possibility.

'At times one also makes mistakes with contracting. For example, in 2011 Heyneke let a bunch of players go who no longer fitted into the culture. Or players don't come through in the way that you had anticipated. They fail to measure up to the expectations you had of them as schoolboys. In such cases, the players in certain positions in the pipeline aren't up to standard and you have to supplement from outside.'

I was writing this chapter on the same day the BBC announced that Springbok scrumhalf Piet van Zyl had joined the Bulls on a two-year contract. A general response from the fans was that the Bulls were 'poaching' other unions' players again and not developing their own talent.

After reading this chapter, it should be clear that the player market – recruiting, contracting and replacing – is significantly more complex than merely walking into a supermarket where you can easily fill any gaps or make up any deficiencies in your life from a shelf of identical products. On that score, Schwartz was a master.

As Meyer said of him, 'It's an art to spot future Springboks before some of them even have downy beards. Ian perfected that art.'

HEYNEKE MEYER

CHAPTER 5

The DNA of success is people

Start with the foundation

'The job of a manager, like that of a teacher, is to inspire people to be better.'
– Sir Alex Ferguson

One of the most predictable things in professional sport is the need teams have to become the next Manchester United at some or other point in their existence. When a new main sponsor or investor becomes involved in even the most obscure team, one usually finds a man wearing a pink tie and rimless glasses heralding that financial injection as their first step towards world domination – or Man U status.

There are countless examples in South Africa where that dream was put forward but then gradually bit the dust. You don't just become Manchester United because you have money. There is an enormous difference between an impressive brand and merely an impressive kit. The problem often lies somewhere between administrators who cut their teeth in the amateur era and businesspeople whose knowledge and experience of rugby are limited to the biltong and beer enjoyed in a stadium suite at weekends.

Manchester United's turnaround in the mid-1980s and subsequent sustained success can be attributed largely to Alex Ferguson's arrival as manager of the team. His job title of 'manager' is a much better description of what he did at the club from day to day and in the long run than the term 'head coach'.

Ferguson managed the team for 26 and a half years before stepping down after the 2012/13 European season. His tenure was longer than the period during which rugby has been a professional sport and it is, therefore, not possible to draw a comparison in this sporting code with a team that did manage to reach Manchester United status.

THE DNA OF SUCCESS IS PEOPLE

Nonetheless, on a small scale there are similarities between what Heyneke Meyer did with the Bulls in the 2000s and what Ferguson achieved with the English football giant from 1986. What these two coaches primarily have in common is not necessarily what they did, but rather the person from whose work they drew their inspiration – Vince Lombardi.

Ferguson researched and emulated this legendary American football coach's work, and Meyer is a self-confessed Lombardi disciple. Lombardi had transformed the Green Bay Packers into the sporting aristocracy to which many sports teams aspired before Manchester United became the 'next big team'. The Packers' 1958 season had been the worst in their history. Lombardi was appointed as head coach and general manager in February 1959, and during his nine years with the team the Packers played in the Super Bowl (the National Football League final) seven times and won five of these contests.

The crux of what Lombardi, Meyer and Ferguson did is best encapsulated in Ferguson's words: 'It was about building a club, not just a team.'

In 2012 Professor Anita Elberse and Tom Dye (MBA 2012) of the Harvard Business School wrote a case study about Ferguson titled *Sir Alex Ferguson: Managing Manchester United*. As discussed earlier in this book, there are always factors outside of a person's control that contribute to his or her long-term success. Although it was no different in Ferguson's case, it is almost inconceivable that the Manchester United era would have been possible without him.

Elberse and Dye summarise his early career as follows:

> Ferguson started his managerial career in 1974, aged just 32, at East Stirlingshire FC, a small club in Falkirk, Scotland, for a weekly salary of $95. He was there for 117 days before accepting an offer from a larger club, St. Mirren FC, where he would stay for four years, and would assume a high level of control over all of the club's football and administrative functions. In his third year, he won promotion to the Scottish Premier Division with an exceedingly young team that he had put his trust in. 'It was about building a club, not just a team,' said Ferguson. However, a clash with the club's new

chairman led to Ferguson's firing. 'It taught me a big lesson. Before that, I did not believe I could ever get the sack,' he said. He would not allow the same situation to arise again.

Aberdeen FC, a stronger club from Scotland's North East, immediately moved to install Ferguson as its new manager. He would form a strong bond with the club's chairman, Dick Donald. Ferguson's tenure at Aberdeen would not only be the most successful in the club's history, but also remarkable in the history of Scottish football itself. With Ferguson at the helm, Aberdeen won three Premier Division titles, four Scottish FA Cups, one Scottish League Cup, and the European Cup Winners' Cup, beating European giants Bayern Munich and Real Madrid along the way.[12]

These experiences laid the foundation for what Ferguson would ultimately achieve with Manchester United. It is stories like these that served as encouragement and examples to Meyer when he was driven by necessity to search for answers to his rugby questions internationally and in other sporting codes, such as football and American football.

The following paragraph from Elberse and Dye's case study sums up Manchester United's success under Ferguson and also describes in a nutshell how he achieved it:

> During his time as manager of Manchester United, Ferguson had won almost every honor in the club game. He had taken over at United when the club was at perhaps its lowest point ever, having experienced a startling fall from grace and not won an English league title in nearly twenty years. By prioritizing youth-player development, rebuilding the team, being shrewd on the transfer market, emphasizing attacking football, and bringing the best out of his players, Ferguson turned United's fortunes around. Now, United was the most successful club in English football with nineteen league titles, and had reclaimed its place among Europe's elite clubs with two Champions' League trophies. Millions of fans around the world idolized former and current United players such as Eric Cantona, Cristiano Ronaldo, and Ryan Giggs. Revenues had soared, too, and by some estimates United had become the world's most valuable football club in 2012.[13]

The writers refer briefly to the 2011/12 English Premier League. In that season United's so-called 'noisy neighbours', Manchester City, then under new ownership, snatched the league title from under United's nose after massive investments in players and thanks to a better goal difference. Ferguson's reaction to this: 'Another day in the history of Manchester United, that's all it was.'[14]

To Ferguson, sustained success was more important than sporadic victories and titles. There might be disappointment and bad times, but in the long run United's performance graph had to show more peaks than dips. That is what teams must aspire to when they want to become the next Manchester United; that is what Meyer achieved with the Bulls in South African rugby; and what Western Province and the Sharks are increasingly striving for in a resolute fashion.

As a follow-up to her case study of Ferguson, Elberse co-authored an article with him that appeared in the *Harvard Business Review* of October 2013. In the article, titled 'Ferguson's Formula', she and Ferguson identified eight leadership lessons through which they explain his management approach. Elberse was wary of taking leadership lessons from a sports context and proclaiming them as universal principles that can be applied in any context. But these eight lessons can certainly be tested and applied more broadly, which is why I will use them to conclude this section about Meyer.

The eight lessons are:
1. Start with the foundation;
2. Dare to rebuild your team;
3. Set high standards – and hold everyone to them;
4. Never, ever cede control;
5. Match the message to the moment;
6. Prepare to win;
7. Rely on the power of observation;
8. Never stop adapting.

---

1. Start with the Foundation

'From the moment I got to Manchester United, I thought of only one thing: building a football club. I wanted to build right from the bottom. That was in order to create fluency and a continuity of supply to the first team. With this approach, the players all grow up together, producing a bond that, in turn, creates a spirit,' states Ferguson.[15]

This was the rationale behind the two 'centres of excellence' Ferguson established immediately after his arrival at Manchester United in 1986. He modernised the youth structures and identified talented players from as young as nine years old, who could play for the senior team in time to come. It was a player pipeline, and future stars such as David Beckham and Ryan Giggs were developed there before they formed the core of the dominant senior teams of the 1990s and early 2000s.

This is precisely what Heyneke Meyer had in mind with the youth structures at the Bulls – in other words, the second pillar. His earlier experience at the SWD had taught him that a coach could also achieve a tremendous amount with young players if he put his trust in them – as proved by Derick Hougaard in the 2002 Currie Cup competition.

There are obvious advantages to a strong youth system, such as identifying and developing players at an earlier stage, and thereby, if all goes well, advancing them more quickly from junior rugby to the senior team. The senior team and its balance between more established players and a few young turks will always be the rugby union's main focus and the factor that drives long-term planning. However, identifying and preparing players for that team is an essential task for a coach who aims to build a club, not just a team.

Ferguson says in this regard: 'Winning a game is only a short-term gain – you can lose the next game. Building a club brings stability and consistency.'[16]

That consistency is not solely the result of a clever logistical model and continuous skills development. At any rate, not as far as the role of a manager or head coach is concerned.

'The job of a manager, like that of a teacher, is to inspire people to be better,' Ferguson states in the *Harvard Business Review* article. 'Give them better technical skills, make them winners, make them better people, and they can go anywhere in life. When you give young people a chance, you not only create a longer life span for the team, you also create loyalty. They will always remember that you were the manager who gave them their first opportunity,' he concludes.[17]

That particular loyalty is the crucial notion in the Blue Bulls' second pillar: recruiting, retaining and developing the most talented players. When Victor Matfield, Danie Rossouw, Fourie du Preez and Bakkies Botha left the Bulls in 2011, it was after careers that had spanned ten years. Such loyalty can only be inspired if a coach sees his responsibility towards players as much greater than merely providing technical coaching. This factor filtered through constantly in Meyer's interviews for this book.

He said, 'Do you know what I find so beautiful about rugby? I've never coached for the sake of the trophies, but to see what kind of person the player has become by the time he retires or leaves. I've never watched the 2007 Super 14 final again. To me, rugby is about the people – it's the only thing rugby is about. It's the only thing life is about. And a rugby player comes into his own when he experiences that you, as coach, are more interested in him as a human being than in his skills.'

To him, there are two principles underlying the way he works with people. 'I did a PTI course [physical training instructor] during my first stint in the army. There you run the guys into the ground. You break them. And you don't feel a thing because there are thousands of troops.

'I can't recall the name of the man who presented the course, but I'll never forget his words. He said we should always remember that we're dealing with another man's child. That has stuck in my mind and I've used it since I first started coaching. I'm not the kind of person that yells and swears at a player. I treat him as I would like someone else to treat my own child and I have three sons.

'That is also why I'm blatantly honest. If I tell a player something, it is sincerely meant and the players know it too. Even when I have to say things that players won't want to hear, I always do it as if I'm talking to my own son and that is a relationship that is not only based on honesty, but also on respect.

'I don't care if people don't like me. It's nice to be liked and I admit that I'm a sensitive person, but it doesn't matter to me if people don't like me. But they do have to respect me because I'm 100 per cent honest with people. It also applies to the reasons for leaving a player out of a team.

'When I talk to young coaches, I tell them it's like chopping off a puppy's tail. It's horrible, and especially for an emotional guy like me it's a very unpleasant task. But you can't chop off a puppy's tail piece by piece, because then you will kill him. You have to chop once and get it over with. That's how I am – I will tell you frankly that you should go and study because rugby is not the career for you, or that you only have one season left to play before I can foresee a role for you off the pitch.

'Players are frequently angry with me in such cases and they want nothing more to do with me. But then they come back ten years later to thank me for having been the only guy who was honest with them at the time.

'So, that's my first principle: treat players as I would like my own children to be treated by others. It is therefore an educational task.

'The second principle I learnt from American steel magnate Andrew Carnegie, who said that dealing with people is like digging for gold. His words were: "When you go digging for an ounce of gold, you have to move tons of dirt to get one ounce of gold. But when you go digging, you don't go looking for the dirt, you go looking for the gold."

'That is how I coach – I believe that there's a bit of gold within every guy. Something beautiful. Something good. And that has to be nurtured. If you can work through the dirt and stones to get to a person's bit of gold and nurture it, that person will come into his own and will do anything for you. That's my second principle.'

According to Meyer, a good system provides a coach with the opportunity to build a relationship with a young player that has those two principles as its foundation and mutual respect as its cement.

'Game plans are important, but people put too much emphasis on that. Everyone actually plays in the same way nowadays and there is very little that is new in rugby. The difference lies in people management and guys who play for their coach.'

At this point in our conversation, Meyer had to fight back his tears … 'Before the 2007 tournament, each of the World Cup Boks could invite one person and give him his jersey. Most of the guys invited their dads. And, to me, it was the greatest thing when Bakkies gave me his jersey that day. He said I was the person who had made the biggest difference in his life.

'This means much more to me than winning Super Rugby. Because Bakkies had been an untamed bird when I got him: he was 20, he was wild. He was an eighth man. I told him that lock was his position if he wanted to become a Springbok.

'In 2002 the players returned to Loftus after a short break. Bakkies was so unfit that I chased him away. So instead of playing Super Rugby, he played in five Vodacom Cup matches. I told him that this was the kind of lesson he had to learn if he wanted to become a Bok. In September that year, he became a Springbok and Bakkies still thanks me today. Relationships like that (and to witness what Bakkies has managed to do in and with his life since 2001) are worth more to me than anything else in rugby. And *that* is what coaching is about,' Meyer said. His eyes glistened. His voice was croaky. Like a proud dad.

This is how Ferguson describes such experiences and the need to build a club right from the bottom: 'Once they [the players] know you are batting for them, they will accept your way. You're really fostering a sense of family. If you give young people your attention and an opportunity to succeed, it is amazing how much they will surprise you.'[18]

---

2. Dare to rebuild your team

The Blue Bulls' third pillar is to create a professional environment in which players can develop into world-class players *and* human beings. Although there are five pillars, in the greater whole each represents just one component of the same machine.

The pillars are interdependent and this becomes particularly evident in the way in which this third pillar helps realise the ideals of the second, that is, players. As is the case in the story of Bakkies Botha.

This professional environment has more to do with a professional mindset than with infrastructure. It stood to reason that the Bulls would eventually acquire a world-class gym, medical centre, and training and recreational facilities. But, in Meyer's view, in spite of all this wealth, a team would still be poor if a healthy culture was absent.

'When I arrived at the Bulls, the culture was about sleeping around, boozing, not training, postponing and cancelling training sessions. A youngster may still be bright-eyed when he enters such an environment, but over time he becomes just like the other players.

'A young player isn't going to stand up to these guys. When I see that someone won't fit into my culture, I tell him straight out. I see it in my sons' school environment. If 90 per cent of the pupils are good kids and 10 per cent of them are bad for the environment, that 90 per cent squeeze out the bad 10 per cent. But once it becomes acceptable to have guys like that around you, the culture goes bad,' Meyer reckoned.

Earlier in the book, I referred to his initially small player budget – the reason why he had to let even some of the Bulls' Springboks go. In order to build a team, he had to use what was available in the constraints of the budget. However, apart from the financial considerations, in his first season as a Super Rugby head coach, Meyer had already experienced conduct on the part of some senior players that prompted him to get rid of them for the sake of the culture and that third pillar.

Culture is a wide-ranging concept and, in Meyer's definition, character is the key ingredient – something that he reckons was lacking in the generation of Bulls he inherited.

'When I let those players go in 2000, most of them joined the Pumas, who then beat the Bulls three times the following year. They were angry with me and they were out to get the Bulls. But the Pumas weren't as angry in any of their other matches and they didn't beat us again after that.

'I think that we are too soft on players and life is about lessons. Many of those Pumas came to me a few years later and told me I had been right – they had been slackers and there had been a drinking culture.

'There was no way that I could create the right culture with those guys in an environment where I wanted to develop a crop of young players. That was a very difficult time for me. In 2000 I was appointed on a six-month contract to coach the Northern Bulls. SA Rugby appointed me from the SWD but when I arrived in Pretoria, no one wanted to accept me.

'I was still at the Stormers the previous year when they created the "men in black" identity. It was a totally new identity and immensely impressive. When I was appointed at the Bulls, some of the players and officials regarded me as a Western Province import and an enemy.

'I had to work with four teams: the Pumas, the Leopards, the Falcons and the Blue Bulls. None of those teams had done well in the Currie Cup and now I had to pick a team from them. The Blue Bulls no longer wanted to play in a light-blue jersey: they said that the Northern Bulls was a regional team that kept losing and because of the jersey their pathetic track record was associated with Loftus.

'They wanted to play in another jersey. I was young and naive, and Wynie Strydom told me we would be able to play in an alternative jersey, a white one with green sleeves. So we created this neutral identity and played our first match of the season against the Cats at Loftus on 26 February. Mr Price sponsored both teams. The Cats played in something that resembled a Blue Bulls jersey and we were in the white jersey with green sleeves.

'A certain Afrikaans rugby commentator declared on TV that we had used SWD green because I came from there. That was ridiculous – the Leopards, one of our four teams, also played in green; the Springboks were green. But apparently I was the person who had the temerity to meddle with a tradition-laden jersey.

'At the time, the media still saw me as a Western Province guy because I had been with the Stormers. That other man claimed that I was pursuing an SWD agenda. For a good three months, I was criticised and personally attacked about that jersey. Not one of the players stood up to say that they had taken the decision about the jersey and to explain the reasoning behind it. There was no integrity or honesty, and you can't change a culture like that.

'It's like a greenhouse, one rotten plant makes all the others go bad. I realised that I would have to remove those guys and so I simply cut out the Blue Bulls that were bad for the culture and long-term goals that we envisaged for the Bulls.'

Joost van der Westhuizen also threatened to join the Pumas, but ultimately stayed with the Bulls on about half his salary. Although his questionable lifestyle off the field eventually hit the headlines, Meyer reckons that this legendary rugby player did appreciate the professional environment and mindset. 'Joost also worked incredibly hard and this inspired the young players.'

Meyer was then sacked as Super Rugby coach, but the following year he won the Vodacom Cup. Out of the squad of the 36 players he selected, 26 made their provincial debut for the Blue Bulls.

Those players formed the core of the teams that made the Bulls such a powerhouse in the Currie Cup and Super Rugby competitions, and the Springbok team in the decade that followed.

So when Meyer, his initial management team and these young players first came together, they found themselves in quadrant one of the cyclical planning model (Figure 3): high work ethic, little experience, individuals, few successes, talented, hungry for success and – with Mr Price's departure – literally without sponsors.

This fresh start made it possible, however, to think in terms of performance cycles and to plan for the future using those models as tools – something that Meyer and Schwartz did to very good effect.

Alex Ferguson followed a similar approach:

> We identified three levels of players: those 30 and older, those roughly 23 to 30, and the younger ones coming in. The idea was that the younger players were developing and would meet the standards that the older ones had

set. Although I was always trying to disprove it, I believe that the cycle of a successful team lasts maybe four years, and then some change is needed. So we tried to visualize the team three or four years ahead and make decisions accordingly.[19]

Victor Matfield would eventually play a vital role in the Bulls' Super Rugby successes in particular. Although he had been with the Blue Bulls from 2001, he was not Meyer's logical choice as captain – that man was Anton Leonard. He had been Meyer's captain at the SWD and, in time, also became one of the great Blue Bulls captains. Matfield still captained the Super Rugby team in 2004 under Rudy Joubert, but when Meyer took over from Joubert in 2005, Matfield was captain in the first game and thereafter Leonard led the team for the rest of the season.

One may get the impression that Meyer summarily gets rid of people with whom he does not have an instant rapport. But that is not the case.

'I liked Victor very much as a captain, but he was always really Rudy's man. Anton was my captain. And once Rudy had left, I asked Victor what kind of a person Rudy was. I'm sure that 99.9 per cent of people will tell you negative things in order to get into your good books. But Victor had only nice things to say about Rudy, and I respected him enormously for that. He and I developed an exceptional relationship and over time Victor became that extension that I wanted on the field as a coach,' Meyer related.

3. Set high standards – and hold everyone to them

When I asked Meyer about that first Currie Cup title of 2002 and the Super 14 trophy of 2007, he summarised the road to those successes in just two sentences: 'It was tremendously important to me that players should enjoy their time at the Bulls. But that definitely didn't mean that it should be easy.'

He did not find that kind of environment at the Bulls, however.

'The players were nowhere! Some of them did their gym work together with their wives and girlfriends at Virgin Active. Being a Blue Bull was a holiday. Therefore, three things demanded attention: the culture, work ethic and facilities.

THE DNA OF SUCCESS IS PEOPLE

'I acquired the right players for the culture, and it wouldn't take us long to get that work ethic instilled. But if we wanted to lure the most talented young players in the country to Loftus, I knew that I needed to be able to convince a child's parents that the facilities and accommodation – the infrastructure – were the very best on offer. A mother wants to know that her child will sleep comfortably, eat well and have a nook where he can study. Most dads just want to know whether the boy is going to play good rugby and whether you will give him the best chance to do so.

'However, the players could do whatever suited them. They didn't really do any gym work. The junior teams' office is now where the old gymnasium used to be, underneath the south stand. It was a tiny room with five loose weights lying around.

'I then told Barend that we couldn't work with that and requested a small sum for weights. We broke down one of the gymnasium's asbestos walls and simply created more order and a structured training programme, which Hennie Kriel got the guys to follow. The guys hadn't been training correctly and they were overweight. Hennie did an incredible job to get those things in place. He was experienced; he was my right-hand man.'

The Bulls would not get a new, world-class gymnasium overnight. The fifth pillar – a brand of rugby that is marketable, fills stadiums and attracts sponsors – had to assist with that. By the time that Vodacom replaced Mobil as the Blue Bulls' main sponsor in 2005, the Bulls had already won a Vodacom Cup, had a shared under-21 title, two under-20 titles and three consecutive Currie Cups. The new sponsor asked Meyer in 2006 what he still needed to realise his vision of making the Bulls the best rugby team in the world. The gymnasium was among the matters discussed, a few million rands was granted and the financial boost contributed to excellent training, recreational and gymnasium facilities next to Loftus's B field. The facilities were on a previously unused piece of land, where Meyer had asked Vlok Cilliers to kick a drop goal through the posts with each foot in turn.

Barend van Graan and the Bulls' newly appointed high-performance manager at the time, Xander Janse van Rensburg, visited Britain on a so-called 'learn-and-live tour' at the end of 2012. Their trip included visits to Saracens rugby club and the English Premier League football club Tottenham Hotspur, among others.

About Spurs, Van Graan said, 'Of course, we're talking about money that we in rugby can still only dream of. Everything at Tottenham was bigger than ours, but I can say in all honesty that there is not a single thing at that club that we don't also have at Loftus. Our facilities are truly among the best in the world, and little of them existed or were of the same quality before Meyertjie requested them in 2000 as part of his long-term strategy.'

The facilities were a long-term project. The players' understanding of professionalism, however, required immediate attention.

'We were revolutionary in that regard,' reckoned Meyer. 'The guys were supposed to be playing rugby full-time, but they would come in for an hour, rush through an afternoon session and go home again. So I told them that they had to report at Loftus at 08:00 in the mornings and they could leave again at 20:00. Nowadays they finish earlier, but it was necessary at the time to bring that sense of professionalism home to the players loud and clear.

'Their wives complained of having to eat alone in front of the TV in the evenings, because the players got home late. For us, it has always been about the family, however, and over the years we have also built wonderful facilities where the wives and kids can relax – on match days as well. I was very keen to build a crèche before I left. About two years ago, I saw the most incredible player room in America. I submitted the idea to the board and it was approved just before my departure. It's a place where wives and children can be comfortable and socialise. The environment has to be pleasant for everyone, but for the players it's still a job.

'In 2001 rugby hadn't been a professional sport for long. The players needed to learn that they must clock in at 08:00 and I always started my last fitness session at 17:00. Barend really supported me right from the start and I asked him whether we could give the players meals as well because in those days they would go home in the evenings and eat the wrong stuff. We appointed someone who prepared meals.

'Loftus became a one-stop sports complex. The players could eat, sleep and train there. Today these are very basic things and everyone is doing it now. But in the early professional years, this approach gave us that vital advantage.'

The facilities and a weekly schedule also brought about an attitude change that made it enjoyable to be a Blue Bull, yet hard work at the same time.

By that time, therefore, the players who made it through from the junior structures into the senior team were the ones who could measure up to Meyer's standards. That tipped the scales in the Bulls' favour in crucial games and finals.

4. Never, ever cede control

Meyer frequently starts his sentences with the words, 'I don't want to sound arrogant ...' He is a modest man who knows himself very well and he has confidence in his own capabilities. For some reason or other, self-confidence and the ability to express one's ideas and plans well tend to be viewed as a form of arrogance in South Africa. Often, though, the opposite applies: people who feel strongly about certain issues and can make things happen are not necessarily arrogant.

Meyer certainly is not – and modesty was probably the most striking feature of the 2013 Springbok rugby team as well. This suggests that Meyer may quite possibly be right when he says, 'I don't want to sound arrogant, but a player doesn't play for a rugby union or for a jersey. He plays for his coach. When a coach tells him that he has played well, he believes it. See for yourself: any player, any team is an extension of the head coach's personality. A backline coach who likes flashy cars and watches will have a team like that. Pote Human is hard and honest, and so are his teams. If a guy is devious and messes around, his team will do the same.'

Ferguson had something similar in mind when he said: 'For a player – and for any human being – there is nothing better than hearing "well done". Those are the two best words ever invented in sports. You don't need to use superlatives.'[20]

To put it in context, Ferguson made this observation when he said in the *Harvard Business Review* article that few players improve as a result of criticism, and that encouragement is a much sharper arrow in a coach's quiver.

This corresponds with what Meyer said. Suppose it is true that a coach can exert such a huge influence on players through his words and actions – in which case, doesn't he have an enormous responsibility resting on his shoulders?

'What it boils down to for me is that a coach has to be blatantly honest in order to keep control of a team,' Meyer explained. 'You take that responsibility, you don't blame the referee, you don't look for excuses. You are in control, and you can only retain that control if you live with integrity, treat players humanely, and work at establishing and maintaining mutual respect between you and the players.

'I've had to deal with players whose mothers have died. I took Ettienne Botha from the wreckage of his car. I addressed the players about it and phoned his mother because I didn't want her to hear the news of her son's death on the TV or radio. I stood by Richard Bands when his dad died. Those guys play for you – there is a relationship. And then there's no way you can take people for fools.'

Meyer reckons that in spite of, and indeed on account of, that fatherly relationship with players, a vital distance should be maintained.

'Anton Leonard and I were very close to each other, yet he and I have never had a beer on our own. We would socialise in the company of other people at a function and then go home.

'Once players lose respect for you, you never regain it. You may think that you're a fun guy and booze with the players. They knew that if they started boozing, I left. No one came to talk to me about team selections. And if they partied hard, I told the players that it was wrong. If there was something wrong with their lives, I told them so.

'As a coach you have to remember that you're dealing with young people – children, in fact. Coaching is not about the game, it's about coaching people. Therefore, I have no problem with it when someone makes a mistake. But when a person has no integrity, I'll excise him from the system. A coach has that responsibility towards individuals, the team and the rugby union. And you have to act fast when someone threatens to disrupt the harmony in a team.'

According to Ferguson, dealing ruthlessly with troublemakers is sometimes the only way to protect the integrity of a club. He sees the manager as the central figure in this: 'The long-term view of the club is more important than any individual, and the manager has to be the most important one in the club.'[21]

While this may sound somewhat presumptuous to a South African ear, it cannot be denied that this approach worked for Manchester United – and the Blue Bulls. An alternative approach will be examined later, in the chapters that discuss Gary Kirsten, Paddy Upton and Michael Jordaan.

But, to Meyer, this approach, namely nurturing a close relationship with the players and yet maintaining a vital distance from them, gave him the kind of control with which he could maintain the Bulls' vision of world domination. And no one was exempted.

'I was sitting at home one day when the phone rang. I knew at once that someone had messed up and it turned out that Danie Rossouw had punched someone. I was livid. My vision was to make the Bulls a global brand and things like that weren't in keeping with what I expected from the players and management.

'Danie was summoned to my office and I was ready for him. I had a reply to any excuse he may have had. If he should say that the guy bumped into him on purpose, I would ask why he didn't just walk away. I had a hundred replies ready and was determined not to let Danie get off lightly.

'So he sat down and I said, "Now, really, Danie! What the hell have you done now?"

'He just looked at me and said, "I can't remember, Coach." He could have told me anything, but not that. I asked him again, but his reply was the same. "I can't remember, Coach."

'I know Danie; I know he's a team man; I know he's a good person. At that time he could have gone to the Sharks for R1 million per year, but he decided to stay with the Bulls at half that salary.

'So that was the situation I was faced with. My intention had been to give Danie a good dressing-down. I had immediately taken control of the situation when I heard about it, but then he had no recollection of the incident. Because there was absolute honesty between me and the players and, therefore, a strong mutual respect, I believed him and said that we would put it behind us but stressed that something like that was not allowed to happen again. Maybe the player just needed a bit of help with keeping his temper in check.

'So the players make mistakes and I have on occasion got rid of players who had gone too far. In 2010 I asked a few management members and ten players to leave. But, ultimately, it's about managing people correctly and once you help people or are simply honest with them, they play for you and you will never lose control of the dressing room.'

---

5. Match the message to the moment

Heyneke Meyer's partiality for stories, and the right story at the right moment, has become common knowledge by now. His motivational stories alone would provide material for a fairly hefty book.

The principle that every player should get a training and rehabilitation programme to suit his unique physiological make-up and needs, and a custom-made diet applies equally to the way in which different people should be uniquely encouraged and psychologically conditioned. Because in the end it is about the human being before the group and this demands an individual approach from a head coach.

Ferguson noted in this regard: 'As a manager, you play different roles at different times. Sometimes you have to be a doctor, or a teacher, or a father.'[22]

Meyer has very good interpersonal relationships and he is quick to sense what the needs of every individual are in the coach–player relationship. But he is also a great believer in science, which is why he started working with brain profiles together with Dr Kobus Neethling during his tenure at the SWD (he later also used this tool at the Bulls). (The chapters on Paul Treu deal with brain profiles in detail.)

'With young people, you have to know which buttons to push,' Meyer explained. 'And that's where I used brain profiles. I knew that at half-time I shouldn't talk about a lot of emotional heart stuff with Victor. He's left-brain dominant: clinical, rational and analytical. When I did those brain profiles for the first time, I saw that 60 per cent of our team were left-brain dominant. I'm right-brain dominant, but I couldn't necessarily apply what would work for me willy-nilly to the majority of the team. I shouldn't bombard them with motivational messages only. At half-time I needed to use a clinical analysis of the first half to prepare a player for the second half. I would say, for example, that we must do this and that on a left shoulder in the scrum, and this and that on a right shoulder. If such and such happened, we must react in this particular way.

'Then I would call Gary Botha, Bakkies Botha and Fourie du Preez. Fourie is right-brain dominant. Long before anything went wrong on the field or in the team, Fourie would have started sensing it. He's the most emotional rugby player with whom I've ever worked. He is technically the best analyst I know, but it's done purely on gut feeling. So I know that I have to motivate guys like that from the heart. *That* is coaching. Not the technical stuff.'

A good example of this is once again the way that Meyer conditioned the Bulls before that 92-3 victory over the Reds in 2007. For the right-brain players, he had the story of the little deaf bull. For the left-brain players, he broke down the target of a points difference of 76 and quantified it point by point, scrum by scrum and lineout by lineout, until he had everyone on the same page.

This approach was particularly useful in the short term, but, as gleaned from the interviews conducted for this book, players remember Meyer's stories better than anything else. With this in mind, he tried to illustrate to the players things like team culture and the pursuit of a long-term common goal through stories.

'I would regularly ask the players during our individual conversations to explain the Bulls' culture to me. You can't possibly expect most rugby players to explain it to you in psychological terms and the intention was never to quiz people. To make it easier for the players, I told them stories, which they then usually repeated to me almost word for word after I asked them how they understood the Bulls' culture. Players remember stories.'

Meyer explained the Bulls' culture and his rotation plan to Bakkies Botha, Danie Rossouw and Victor Matfield using the following story: 'A man could choose whether he wanted to go to heaven or hell, and he wanted to investigate both possibilities beforehand. So he first went to hell and saw that the people there looked neither healthy nor happy. Then he went to heaven and saw that everything there looked more or less the same as in hell, except that the people were healthy.

'He couldn't see any reason for that one difference and asked whether he could pay another quick visit to hell. This time he noticed that everyone in hell had long knives and forks attached to their hands. When he got to heaven again, he saw that the picture was the same there. Long knives, long forks. But everyone was happy. For some or other inexplicable reason it was nicer in heaven than in hell.

'Then the man stood at a distance so that he could have a good view of both possibilities at the same time before making his choice. At that moment, everyone sat down to dine at long tables and the most delicious food was brought out – exactly the same in heaven and in hell: steaks, prawns, roast potatoes, all the most delectable dishes imaginable.

'When the food was put down in the middle of the tables, each guy in hell went for the biggest and tastiest pieces of meat. But no matter how hard they struggled, they couldn't get the food into their mouths because the knives and forks were too long. Because the people in hell were egocentric, they were also emaciated.

'But in heaven everything was going smoothly. One guy would cut up the choicest piece of steak and feed it to the guy sitting opposite him. That was why they had such long knives and forks – so that you could help someone else, and so that they could help you in turn. That was why the people in heaven were so healthy and happy. It was a win–win situation.

'And that was the Bulls' culture. You had Bakkies, Victor and Danie. All three of them wanted to play. All were Springboks, but only two of them would have a chance to play at a time. So I told them that for us at the Bulls it was about a common goal. We'll go on this journey together, everyone gets a contract and everyone gets a chance to play. But we first seek the best for each other and for the team before we look after our own interests.

'This wasn't only good for the team, but it was also a win–win situation for the players. I told them that I would devise a rotation plan for the three of them so that they played fewer games per year but would, at the same time, be able to play until the age of 38. And that is exactly what happened. Bakkies and Danie are still playing in France for Toulon, and although Victor did some coaching in between, both of us knew that he was still good enough to play. That is the Bulls' culture – one for all and all for one,' Meyer explained.

When it came to motivating players, he followed Ferguson's principle: that you get more from a player with a timely 'well done' than by criticising him. There was one exception, though: Pedrie Wannenburg.

One of Meyer's goals was to have the best-disciplined team in the world, but with players like Wannenburg it was not feasible. With the right approach, however, it was indeed possible to make even some of the more wayward players part of the greater goal of world domination.

'Pedrie played his best rugby for me,' Meyer said. 'It is something I never do, but Pedrie was the only player with whom I used negative motivation. Danie Rossouw was a lock and loose forward, and when Danie was injured, Pedrie played. But then there would be a slight chance that Danie could play again the following week, so I would tell Pedrie that he should enjoy himself on the field but that this was his last match. Boy, then that man would play a cracker of a game and we would give Danie more time to recover. So I would tell Pedrie that he was going to play another match, but that this would now really be his last match. And once again he would have a good game.

'Those players I got as 20-year-olds all became Springboks – like Pedrie. He's an incredible rugby player but I didn't put up with his nonsense. Because if you overlook it once, it becomes a habit, but if you manage a player with a discipline problem correctly, even he comes into his own. When I became involved with the Bulls again in 2010,

I removed a bunch of players from the system who had kept messing up. As with all these things, it's about culture and people management.'

The way that Meyer and his management team wanted to improve this kind of communication at the Bulls was in line with the Bulls' fourth pillar: to establish a science-based programme that would allow the players to develop to their full potential. It included the training, approach, and recreational and medical facilities used by the Bulls. But psychology, too, was a very strong component of this pillar. The Bulls appointed Jannie Putter as their mental coach from 2006 to 2010. Putter was a provincial sportsman with an honours degree in sports science and a master's degree in sports psychology.

Springbok flanker Arno Botha maintains that Putter and Meyer were the two biggest influences on his life after he moved from a small school in Nylstroom to Pretoria to become a professional sportsman. According to Botha, it all had to do with the right message that Meyer and Putter gave him at the right time. That, rather than technical coaching, enabled him to make better decisions at crucial times in his young career and ultimately to become a Springbok.

6. Prepare to win

One of the most famous sayings in sport is that winning is a habit. These words are pasted on the walls of countless dressing rooms and player lounges. They come from a speech given by Vince Lombardi, and that sentence represents Meyer and Ferguson's approach to the training and conditioning of players in all their facets – in other words, everything that has to be done before a match in order to be able to win.

Here is the full version of Lombardi's brief yet powerful speech:

> Winning is not a sometime thing; it's an all-the-time thing. You don't win once in a while; you don't do things right once in a while; you do them right all the time. Winning is a habit. Unfortunately, so is losing.
>
> There is no room for second place. There is only one place in my game, and that's first place. I have finished second twice in my time at Green Bay, and I don't ever want to finish second again. There is a second-place bowl game, but it is a game for losers played by losers. It is and always has been an

American zeal to be first in anything we do, and to win, and to win, and to win.

Every time a football player goes to ply his trade he's got to play from the ground up – from the soles of his feet right up to his head. Every inch of him has to play. Some guys play with their heads. That's OK. You've got to be smart to be number one in any business. But more importantly, you've got to play with your heart, with every fiber of your body. If you're lucky enough to find a guy with a lot of head and a lot of heart, he's never going to come off the field second.

Running a football team is no different than running any other kind of organization – an army, a political party or a business. The principles are the same. The object is to win – to beat the other guy. Maybe that sounds hard or cruel. I don't think it is.

It is a reality of life that men are competitive and the most competitive games draw the most competitive men. That's why they are there – to compete. To know the rules and objectives when they get in the game. The object is to win fairly, squarely, by the rules – but to win.

And in truth, I've never known a man worth his salt who in the long run, deep down in his heart, didn't appreciate the grind, the discipline. There is something in good men that really yearns for discipline and the harsh reality of head-to-head combat.

I don't say these things because I believe in the 'brute' nature of man or that men must be brutalized to be combative. I believe in God, and I believe in human decency. But I firmly believe that any man's finest hour, the greatest fulfillment of all that he holds dear, is that moment when he has worked his heart out in a good cause and lies exhausted on the field of battle – victorious.[23]

Ferguson echoes this thinking in the *Harvard Business Review* article when he says:

Winning is in my nature. I've set my standards over such a long period of time that there is no other option for me – I have to win. I expected to win every time we went out there. Even if five of the most important players were injured, I expected to win. Other teams get into a huddle before the start of a match, but I did not do that with my team. Once we stepped onto the pitch before a game, I was confident that the players were prepared and ready to play, because everything had been done before they walked out onto the pitch.[24]

That sense of preparedness was precisely what the Bulls players had when they ran onto the field to face the Reds on 5 May 2007. The work had been done beforehand, and two hours later the final score was 92-3. It was the result of that third bleep test, which Meyer had insisted on after Basil Carzis had told him it was impossible. It was because of the story of the little deaf bull and the quantifying of the 76 points. And, above all, it was the outcome of those Blue Blood sessions where the players had to work unremittingly for ten minutes after Derick Hougaard, Morné Steyn or Jaco van der Westhuyzen missed a goal kick from the touchline. Meyer is firmly convinced that this was the factor that tipped the scales in the final, two weeks later.

The best generic term for training sessions like those Blue Blood ones is 'situational training'. It describes the sessions exactly – to practise being in a specific situation so that you can be ready for that situation in real life.

Meyer believed that if winning is a habit, it should also be a habit to do the right things that enable you to win.

7. Rely on the power of observation

As mentioned, as a young coach at the SWD Eagles, Meyer even watered the pitch himself, while his right-hand man and fitness specialist, Hennie Kriel, sewed the numbers onto the players' jerseys.

'We did everything, and the workload just became greater and harder when we started working for the Blue Bulls at the end of 2000. We had to do everything ourselves – and we did. Those were tough times,' Meyer recalled.

Over the years, the Bulls' infrastructure and their management team developed to such an extent that he could gradually delegate some of those responsibilities to other members of the team. In 2005 Pote Human took over the Currie Cup team from Meyer after they had won three consecutive titles. After Meyer's return to the Bulls as director of rugby, Johann van Graan started doing much of the coaching in his capacity as forwards and attack coach. Meyer could then focus on the business of rugby; Frans Ludeke could focus on the senior team as a whole; and the order that had been brought into the coaching structures enabled the top management to observe matters from a necessary distance.

Being able to do this is one of the great advantages of a strong management team that can function interdependently. 'Once you appoint a strong management team, it's very easy to trust those people completely,' believes Meyer. 'I know that everyone is facing in the same direction. I know that all of them are capable and even among the best in the world in their field. When you have a team of that calibre, you can confidently take a step back without ceding any control. And that gives you the opportunity to observe things in a different way, reflect on them and then go back and make the necessary adjustments,' Meyer said, as he elaborated on the luxury of being in such a position.

After winning the Super 14 trophy in 2007 as coach, Meyer wanted to work full-time as the rugby executive. It was partly because of this that Frans Ludeke was not appointed in this position, but rather as head coach of the Blue Bulls and the Bulls. However, when Meyer left the Bulls and entered the business world after Ludeke had already been appointed as head coach, Ludeke and Schwartz were obliged to take over some of the responsibilities that Meyer was supposed to have shouldered, and still make the structure work.

The initial plan was realised in 2010, though, when Meyer was appointed in the executive position – a timely move.

He said, 'When I joined the Bulls for the second time, Ian was occupied with rugby business at such a high level that he no longer had the time to do thorough recruitment. They then started taking in more and more players only from Pretoria, not because they didn't want to look more widely, but because there was simply no longer the time.

'I then appointed Xander Janse van Rensburg. He was an agent with a good knowledge of rugby, and my instruction to him was that we had to identify and draw in players at an even younger age. I had wanted to sign Pieter-Steph du Toit at that stage, but he was already enrolled at the Sharks Academy.

'We definitely did the right thing when I appointed Xander and Werner de Beer as full-time recruiters. Once again, the Bulls needed a very strong line-up of young players. A number of the Bulls' Boks were on their way out and a bunch of second-line players had started coming through – nice guys, all of them, but not good enough. I told the management we would struggle if we tried to contest for trophies with these players.

'My proposal to the board was that we should go for even younger guys. It's a risk, but I would rather make a few mistakes than lose another Pieter-Steph. Jan Serfontein was one of the success stories.

'Ian had spotted him in 2008. We offered him more than we had offered any young Bull before him. The Sharks wanted to offer him the same, but in 2009 I went to talk to his dad to make sure that we got this guy to join the Bulls. I had decided that we wouldn't lose guys again, and Ian and I already knew in 2008 that 15-year-old Jan Serfontein would become a Springbok by the age of 20.'

In addition to the junior structures, overtures and contracting that were improved within a high-performance programme in 2010, Meyer also had the opportunity to inspect what was happening with the senior players – except for the second line, which did not measure up to his standards at that stage.

'On my return, I was only with the juniors. And I think it was good because I could focus all my attention on junior rugby and recruitment. When I was also appointed as the rugby executive in 2010, Frans said he had no problem with that, but he still wanted to have the final say on team selections. I told him that was absolutely fine – I would never question his team selections and I wouldn't even talk to the team. My job was to safeguard and regain the culture. He bought into it completely and that's why the board was upset with me when I accepted the Springbok position.

'The wonderful thing about that executive position was that I was no longer involved with the team. There was distance between me and everything that happened on the field. During that time I got rid of ten players and a few management members who no longer fitted into the culture.

'When we failed to reach the Super Rugby semifinals in 2011, one player went on an all-night drinking binge and arrived drunk at a photo session the next day. I summoned him to my office, asked him why he had celebrated after the team couldn't even make the semis, had his blood tested and decided not to renew his contract.

'A lot of people were angry with me, but my approach was that *this* is our culture – with or without you. And that's why I let players go – average guys who boozed and with whom we wouldn't win trophies. I told Frans I wasn't going to budge a millimetre on the culture that had brought us to where we were. There was no way I would do that.

'It was necessary for me not to be involved directly with the team because then you notice things that are hard to spot otherwise: structures, management, culture.'

Ferguson, too, delegated more and more of the physical coaching to his management team. 'Once I stepped out of the bubble,' he said, 'I became more aware of a range of details, and my performance level jumped.'[25]

8. Never stop adapting

In his late twenties, Heyneke Meyer worked for the Woolworths group. He opened new shops and appointed staff. That has always been typical of him: getting a project – a shop, team or rugby union – that is still in its infancy and striving to turn it into the best. He is entrepreneurially minded, both as a person and as a coach.

Meyer regards even unrelated experiences as learning opportunities, as useful for whatever he could find himself doing next. He never sits still – it goes against his nature. Even he was surprised at the long period of seven years that he spent at the BBC. Three years at Woolworths, three years at the SWD Eagles, seven years at the Bulls, six months in the business world, seven months in Leicester, then another three years at the Bulls. And at the time of writing, he is in his second year as head coach of the Springboks.

It is not because he gets bored or lacks the loyalty he demands of his players that he has moved around so much. To him, loyalty is an inextricable part of one's honour and integrity. However, in his view, loyalty is not connected to time but to dedication and the quality of a person's contribution, regardless of the period. For him, everything revolves around a central question and a reluctance to become comfortable with the status quo: 'How can I improve something?' Whether it is a human being, a team, a structure or even an entire industry.

'At Woolworths I learnt how to appoint the right people in the right place. These were basic things but, in the end, details matter. There's a specific kind of person you look for to man a cash register. You want a specific kind of person to pack shelves. It's about personality types. The one person is outgoing, the other may be reserved but have a good work ethic and eye for detail. That principle applies anywhere in life – the greater whole can only become and remain the best if nothing is regarded as insignificant or unimprovable. These are the things that continuously add value,' reckoned Meyer.

He has always known where he wanted to add value and that there were no short cuts, but that he would often have to carve out the roads and tar them himself in order to get to where he is now – Springbok coach.

'I still remember that in 1995 there was a Sanlam policy you could buy that would enable you to go to the 1999 World Cup tournament. I didn't have money, but I knew that I was going to be at that World Cup too. In 1995 I was a coach at school level, and in 1999 the Springboks' forwards coach. Nothing is impossible.

'Everyone always told me that coaching would never become a professional job, but I knew that it was due to happen eventually and that's why I studied the things I did. That's why I did the kind of reading I did. That's why I tried to draw lessons from everything I embarked on, which I would eventually be able to use in the professional era. You just have to work out these aspirations for yourself in your head. You have to wonder what something will look like in the future – not whether someone else will make it happen for you, but how you yourself can be the change.

'It's simple. I always tell the players that 97 per cent of people don't write down their dreams, but the 3 per cent who do write them down achieve much more than the majority of people who think that they are dreaming, but do nothing about it. My whole life I've wanted to coach. I wrote down that dream. And the route I carved out for myself towards that destination was not the fastest route, but the one that would prepare me the best for the day I would make that dream a reality.'

Meyer has coached at every level where a South African coach can ply his trade: primary school, high school, university, club, provincial and national. And at almost all of those levels he came up with something new.

'People laugh at me now when I talk on a two-way radio in the coaches' box as if it's a novelty to me. But Ian and I did many things for the first time, and back in the day at the SWD we were the very first guys to use radio contact. Ian McIntosh gave us a tongue-lashing and said we were cheating.

'I also wanted to appoint Tommy Smook as the SWD's full-time team doctor. It would have been another first in South Africa. There was no money for that, however, and so we told the board that we should at least pay the players' medical-aid contributions. So the SWD Eagles became the first rugby team in South Africa with medical aid for the players. Today this is a non-negotiable part of professional players' contracts.'

When Meyer joined the Blue Bulls, he again insisted on appointing Smook as the team's permanent doctor. Smook secured the job – a first for professional rugby. Today the BBC is still the only rugby company in the country that employs two full-time doctors.

Meyer was the first coach in the professional era to dump the unsustainable contracting model that revolved around senior players. The pipeline in rugby was his brainchild. Nowadays all the big rugby unions have similar models.

Meyer was the first coach to appoint an extended management team and specialist coaches. He recalled, 'I still remember that time in 2001 when we went to play against the Pumas. They beat us on that occasion with all those former Blue Bulls in their ranks, and afterwards they laughed at me and my big management team as we boarded the bus.' Today big management teams have become the norm.

Moreover, the work of that management team and specialists was supplemented with applicable alternative disciplines such as Pilates, karate and the combat skills that the Special Forces are trained in.

Meyer was also the first rugby coach to apply specific skills from American football, Australian rules and rugby league in rugby. The Bulls' defence system was developed from rugby league and in the process John McFarland also became the world's first specialist defence coordinator. This, too, is a common phenomenon nowadays, and their sound defensive game is what has enabled the Stormers to become a consistent and competitive Super Rugby team again.

Meyer and Eddie Jones, then at the Brumbies, were the first rugby coaches to employ structured patterns of play. Meyer said, 'People shot down those patterns at the time, but today the whole world plays like that. I still remember how we were the first rugby team in the world that got the hooker to do the scrumhalf's work from a lineout. The Bulls' rugby committee summoned me at the time and said that a hooker couldn't pass. But those things worked for us.

'Ettienne Botha scored most of our tries in those days and there was a simple explanation for this – patterns. Within a 5-metre radius, no one could touch Ettienne. Not even Bryan Habana. His feet were too good. Everyone said at the time that I "overcoached" the guys. But that wasn't the case, I said. You simply take your best guy and put him down opposite your weakest opponent, thereby giving him an even better chance to score tries. So I ran a pattern with Ettienne. When we had a lineout or scrum at a specific place, we first took the ball up to the advantage line. Then a second ball carrier would come in while Ettienne had moved to inside centre by the time he got into a one-on-one situation with a prop. He invariably won the contest and scored tries. That was the only thing we did with patterns and it was the reason we won.

'American football utilises patterns, American soccer utilises patterns, netball has patterns. You can look at so many sporting codes because what you achieve with patterns is to disrupt your opposition to such an extent that you create space and opportunities. Most tries are scored from broken play, but we don't practise that. At the Bulls we wanted to gain that advantage with pattern play, and we did.'

After this explanation, Meyer paused for a moment, burst out laughing and remarked, 'I read newspapers. People think that I'm this dumb, narrow-minded Afrikaans guy, but there was much more than just brawn involved in the way that the Bulls dominated rugby. I never said that there was only one way of playing rugby. But at the Bulls we examined trends in the game, learnt from sources beyond the confines of the game and ended up playing a brand of rugby that we called winning rugby. Winning rugby is a mindset, it's a science, it's psychology, it's about people. And we won trophies with it. Supporters don't care about what was done behind the scenes when they watch rugby. When they sit in the stadium or in front of the TV, they aren't wondering about everything the team has done to prepare, but whether the team will win. That's all you have to do to attract more supporters and sponsors. People want to win and we made winning a wonderful habit.'

That brand of winning rugby represents the last pillar in Meyer's business plan. Market-research agency BMI conducted research for the BBC in 2012 and compiled a very interesting demographic profile of the Bulls' supporters across South Africa, which indicates that a winning culture and the need to identify with it transcend racial stereotypes. The gender ratio of the respondents was 56 per cent male to 44 per cent female.

Ultimately, the crux of sustained success lies in embracing the *kaizen* culture of continuous change and progress. The time when it matters

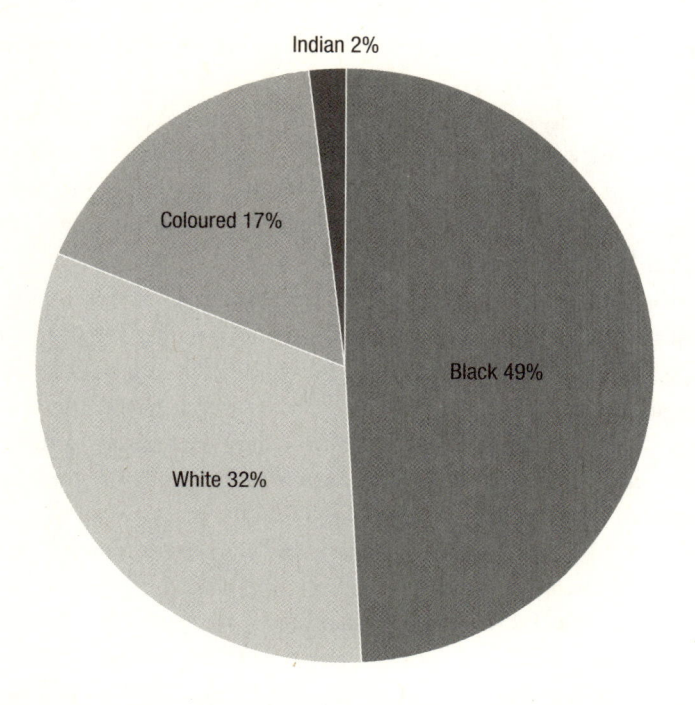

Figure 5: Demographic profile of Blue Bulls supporters, end 2012 (Source: BMI)

most of all is when a team is at the peak of its performance cycle – at 12:00 on Wayne Goldsmith's performance clock.

Ferguson summarised the role of a manager at this stage in the cycle as follows: 'Most people with my kind of track record don't look to change. But I always felt I couldn't afford not to change. We had to be successful – there was no other option for me – and I would explore any means of improving. I continued to work hard. I treated every success as my first. My job was to give us the best possible chance of winning. That is what drove me.'[26]

In conclusion

'Heyneke was a generation ahead and he put professional rugby on a completely different course. We've been together since the SWD days and he could see these things in his mind's eye – he was visionary,' said Frans Ludeke.

We were sitting in Ludeke's office in the grandstand of Loftus Versfeld. In any other stadium, this office could serve as the presidential suite. There are three walls and one enormous glass panel that offers an unsurpassed view of the field where Ludeke won the first of his two Super Rugby crowns as coach.

He was also supposed to feature in a leading role in this narrative. But the most successful Super Rugby coach in South African rugby history is a pious man, a humble man. Instead of seeing himself as a trailblazing sports leader, Ludeke prefers to give the credit to his predecessor and to God.

'I came after Heyneke and built on what he had created. That was truly pioneering work and I'd be happy to talk about Heyneke, but the focus of the story can't be me. I have a servant's heart. I have an eye for detail. Heyneke changed an industry. He's an entrepreneur. He starts things and then, after a while, he sees the next big thing and moves things around again. He's a starter,' Ludeke remarked.

In front of him was a page from the presentation he made during his interview for the Bulls' head-coach position in 2007. The teacher in him came to the fore as he made notes with his purple pen and underlined words twice to emphasise them.

The page read as follows:

VISION: Be a World Class Sports Brand
MISSION: To keep a winning edge on our competitors
FOCUS: Understanding and Small Adjustments
CULTURE: Trust, Family, Learning, Work Ethic, Respect

At the bottom of the page were three pictures, with the word 'winning' written above each of them. Below the first picture was the word 'yesterday'. It showed Buurman van Zyl, the most successful coach in the history of Blue Bulls rugby, holding the Currie Cup. The second picture, 'today', was one of Victor Matfield holding the Super 14 trophy in the air in 2007. And below the third picture was the word 'tomorrow' with the picture itself showing only an exclamation mark above the dates 2008–2010.

Ludeke has since added one Currie Cup title and two Super Rugby titles to that third picture. He humbly shared another piece of wisdom:

'People often say that it is only after a leader's departure that one can really see for the first time how good he was – if things continue to exist and keep working.'

It has frequently been claimed that Ludeke ploughed with Meyer's ox. There are two reasons why this is a ludicrous statement. To start with, his first year at the helm was less successful and a tremendous amount of work had to be done to get the Bulls back on track. Secondly, that statement is indicative of a lack of understanding of what it takes to achieve sustained success. After all, the idea behind good structures is the pursuit of sustainability and not needing to rebuild from scratch each time a leader leaves an organisation. The fact that the system could go through a period of adjustment under a new leader and subsequently help bring about the two biggest successes in its existence was a tribute to the good structures and the new leader, who had not been part of their development but nonetheless took them to a next level.

When Ludeke moved across the Jukskei River at the end of 2007 after his seven-year stint at the Golden Lions, he initially found his new working environment intimidating – especially when Meyer did not stay on in his executive capacity but instead left the organisation.

'I had to shoulder a bigger yoke, but I had no idea what that yoke looked like,' Ludeke recalled. 'Also, that first experience of Loftus was overawing. The traditions and history of success are in your face when you walk in here for the first time. All the photos; all the memories. And there were *big* moments. Not one – many of them. The Bulls were successful.

'When you walk into the dressing room, you see the boards with the names of guys who played the most matches, scored the most points. There's history wherever you look. I found it intimidating at first. You think to yourself that you've come from the Lions' structures. I played in the days of Doc Luyt and Kitch Christie. There was success, but as a player, I never really understood what lay behind that success.

'Later I started coaching at the Lions after the successful era of Laurie Mains. We played in finals, but never won enough games in Super Rugby to reach the play-off rounds. So I came from the Lions and walked into this environment where there was success, and the expectations were that this success would be sustained. There was enormous pressure on me.

'But the legacy Heyneke left here, the people he left here, were incredible. I received guidance from the Lord, read books, listened to people. And my eyes were opened so that I recognised what I had to do: basic things, such as ensuring that relationships got back on track.'

Barend van Graan has at times referred to Meyer's strong management team as his greatest legacy – the people who immediately took Ludeke under their wing during his introduction to the players at their training camp in George for the first time.

This helped a lot to relieve the pressure on Ludeke. Another big difference was that, despite the departure of several prominent players, he still had a very strong group of senior players to work with.

And it was because of these players, among other reasons, that Meyer asked Ludeke to take over the head-coach position from him – interpersonal relations and a strong analytical approach are Ludeke's strong suits. Therefore, he was not an entrepreneur par excellence like Meyer, but someone who would be able to build good relationships with the players and management in the first place, and who could also make vital improvements to the Bulls' structures thanks to his critical-analytical approach.

Despite their dissimilarities, Meyer and Ludeke have some very important traits in common, and it was this commonality that caused Meyer to call upon his old rugby friend again when he foresaw change for the Bulls.

Ludeke explained, 'Good leaders know that the tiniest things can make a big difference in an organisation's success. If he has a vision, the next important question is whether he has time and a unique vision for you as an individual. Does that leader make time for you? The kind of leader who does that has a powerful influence on an organisation because he wins people's hearts as well as their minds, and then he can take them anywhere. Also, you have to be sincere, otherwise people will see through you. Those who don't know me well think that I'm only analytical. They think I'm just a manager. But people are immensely important to me and if you understand people's hearts, your style is what makes them click with you, not your technical knowledge.'

Meyer and Ludeke's shared philosophy of life encapsulates what Meyer considered the Bulls' biggest success factor – a people-oriented culture. And Ludeke is very good at that.

'When it comes to anything new, my point of departure is the following: seek to understand before you want to be understood,' said Ludeke. 'I understand what culture is, and culture demands that you learn to speak to people in their own language. On my arrival at the Bulls, I first learnt to understand and speak the right language before I could make changes of my own to the structures. That was where my growth started and it's probably the most I have grown in my life.

'I knew Heyneke well, and knew that continuity was the important thing for him and that I, therefore, would only have to make minor adjustments. So I first set out to establish relationships because that is how you learn how people communicate here, what the language is and what makes people tick. Listen to them. Try to understand their heart. What are their needs, and what are the handbrakes that we would have to release – things that hold us back? What do they find frustrating? What excites them? What works in the structures?'

Ludeke is the antithesis of an autocrat and his leadership style is based on the participatory management style he learnt from former Crusaders coach Robbie Deans in 2006.

Ludeke remarked, 'I wanted the players to take ownership of the way we play. It's the only way to give them the freedom to make decisions within a certain structure. That's how the Brumbies and the Crusaders operated at the time. I spent a week with Robbie Deans in 2006 and it was a life-changing experience. I saw how he managed his senior group and it changed the way I thought about senior players. I knew that kind of empowerment would work for players such as Fourie du Preez as well because they would take that responsibility and do something exceptional with it.

'I have a servant's heart and it wasn't a problem for me. I had enormous respect for people who had played more than 100 Currie Cup and Super Rugby matches. I had respect for what those people had achieved and I wanted to know what had driven those successes and what the key factors were.'

In the first few days in George, therefore, Ludeke had individual conversations with the players.

'I could gather immediately what made the players' hearts beat faster, but also that there were a number of handbrakes. Some guys didn't know where they stood in the team and there were players who didn't know what their roles and responsibilities were. We identified five or six short- and long-term goals straight away, and it was extremely important to me to just get that unity in the group as a first step – there was edginess among them.'

Ludeke was reminded of his experience with Robbie Deans after his conversation with Fourie du Preez in particular, and it convinced him that the senior players needed a big say in the management of the team. For the first time in his life, he was faced with the challenge of thinking strategically about the future, and how he and his team would get there. It was a vital decision that he took deliberately, which made it possible for Ludeke to eventually give expression to his more analytical qualities with greater passion.

'I started the GPG – the Game Plan Group. I started it so that there could be a forum where senior players and management would be able to give their input and question anything they wanted to. We reviewed things, made changes and put stuff in place that had been discussed there. This was also where the Bulls' structures, processes and way of doing things started making more sense to me.

'It was incredibly important to empower all these people. It was a priority for me, and the things that worked at the Bulls over these few years were often the important suggestions made in the GPG. It was a question of drawing on other people's input, different ways of thinking. It comes back to Heyneke's ability to put things in place and get the right people there to drive the culture. When I arrived here, I didn't just feel it, I could see it,' Ludeke added.

In 2008 the Bulls won only 6 of their 13 Super Rugby matches and finished tenth on the log. Ludeke had to face scathing criticism and his participatory management style was viewed as a weakness. The players responded well to his style, however, and came to trust, understand and appreciate him as their new coach – because that GPG was certainly no tea party.

'There was no hierarchy, but if you were there, you had to speak your mind. When we walked out of there we had to be a unit because we were the leaders. Honest, and sometimes harsh, feedback is the only way of making something grow. It's the kind of thing that sometimes hurts people's feelings. But we held each other accountable there,' said

Ludeke, describing another of the principles he shares with Meyer — blatant honesty and mutual respect make for sound relationships.

After the chastening season of 2008 and thanks to the relationships that had been forged during that time, in his second year Ludeke could focus more on the detail of the five pillars and make the adjustments he had promised at the end of 2007. In 2009 the Bulls experienced the best year in their history when they won both the Currie Cup and the Super 14 — a year before they defended the Super Rugby crown successfully.

'It was wonderful to see how we progressed year after year and developed things further,' said Ludeke. 'I could take a season to get to know and understand the structures. There were so many things in place — blueprints of everything: defence, attack, kicking plan. It was all part of the structures and initially I didn't make any changes.

'Then we all looked at those things together, proposed changes and made small adjustments. This created energy for the new season every year and undoubtedly contributed to the bumper years we had in 2009 and 2010.

'Detail has always come naturally to me and I was in my element. It gives me energy and it's a big focus of mine. I like taking things apart, asking why they work and then putting together an improved model for the following season. We're talking much more widely than just the things that happened on the playing field.

'There was a different focus in how we played: protocols, blueprints … And with that emphasis on the details, we could tweak the already established structures and the five pillars in just the right places to make sure that we retained that advantage over other teams. If a new player joined us, for example, we could immediately say how we played. Here are video clips, here's a book — and then we put that youngster in the fast track of the player pipeline. We were able to bring the junior players through systems at a faster and faster rate. It's also important to me that everyone should know exactly what the details are of what we do. Everyone: coaches, players, the lot.'

When Ludeke, the analyst and critical thinker, started examining the structures in finer detail, he was surprised at what he found — something he had not foreseen as an opposing coach.

'I still find the simplicity of things here incredible. Heyneke created such an impressive system that one assumed it had to be a complicated affair. But it isn't – the success of the system lies in its very simplicity: honesty, compassion, don't do to another guy what you don't want to have done to you, hard work. Rugby is simple – it's won in the hearts of players. Everyone has a plan and everyone has achieved success with their plan at some or other time. However, getting people's buy-in with just a simple plan is often the difference between a plan that works only sporadically and a plan that makes sustained success possible. And that's something that strikes me about Heyneke – he has big visions and he realises those plans by putting in place a few simple things and then persuading others by means of that big vision to join him in pursuing it and turning it into a reality.

'I don't cajole people. If a guy says no to me, that's that. But a guy like Heyneke will persist and persist until he gets to where he wants to be. Despite being primarily task-oriented, he has a very strong human side to him. He understands people and that's why he can convince them to join him by refusing to take no for an answer.

'When he finds himself under pressure, he becomes purely task-oriented because he knows what the job requires and that's what he will do. He gets the job done. I had to learn to become more like that too. We all grow. I'm here in my little analytical box, but I see what's happening in those places where Heyneke has spotted the next big move. It stimulates me and I know it's wonderful – I have come a long way in this culture. As a good leader, you need to know when to be what – and that's emotional intelligence.'

There is an exceptional interplay and understanding between Meyer and Ludeke. It's almost as if Meyer, the right brain, had to be there first to elevate the Blue Bulls from the valley of rugby death to the peak of rugby aristocracy. Then Ludeke, the left brain, had to come in to maintain that new status with the precision and care of a watchmaker, and keep it in step with the changing times.

'It's incredible to think of what we talk about nowadays,' said Ludeke. 'The pillars will always be there, but the growth that has occurred has steered the conversation in a more psychological and spiritual direction.

We'll always ensure that the pillars remain strong, but the language we speak — what currently gives us the edge — is not about the pillars as such, but about the level we operate at from day to day to ensure that we remain successful. No one can exist in our industry nowadays without those five pillars. But how have they developed continuously and what keeps them upright?

'It comes down to the quality of the people in the system. Everyone may have the same structures, but it boils down to the people. *They* are the DNA that gives this thing its unique personality. You can imitate anything, but not DNA. The culture is about people. Heyneke Meyer's ability to invest in the right people and to let people become the best that they can be are the biggest reasons for the continued success that South African rugby has experienced over the past decade.'

BRENDAN VENTER

CHAPTER 6

Giving more than you take

'The great essentials to happiness in this life are something to do, someone to love and something to hope for.'
– Joseph Addison

If life is a collection of memories, Brendan Venter will never be able to touch an oatmeal biscuit again without thinking of 29 May 2010.

That was the day the rugby clubs Saracens and Leicester Tigers played in the final of the English Premiership at Twickenham. Leicester were defending the title, while for 'Sarries' it was their first Premiership final since the club was founded in 1876. Venter had been appointed as the Saracens director of rugby at the beginning of that European season, and for him, too, it was supposed to be a glorious day.

With three minutes left on the clock, his troops were leading by 27-26, and it seemed as if the near unthinkable was about to unfold: the team that had finished the previous season in the ninth spot were well on course to defeat the defending and five-time champions. The Tigers had been behind five times during that final, but also regained the lead five times. Venter, however, was not on the field afterwards to congratulate his opposite number, Richard Cockerill, on his 33-27 victory. Not because he didn't want to be there, but because he had to watch the match on TV on account of an oatmeal biscuit.

Shortly before that match, a disciplinary committee of the governing body of rugby union in England, the Rugby Football Union (RFU), had banned Venter from attending the final. The original charge against him was that he had allegedly been involved in an altercation with Leicester supporters. A light reprimand was anticipated, but for the chairman of the disciplinary proceedings, Judge Jeff Blackett, the gravity of the case increased drastically when Venter came back into the venue to hear his sanction while still munching on an oatmeal biscuit.

Although the RFU had provided the biscuits, Venter's last mouthful in front of Blackett was viewed by the disciplinary officer as evidence of his disdain for the disciplinary process. Hence the offending biscuit was specifically cited in Blackett's judgment. Consequently, Venter was banned from the biggest day in Saracens' rugby history, and the petty reaction of the RFU's stiff-upper-lip brigade was dubbed rugby's own Biscuitgate by the British media.

That was not the end of his disciplinary woes. In October 2010, Venter was fined £21 850 for having claimed that the European Rugby Cup had failed to properly prepare its referees to ensure a uniform interpretation of the breakdown laws. An independent disciplinary panel found him guilty of misconduct and described his comments as 'inappropriately critical'.

A portion of the fine (£13 000) was suspended until June 2012, on condition that Venter refrained from giving verbal expression to the courage of his convictions and speaking his mind. Somewhere between biscuits and Venter's convictions a golden mean had to be found.

Saracens lost 21-24 to Racing Metro on 11 December 2010. In Venter's post-match interview with Martin Gillingham of Sky Sports, the South African answered nine questions in 57 seconds without saying anything. But the interview became an Internet sensation – as evidenced by the more than 700 000 hits it has received on YouTube. The interview went as follows:

> **Martin Gillingham:** How disappointed are you?
> **Brendan Venter:** Disappointed – very disappointed, very disappointed.
>
> **Martin Gillingham:** What went wrong, because you got off to such a wonderful start?
> **Brendan Venter:** Yeah, interesting. I wonder what went wrong. Have to think about it.
>
> **Martin Gillingham:** But what did go wrong?
> **Brendan Venter:** I'll have to look and think. Think about it deeply. Very deeply.
>
> **Martin Gillingham:** Did it hinge in the end on a bit of genius from Sireli Bobo?
> **Brendan Venter:** Bit of genius, bit of magic, Sireli Bobo, very interesting, very good, yeah. Three cheers for Sireli Bobo. Very good. Very good.

BRENDAN VENTER

Martin Gillingham: What were you happy with about your side?
Brendan Venter: Happy? Everything. Very good, very happy with my team.

Martin Gillingham: But you didn't win, did you, Brendan?
Brendan Venter: No, well, we didn't win. It's true.

Martin Gillingham: Why didn't you win?
Brendan Venter: Good question that, very good question. It's important to win, it is. We must try harder, absolutely, yes.

Martin Gillingham: Do you think it's a lack of effort?
Brendan Venter: Lack of effort, lack of effort? I can't think it's a lack of effort.

Martin Gillingham: So what is it, Brendan?
Brendan Venter: What would it be? Let me think. I'm not sure. I'll have to think about that one. Think about it deeply.[27]

This deliberate attempt at avoiding any possible controversy by not stating any opinions, which was inspired by a scene from the spoof film *Mike Bassett: England Manager*, was also met with disapproval in some quarters.

But this is exactly why one enjoys being in Venter's company. He, too, enjoys himself. He enjoys life. In an interview with British tabloid the *Mirror*, he explained Biscuitgate and the Gillingham interview as follows: 'Look, I agree I've got a mischievous streak in me. But that's because life is a privilege to live. There are a lot more serious things out there than rugby. It is a game, it is not life and death.'[28]

This has been the attitude to life that Venter has had since his days as a medical student at the University of the Free State. For him, rugby was a way of paying for his studies. But too much fun and games in his first year at Kovsies almost shot down his dream of becoming a doctor. Hence he took a decision that rugby would always come second.

On the face of it, therefore, it is hard to understand the following successes in his rugby career – whether as player or coach: 120 matches for the Free State; 17 tests and 24 matches in all for the Springboks; won the World Cup tournament in 1995; 86 matches for London Irish; won the Anglo-Welsh Cup (Powergen Cup) with London Irish as coach; English Rugby Coach of the Year; final of the English Premiership in 2010; won the Premiership against Leicester Tigers in 2011; won the Junior World

Championship as assistant coach of the Junior Springboks in 2012; and won the Currie Cup with the Sharks as director of coaching in 2013.

In between, Venter still runs his own medical practice in Strand, near Cape Town. That's why some people are of the view that he can afford to be controversial: precisely because he does not need rugby. There is some truth in this, but not because Venter has another profession to fall back on. Rugby will never be the most important thing in life and this has been pivotal to Saracens' rise as a super club since he became involved there in 2009.

Former Springbok scrumhalf Neil de Kock has been playing for Saracens since 2006. In response to my question about who Brendan Venter is, he replied unhesitatingly: 'The very first thing that comes to mind when I think about Brendan is that he's incredibly passionate, and competitive to the marrow. But, at the same time, he's astute and technically very good in his approach to rugby. He encourages conversations about anything, but especially about rugby. And, on occasion, there have been some fierce debates between him and certain players about technical issues. The important thing in this regard is that he is prepared to listen to you. For me, what is most important about Brendan is that he's the key person who drove the plans, values and culture at Saracens – day in and day out. And he not only talked about those things that characterise the club, he lived them. Because of that example, anyone who plays for this club truly wants to be part of this group of people.'

In Venter's mind, people – nuanced beings – are what rugby is about. We met at a coffee shop in Somerset West, near where he trains. This first conversation lasted only 36 minutes before Venter had to join Dawie Theron and Nazeem Adams to plan for the Junior World Championship in France. Nevertheless, after just 36 minutes you understand who the person is that De Kock described, and Saracens makes sense to you.

'I think our model is completely different. Completely,' said Venter, who is still the club's technical director. 'Our model is much less about the result of a match, and people don't understand that.

'There is a greater plan in what we do. To us, it's about relationships that are forged over the long term. We feel that it doesn't matter what cups you won – those things will be forgotten, because you have to give a cup back. If the object of rugby is to win cups, you only get to keep it for one year before someone else possibly takes it from you again. So, what did you get in the process? You made memories. And if you know from the outset that you're playing for friendships and memories, you yearn less for cups and more for those things that have real meaning in your life. What makes memories precious is people. Memories are not about what you achieved.'

Venter often refers to experiences in his medical practice, and it is clear that they have had an influence on his outlook on life and his approach to rugby.

'I've seen it many times. Rich people reach the end of their lives and they are lonely. They don't have people around them. It is about people. That's all that it's about. Our early choices in life between money, cups and people have an enormous influence on how we will feel one day.

'That's why at Saracens we ask what we can do for you as a player and a member of the management staff that would develop you as a human being. Because we believe that happy people perform at a higher level. And there are certain things that make all people happy. There are commonalities.

'A wise man, Joseph Addison, once said that everyone needs three things to be happy: someone to love, something to do and something to hope for. In my practice, these are the things people deal with on a daily basis. The people who recover and get well are people who are happy. Those who never get well — even if we take their illness away — are unhappy people.

'Hence, our primary goal at Saracens is to make people happy. And you don't make someone happy by giving him what he thinks he wants. You make someone happy by discovering what makes him tick as an individual. It lies in those three things mentioned by Addison. Certain things, like family, are important to any person. It doesn't matter if you are a mean gangster — you care about your family. And because something like that is so important, we put a lot of effort into families. We look after them unbelievably well.'

Venter may be excellent from a technical sense, but, for Saracens, technique and strategy are like components that are required to assemble a car — they are not the car itself. The fuel that makes the car go is that culture of people, relationships and being happy.

GIVING MORE THAN YOU TAKE

Happiness: Someone to love

The rugby family

Before Venter joined Saracens on a full-time basis, he had assisted them regularly as defence consultant when Australian Eddie Jones was the club's director of rugby. So he knew the players by the time he took over from Jones.

During this time, South African company Remgro acquired a big indirect stake in Saracens. On top of that Venter decided to let 14 players go, and there was great concern in local rugby circles that the club would lose its English character. A South African takeover was never the motive, however, even though there were seven South Africans and one Namibian in the senior contracted group of 2013/14.

Said Venter, 'I got to know the people and understood their temperaments. You win matches with fighters – with guys who never give up and never give less than their all. And I knew that some of those players weren't fighters. A guy like Glen Jackson had been with the club for a few years by then, and when the two of us had our conversation, he told me he knew that he could just as well pack his bags and go – surely I wouldn't want him. But he was wrong, and so I told him: "Glen, I really want to have you here. We will disagree at times, but you have a fighting spirit within you." There were great contrasts between the two of us. He was a typical New Zealand flyhalf and, before my arrival, Saracens had played beautiful rugby, but won bugger all. But Glen had something in him that I respected immensely.

'For me, that's the thing about family. There will inevitably be differences, but just because we disagree it doesn't mean that we don't respect each other. And where there is respect – for each other and for differences – relationships develop between people. And with that you can accomplish a tremendous amount in a rugby team.'

That is why Venter, just like Meyer, got rid of players who wouldn't fit into the culture that he wanted to establish at the club.

'You end up coaching according to what you were like as a player. I had shortcomings, but I was a fighter. It's what you see in people. Heyneke will tell you that you win games with people and with personalities. Joost van der Westhuizen had many flaws. He was a left-footed scrumhalf, and his passing from his right hand wasn't wonderful.

But Joost was unbelievably successful because he was a fighter. He just never gave up. And when you played against Northern Transvaal with Joost in their team, you stood a much better chance of losing than on the occasions he didn't play. It had nothing to do with his speed or his size; it was due to that something extra within him.

'And that's what makes us South Africans such good rugby players. There are certain skill sets that everyone must have, yet we South Africans have many deficiencies – our skills and decision making aren't always up to scratch, but we fight like hell.

'So, when Jacques Burger became available in the market, I knew we had to get hold of that Namibian. He's a fighter. Neil de Kock is small, but he's a fighter. Bradley Barrett is small, but he's a fighter. Schalk Brits is a fighter. With that attribute, seemingly average guys can become world-class people and players. In the eyes of many, a guy like Mouritz Botha was average. But we saw a hunger in him, and everyone respects and admires him for that. It is what made him a test player. And Mouritz is held in extremely high regard in the Saracens environment because he gives credit to the group.

'I look for those things in players, and I can't bullshit them: I won't be able to make them happy if they lack certain things that the club needs. For us, it is very much about self-awareness and being honest with yourself, and you must be conscious of what you have. Jacques and Mouritz have certain shortcomings but I don't focus on the fact that they will make mistakes, since I know they will do many things right because they are fighters. So if they knock a ball or miss a tackle, it's not a big deal. Their presence and work rate compensate for errors like that, and *that* is what tells me something about their attitude and the kind of people they are. When you have a team where everyone has the attitude of giving more than what you take, and you give because you care about the happiness of the guy next to you, you can go a long way with people.

'Those 14 guys who were let go wouldn't have been able to play well for me because they weren't fighters. Essentially, they couldn't do what I expected of them. Relationships between us would always have been bad, and this was not what we wanted to build the club on. It's about relationships.'

According to De Kock, every player enters into an unwritten agreement with the club when he joins Saracens: 'You commit yourself to working unbelievably hard for Saracens, and then the club will treat you unbelievably well in return. All that the club asks of you is to be professional and to give your all. It's enriching to work in an environment where every single person truly has that mindset – from management to players.'

Since Venter's arrival at Sarries, the team has engaged in activities such as attending the Oktoberfest beer festival in Munich, skiing in Verbier, Switzerland, undertaking a tour to Miami, doing development work in Bermuda and building sports facilities in Kayamandi, outside Stellenbosch.

'This is partly what our ethos at the club means when we say we give more than we take,' said De Kock.

Derick Hougaard also played for Saracens. To him, the visit to the Oktoberfest during the Premiership of 2010/11 was illustrative of how this club does things differently: 'You ask yourself what makes rugby work, and what distinguishes successful sides from others. I'm reminded, for example, in that year of how Wasps trained in Switzerland in oxygen tanks of some sort. In terms of science, they did everything you could possibly do to get a team to the top position of the Premiership, and from the outside it looked very impressive. But, to us, the family culture was the factor that had to set us apart.

'We went to the Oktoberfest, but we practised in the afternoon. Things rattled a bit – balls were dropped, but what you put in and what you gave mattered more than the mistakes we made. Because when you trained, you worked incredibly hard. You worked your butt off. I had the time of my life, and we ended up winning the Premiership later while Wasps had to fight relegation.'

Venter had the players train for one day less per week than had been the case under Eddie Jones: 'I cut a whole day from the programme because I believe players need to rest and do something else with their lives as well. But I made them train harder at the times when they did train. The English players did an incredible amount of training in those days, but they trained in the wrong way. So I told them it shouldn't be about having programmes to complete just so that you can tick all the boxes. There should be something inside you that wants to get the job done.

'We have a 100 per cent principle. I told the players that they train for five hours on Mondays, five hours on Tuesdays, and three hours on

Thursdays. They get Wednesday, Friday and Sunday off. That's 13 hours in all, and so in a week of 168 hours, I'm asking them for only about 7 per cent of their entire week – I ask little, but what I do ask is that in that 7 per cent of your week you give 100 per cent.

'It took the players a little while to figure out that sum, but that was the only working time I asked of them. And then we give each other our all. You can decide for yourself what you want to do with the remaining 93 per cent of your week, and we encourage you to use that time productively. But it also means that I'm not going to ask you on Saturday whether you're ready. You're always ready to play. It doesn't matter where we play. It doesn't matter who our opponents are. You only need to give yourself to your teammates and your club for such a small part of your week to the extent that you can truly be expected to win anywhere, and we have by far the best record with away games in the Premiership.'

This mindset confirms that competitive nature, which De Kock regards as an integral part of Venter's make-up. He recalled a match against the Cardiff Blues in which Saracens were not up to standard.

'For some or other reason, we were physically exhausted that day, and we didn't play with our usual intensity. Brendan walked into the dressing room and just said to us: "I hope you have a shit evening, because you've stolen my joy!" To us, that was typical of Brendan. The opposite also applied in cases where we lost, but where Brendan believed that we had really given our all. He would thank us for the effort and immediately shift his focus to the next challenge.'

For Venter, there is simply no such thing as excuses – not with the way in which Saracens manages its people and their happiness. He took his team to France for his first away match in the Heineken Cup competition. At 08:00 that morning, they flew from Luton to Bordeaux, spent another two hours travelling by bus to Agen, played the match, won, and travelled home at 06:00 the next morning.

'We did that for a reason,' he said. 'It couldn't be any tougher than that. You can't get up that early, fly to France, take a bus, thrash a team, and after that have any excuse not to win in similar or easier circumstances. It's the same people, the same field, the same lines, the same responsibility. Small things like that bind people together, and if you have a group of fighters fighting together, rugby unites you like few other things can. You become a family. And when you are a family who play for each other, you make memories that you will carry with you for many years after you've long forgotten by how much we beat Agen.'

Saracens beat Harlequins 27-12 on 24 March 2013. Venter was with the team that week in his capacity as technical director, and he led the team talk before the match: 'I told the guys there were only two things they could do about the outcome of the match that day, and determining the scoreline wasn't one of them. There are too many factors that can influence the outcome of a match.

'First, they can do their best and every man can play his heart out. There are parameters for these things. We can sit up there in the stand and measure how quickly you get up from the ground, how hard you chase kicks and how strongly you carry the ball. We can measure it scientifically and draw conclusions.

'The second thing I told them they could do was to ensure that there was harmony in the group. It's your choice whether you want to be good to the guy next to you. But everything works in harmony. And that's it – nothing more and nothing less. If something happens to a teammate – for example, if he makes a mistake – it must feel to you as if you yourself have made that mistake. But if you're going to be angry with him and curse him, you're cursing him because you think it's going to cost you the game. And that's not where our focus is. We want to win, and we hate losing. But our motivation, what gives us strength, is to ensure that the guy next to you is happy. It's not about me. You feel bad for a friend's sake. And the moment you develop that awareness of yourself and of other people, you feel ashamed of your emotions, because your emotions are self-centred. All the time.

'We are people, and every now and again we need to take a little step back to regain our perspective when winning becomes too important to us as a sole objective. There's ego involved. And our culture at Saracens is in fact a spiritual journey. We sometimes have to remind ourselves and each other that we can actually be quite fallible beings. Then you feel ashamed and you start thinking differently about life. You manage to do it for a while, you feel good again for a while, and then you lose perspective again and become big-headed. Then you are ashamed of yourself once more, you manage to keep things in perspective for a while, and then you lose touch with reality again. The difference between a culture that doesn't have people as its main focus and one that does is that the guys in the people-centred culture are aware of it when they lose perspective and can put a stop to it. That sense of being aware of it when you mess up encourages harmony.'

The 2012 Junior Springbok team was the first to win the under-20 World Trophy. Venter was one of Dawie Theron's assistant coaches, and the same team ethos that had worked at Saracens was established at the Baby Boks.

Pat Howard, an outstanding young wing and centre from Western Province, injured his hamstring in the Baby Boks' last pool fixture, against England. I was in the team hotel after the team doctor had informed him that his tournament was at an end. One of the players walked past him, asked what was wrong and just said: 'All the best, mate. That's just bad luck.' The vice captain, however, William Small-Smith, put his hand on Howard's shoulder and told him how much the team was going to miss him not only on the field, but also in the team environment.

To Venter, this is an example of the empathic ethos that bonds a rugby team. 'Not all people are empathic. But anyone can be attuned to others and be interested in them. William is attuned to other people by nature, and that's why he is also an unbelievable human being and was an unbelievable headboy at Grey College, and why he's an unbelievable leader in a team. If you keep emphasising the cultivation of that ethos – in all your players – you will be dealing with a group of happy people who all feel that they are valued for who and what they are. Especially during difficult times. Members of a family not only share each other's joy, but also each other's pain.'

Your family

Families, wives and children are an inextricable part of the Saracens culture.

'I can see my children while I'm at work,' De Kock remarked about the club's crèche. 'How many people can say that? I can't help describing the environment as one where everybody cares for everybody. An enormous amount of trouble is taken to involve our families in the club in so many different ways. Brendan drove this thing and made sure that all the families, old and new, always feel welcome.'

This environment and culture is all-embracing, not just a series of socials and picnics.

'This focus on people is everything. Even when I go to London once a month,' said Venter, 'it's very important to me that Schalk Brits's wife, Colinda, should be able to phone me to say that their little boy, Christiaan, doesn't feel well and ask whether I can suggest something.

'John Smit split open his head when he bumped it once during a match, and when I went to see the players afterwards, I noticed that the wound had been stitched up very untidily. I told him: "Jeez, John, come and sit here." And I took half an hour to stitch his head up neatly. Otherwise it would have left an ugly scar. But it's not about me being this wonderful guy. It's about me wanting to do something for a friend.

'These are small things, but people notice them. We've got an impressive guy at the club, our statistical analyst, Bill Gerrard, from the Leeds Business School. I told him that if it's so simple, then, that people give you so much in return when you treat them well, why isn't everybody doing it? He attended a congress in America and when he returned, he told us the whole model there is about improving the environment because people perform better as a result. And it's the same model that we have in our own little way at Saracens. It works everywhere – whether it's in a medical practice or at a rugby club.

'Bill told me that this model only works if it is authentic. People can see when you don't genuinely care about them. If you create an environment to serve your own needs, people know it. I used to be a player, and I know what I didn't like. So we ask the players what things they don't like, and from our shared experiences we create a people-centred environment where people are happy and hence can be truly successful. This is what Edward Griffiths, our chief executive, is so good at. He cares about others to an unbelievable extent. He has this compassionate, soft side to him. These are the things that people notice. When there is someone in the club who is ill or someone who has a family problem, he solves it for you. He'll drive through the night to help someone – that's him, it comes easily to him. As coaches, we must sometimes allow ourselves to take a step back when we become too focused on winning and are no longer focused solely on the people.

'It's an ego thing: when we lose, our egos are hurt. That's what our culture is about – awareness of your own emotions. Not for your own sake, but if you can't maintain perspective and control your own emotions, you take out your frustrations on others and that causes breakdowns in relationships. At Saracens we cannot allow that to happen.'

Happiness: Something to do

With the never-ending extension of the rugby season in each hemisphere, the need for a bigger player group and a rotation system becomes increasingly important. The obvious reason for this is that no human body can indefinitely endure the blows, bumps and fractures that come with a long rugby season.

According to Venter, a pioneer of rotation rugby at Saracens, there is also a more deep-seated reason for a rotation system, which sits with the club's real focus – people's overall well-being. 'A human being wants to feel worthy,' he said, 'and a rugby player wants to be on the pitch. He wants to know that he is valued and that his existence is recognised by his peers, friends, fans and family. By rotating a team, you're not only giving players the opportunity to rest their bodies and minds, you also create value. By not picking the same team all the time, you have 30 or 35 players who feel valued, and not only 15. Because now guys aren't competing against each other, everyone is respected as a player, all of them will get a chance to play and we remove fear from the equation. There is no greater obstacle in sport than the fear of failure.'

When Venter started using this rotation model at Saracens, some of the players were sceptical. Most of them came from a culture where a player was only considered as good as his last game. If that game had been poor, you were left out and you had to fight your way back into the starting team again. An expected consequence of a rotation system is that players believe they are going to play anyway and therefore don't need to fight for that place.

'But that wasn't how we experienced it, and initially I was also sceptical when Brendan reckoned that this rotation theory was the route to follow,' said De Kock. 'It increased the competitiveness in the squad, however, and thereby had a positive influence on the team's performance. Taking into consideration that injuries could play a role, most players knew long beforehand when they would play and when they would be rested. This sharpened each player's focus for those times when he knew that he was going to play, and then that focus was more on the well-being of the team than on himself.

'In modern rugby you need depth in your squad and the players need to get regular game time for when you get to the play-off rounds. We've been using this rotation policy for more than four years, and I believe we're in a very good place because of it. When we won the Premiership in 2011, 42 players played in the starting team that season.'

The rotation policy and Venter's decision to let the team train only three days a week have had far-reaching implications in terms of allowing the players and support staff to develop beyond rugby. Dr David Priestley is Saracens' head of psychology and personal development. He evaluates each player individually, and together they establish what the player's interests and aptitudes are. Then they draw up a personal development plan with which the player can acquire skills and experience in an appropriate industry outside of rugby.

'The players should be able to switch on and off,' said Venter. 'When you're not at work, you should think of other things. You have a wife, children, friends, hobbies and you're your own person. If you're only thinking of work all the time, you will be an unhappy person.'

This emphasis on personal development is a vitally important part of the Saracens culture, and over the last four years about 85 per cent of the club's professional players have been involved in either formal academic education or other forms of meaningful personal development, such as work experience or charitable work. In a variety of ways, since 2009 every member of the 'Saracens family' has been exposed at some point to activities and processes that encourage their development outside of rugby.

In Venter's view, the club compels players in a friendly way to develop themselves as people. 'Before my time,' he said, 'the players were told that they weren't allowed to study because there was no time for that. But then I went to see Rhys Gill and his mother. I said: "Mrs Gill, Rhys must go back to university." He had just one year of study left to complete his course. So I asked David not to put up with the players' excuses – I said there is time to study. Jackson Ray and Jamie George obtained their degrees in 2013.

'But it's not only about the fact that they must have something they can do after rugby. It's about their sense of self-worth. It's an unbelievably nice feeling when you hang up your boots one day and you already have this qualification under your belt with which you can now pursue another career, and if you have the right motivation, you can get a very good qualification.

'There are also other advantages to allowing yourself to develop into a more well-rounded human being while you are still playing. Suppose you have a poor game and your total sense of self-worth is tied to your talent to play rugby. I can promise you that you'll have a very hard time when people criticise you. It would feel as if they are targeting you on your entire being. But if you're a good husband to your wife, a good father to your children, someone who is studying for a good qualification, it's much easier to be honest with yourself, to say that you've had a pathetic game and then to get over it. Because your worth as a human being is not only defined by your talent for playing rugby. When we encourage people to develop themselves and they do so, it is also a way in which we can help people to be happy. And that establishes the environment,' said Venter.

Former England captain and Sarries lock Steve Borthwick spent a week at Loftus Versfeld in January 2013 to see how the structures work and how coaching is done – mainly how Victor Matfield coaches lineouts. Although Borthwick did this midway through the European rugby season, an advantage of the club's rotation system is that a player will get a week off during the season, when he can use his time as he sees fit. Some players spend that free time with their families; others, like Borthwick, in this case, use it for personal development.

What is impressive about Borthwick is that he obtained a master's degree in business management shortly before his visit to South Africa. He managed to achieve this while playing test and club rugby, and being part of the club's management team to boot.

Borthwick described his strategy to me as follows: 'I plan to start coaching full-time once I stop playing. I'm still playing at present, and it's important to me to start developing myself already as coach so that when I retire, I will be in the best possible position to make a full-time contribution somewhere as a coach.

'I've assisted at times with some of the Saracens Academy's activities, and I try to seize every opportunity to develop myself in that capacity. That's why it's an unbelievable experience for me being at Loftus to see how the top coaches work. Hopefully, it can help me in the short term, but in the long term I hope that many such visits would make me a better coach.

'I'm not going to try to predict the future. At the moment, I'm a player, and my focus is to be the best possible player and club captain of Saracens. It's vitally important for all professional players to learn, to gain experience and to develop new things when the opportunities arise – to grab every chance.

'I'm not talking only about rugby. I've recently obtained my master's degree in business management, and I exposed myself to environments wider than rugby – such as the corporate world – so that I could experience as many things as possible from as many different environments as possible.

'The world of professional rugby can be very, very small. It's critically important to move outside of rugby and to search in the world out there for those things that will suit you and your personality – things that stimulate you as an individual.'

According to De Kock, it will probably take a rugby player a bit longer to obtain a professional or academic qualification. 'But if you're disciplined, there is undoubtedly enough time at Saracens to do it. That personal development is something that is driven very strongly and in which everyone participates,' he said.

It was for this reason that Sanlam Private Investment (SPI) partnered with Saracens as a sponsor in August 2013. Craig Massey, chief executive of SPI, explained the company's decision as follows: 'Saracens is a strong brand with a large South African connection and we feel its talent, work ethic, discipline and values resonate strongly with our culture at SPI. We believe in working with talented people and with the right people, and Saracens' commitment to their players both on and off the field fits well with our core values of passion, innovation, transparency and trust. We have also been impressed by their ethic of reaching out into the community – largely through the work of its sports foundation, community team and school partnership programme.

'For our part, we see ourselves not just as sponsors of the Saracens, but as "wealth partners" – so we will be offering to support the players not just on the field, but in the wider world and in life after rugby – whenever that might be. We will seek to guide on how to structure their financial affairs throughout their careers, assisting them with financial planning and helping them develop other life and work skills by offering advice on careers and training in financial services.'

Happiness: Something to hope for

Aristotle said that hope is the dream of a waking man; for Addison, hope is one of the prerequisites for happiness. But it cannot be isolated from loving someone and having something to do.

In the case of sports teams, hope tends to be focused on winning trophies; in the case of professional rugby, it is on playing tests. These are vital drivers, but neither of these goals can be reached single-handedly: you need a team, and one that does something meaningful together.

This represents in simple terms the foundation on which the culture at Saracens stands. However, the hope to play at a higher level and to win trophies is not the primary reason why the club rests on that foundation. And Venter reckons that few people really understand it: 'This is what makes our model different. The Friday before we won the Premiership final in 2011, I said in a board meeting that even if we should lose the match, we would still have been unbelievably successful. The directors looked at me askance and said that couldn't be the case. So I emphasised that our objective was not to win the Premiership, but to develop people. This is a big thing to say, and people don't understand it.

'I then told Nigel Wray, our chairman, that I wanted to share a nugget of truth with him – if we win the next day, the feeling will be gone in two weeks' time. Remember that. So we won, two weeks went past, and my cellphone rang. I was in South Africa at the time. Nigel just wanted to say that the feeling had gone.

'But it was a nice challenge, because it meant that we had to create the next good feeling. Happiness is a funny thing. You can't survive on yesterday's happiness. Cups and trophies can't determine your happiness because once they are gone, there are long periods between cups that you have to fill with other things. You have to create new memories, new happiness and invest in new relationships.

'Because our focus and our hope are not on cups, at Saracens we keep making new memories on a daily basis. CEO Edward Griffiths is at the centre of this – we have a chief executive who believes in a vision of people. We've known each other since 1994, and Edward was at Saracens before me. So when I arrived there, I had the privilege of living a philosophy of life in the club with a chief executive who knew exactly what it was about.'

Venter admits that it is easy to look at success in the rear-view mirror and then get philosophical about it. Winning remains incredibly important to him, however. It is not a concept that is sidelined for the sake of harmony among people. The focus on the way to winning cups and achieving success is just different: 'If you treat people well, they give back to you abundantly. When you have a bunch of people who treat each other well, they give back abundantly as a team, and with a team like that you will win – you don't have to make cups your main driver. Cups are then just a by-product of a culture where we want to ensure that people are happy in every facet of their existence and that we develop people. Hence the question is not whether we win cups, but whether we add value in people's lives.'

According to Venter, for that happiness to be sustainable there sometimes has to be conflict in a healthy environment to stimulate growth.

'Many people think I'm actually a very difficult guy, because I don't mind getting involved in conflict,' he said. 'But the people around me don't think that about me, because there is harmony where I am. There's a simple reason for that – we don't bend the rules. If I make a rule at the start of a relationship, it applies to me as well.

'And there is only one rule: we respect each other. And we earn that respect. Then we can disagree about technical issues, or whatever, without our differences disrupting the harmony of the team. The sporting code of rugby is too fluid to be subject to rules. If you tell me you don't agree with how we do a certain thing on the field and you have another suggestion, it's absolutely fine if you implement that plan of yours with full commitment. Even if my plan is better, there's a good chance that your less good plan will work if you execute it wholeheartedly. Our style of play is not subject to rules, but our environment is: there is mutual respect and we don't need to agree with each other to respect each other. That's all we ask for,' Venter explained.

He then referred to his medical practice and acknowledged how regular contact with people who are close to the end of their lives has made him look differently at his own life. 'I see it as people get older. It's about relationships; it's not about money. It's not about status. In rugby, it's about what you built while you played – and we rugby players have the most incredible way of building it. We are pals, all the time; we fight together. You have a different kind of bond when you've played rugby together. But then your focus has to be right.

'I see all these elderly people and I realise that all of them chased after something in their lives. They chased after the wrong things while they should have been chasing after relationships instead. I don't want to make the same mistake, and so I say to the players, let me tell you in a nutshell what I see in my practice every day: we focus on the wrong things. I tell them that constantly.

'We then help each other to focus on the right things. None of us are perfect, but we're on this journey together. While I can give you the solution to certain things, I can't make the decision for you. You must make your own decisions. I'll guide you, I'll support you and I'll help you to study, for example, but if you don't take your studies seriously, I'm no longer going to pay. If you don't train, I'm not going to pick you. At Saracens, it all comes down to caring for each other. And, jeez, does this team play! We play our hearts out. So, what we give to the players, they give back to us in multiples. And the nicest thing on this earth is to give someone something. It makes you happy,' said Venter.

His cellphone rang. It was 14:36 and Dawie Theron just wanted to let him know that Nazeem Adams and he were ready for their meeting. 'I'll be there shortly, Dave,' said Venter. Then he said goodbye to me with a parting thought: 'We play for each other.'

GIVING MORE THAN YOU TAKE

John Smit, the controversy and the Currie Cup relief

When Jonathan Kaplan blew the whistle at the end of the Currie Cup final between Western Province and the Sharks on 26 October 2013, John Smit rubbed his hands over his face and head. Relieved. The same head that Venter had stitched up earlier in the year when Smit had sustained a cut while playing in Saracens colours. Many changes had taken place in the meantime. Smit was at Newlands that day as the new Sharks chief executive, and Venter as his director of coaching.

Smit's tenure as boss of his old union got off to a stormy and controversial start when he decided not to renew the contract of long-serving coach John Plumtree. Smit's predecessor, Brian van Zyl, distanced himself publicly from that decision. It was the final straw in a series of issues that had looked suspect to outside observers the whole year. There had been rumours of strife between Plumtree and some of the players. There had been rumours of dissension in the camp, rumours of fist fights. Little of the smoke turned into actual fires, and some of those rumours only brought the players closer together. The players also had great appreciation for the way in which Plumtree had handled the tough season. This was a young team that had started struggling after kicking off their Super Rugby campaign on a good note. Plumtree's message to the players had been that they should simply enjoy themselves.

The Sharks were at a watershed moment in their existence. Smit acted swiftly. He ran into flak just as swiftly.

When Smit appointed Venter as his new director of coaching without a formal contract and only on a short-term basis, they endured personal attacks from some quarters. Venter's background as a coach was questioned and the complete turnaround that the Sharks needed was judged predominantly from a technical viewpoint.

The Sharks had good rugby players and structures. The culture, however, needed work. Smit knew that. He also knew where to find the solution: from Venter.

People seldom pay attention to culture because they wrongly consider it a trivial concept instead of the most important pillar supporting any consistently successful organisation. According to Jannie du Plessis, the Sharks' Springbok prop, there had at times been friction in the past because players' roles and responsibilities in the team were not always communicated clearly.

'In cases in the past, the coach almost seemed intent on keeping people satisfied,' said Du Plessis. 'He supported the players who played while the Boks were away. But when the Boks returned, you felt that that guy was taking your place. There was a bitterness between some of the players who competed against each other, because the guy who had played the whole season was left out of the 22-man squad for the most important matches of the year. It left a bitter taste in the mouth. The reason was that the coach didn't explain his plan clearly from the beginning. In such a case, the guy who was left out didn't respect the guy who was picked in his place, because there were hope and expectations to play in the big games, but then it didn't happen. This causes division, and where there's division, you put your own interests ahead of those of the team. It was never a serious problem at the Sharks, but there was sometimes a slight discomfort about these things.'

Issues like these required attention. When the Sharks lost their first Currie Cup match under Smit, Venter, Brad Macleod-Henderson and Sean Everitt (against Griquas), few people foresaw that they would end up beating the undefeated Western Province team 33-19 in the final at Newlands 11 matches later. And even when they achieved that, people looked for, noticed and lauded Venter's technical and strategic shrewdness in the victory, while even the technical elements actually depended on culture.

Venter immediately introduced a rotation system at the Sharks, and this had a material influence on the way someone like scrumhalf Charl McLeod played in the final. Besides his two tries, McLeod also wreaked havoc together with his halfback partner, Pat Lambie. In 2012 McLeod had been replaced by Cobus Reinach in the starting team before the Currie Cup final. In the event, Reinach had a very poor final, and afterwards, both his and McLeod's confidence took a slight knock.

The moment Venter eliminated the unhealthy competition between these two scrumhalves, among others, and only expected them to perform excellently when they did get the chance to play, they did so. This approach has to do with dignity and a common team focus, a family focus, and not only, as is generally expected, with a strategic decision to rest players. It also proved decisive that Venter did not draw a marked distinction between senior and junior players. He didn't get a group of seniors together for the Monday meetings, for example, though he did consult with them. All the players – from 20-year-old Fred Zeilinga to 30-year-old McLeod – were consulted about the team's vision and involved in the decision making. This way, the younger players were empowered. This contributed further to the success of the rotation policy.

McLeod reckons that the policy had an enormous impact on the team's performance and, in his view, two things were central to it – honesty and a good work ethic. 'When Brendan arrived here, the very first thing he did was to convene a meeting with everyone – the new coaches, the whole contracted group, medical team, everyone,' McLeod said. 'He told us that life is about giving and taking. In other words, what did we want from the coaches, and what did the coaches want from us? Honesty is paramount. With Brendan you knew exactly where you stood and what was expected of you. You could go and talk to him at any time and he would have an honest conversation with you. That made an enormous difference. Everyone knew where he stood.

'The second big thing was work rate. Brendan didn't care if you knocked the ball, but then you had to work very hard afterwards. It established an important sense of duty towards yourself and your teammates. We as players didn't feel that we had let each other down when we knocked the ball, but we did feel bad when we realised that we hadn't given our all and, for example, hadn't chased after a ball hard enough.'

With the rotation policy, the players knew where they stood with each other and with the coach, and since it eliminated unhealthy competition between two players, it had a positive influence, in that players started caring for each other, according to McLeod.

'The rotation policy improved the relationship between me and Cobus by 400 per cent. We're good friends now. And it's not because there used to be some friction in the past, but because you feel so much freer to do something for each other once that competition for one position is removed. And again it comes down to honesty. You knew long before the time that you would start this game and play for 50 minutes, or come on later and play for 30 minutes. So, even if I played badly this week, I didn't feel nervous about losing my place because I knew beforehand that I was going to play for 30 minutes the following week. And in those 30 minutes you do your utmost. It takes a lot of pressure off you, and Brendan also made a great deal of our play happen around me and Cobus. Both of us like to run with the ball, and under Brendan we had a lot of freedom to do what we enjoy. Which is why we play rugby, after all,' McLeod said.

This type of culture made it easier to digest the defeat against Griquas, which had clouded the start of the season. The team had had three weeks before that first match to get on top of a completely new system and style of play. After the match, Venter assured players that he would start the next match with the same team, so that the players could get more game time together. This immediately relieved the pressure and was also conducive to the feeling players had that they were free to enjoy themselves. That freedom was exercised within a certain framework, style of play and team ethos.

The most striking and decisive tactic in the Currie Cup final was the way in which the Sharks outwitted Province with box kicks and long punts. Once again, McLeod and Lambie had been instrumental in this. When asked about his good tactical performance afterwards, Lambie didn't refer to the tactic itself, but to how well his kicks had been chased by his teammates – a feature that is part and parcel of the Saracens culture, and which is based on that 100 per cent principle.

Derick Hougaard explained it as follows: 'Work rate carries much greater weight with Brendan than talent. Just look at how Saracens chase kicks and why teams find it so hard to beat them. The club has big names now, but that wasn't quite the case when I was there. The success of this kicking pattern we used depended totally on the work rate off the ball. We were quicker to reach the ball than anyone else, we allowed no one the space to play with the ball and we worked our butts off for each other. The nice things about teams like that is that you can turn a bad kick into an unbelievable kick by putting in that work off the ball. It is purely and simply a mindset, and when you know that your mindset, rather than technical stuff, is the most important thing by which your contribution in the team is measured, you work extremely hard on it. And that is what makes Brendan's teams so good.'

It was this approach, rather than merely clever tactical kicking, that gave the Sharks the edge in the final. A telling illustration of this mindset was Lwazi Mvovo's decision to continue playing after he had broken his hand in the first half.

'To me, that is still the most beautiful thing about that final,' Venter recalled. 'Jannie du Plessis was due to have an operation on his hand, but he decided to play. Lwazi broke his hand in the first half and suffered incredible pain. At half-time I asked him to please stay on the field, because our entire plan – with him and, later, with the replacements – depended on him being on the field. And that is what he did. I had broken my own hand in the past, so I know how painful it is. I'm not sure whether I would have kept on playing, however. But Lwazi and Jannie did. I don't think many coaches always realise what sacrifices players make, but I like to believe that the two of them saw that day how much it meant to me and to the team. I didn't only appreciate what they did – I admired it.'

Du Plessis, for his part, has unbelievable admiration for Venter's role in that final, and while he would play with a broken hand for any coach out of a sense of duty, to him there was something different about Venter: 'I would play for him with a broken neck if I could. People expect of us rugby players to play in these big matches and to sacrifice something, but for me it was an absolute pleasure and privilege to do it for a coach like him.'

The Bok prop believes that the honesty and work ethic in the team had to be traced back to Venter's leadership style – something in which humility plays a big part: 'Coach Brendan didn't want to be photographed with the Currie Cup after the final, or to let us carry him on our shoulders. He said that he wasn't the one who had played, and I feel that he takes far too little credit for what happened in this final and in the season. I think he took decisions that were at his own cost for the sake of the team, and at his own cost he didn't take the credit for what the team accomplished. And that was the case from the outset.

'He came in and didn't let himself be dictated to by players with strong personalities. He took control and told us what he wanted from us. There was clarity about his plan, and honesty, and no one had any reason to have doubts about it. In cases where you have a coach who comes in, lays down the law and does it for his own good, you're sitting with an unhealthy autocratic management style.

'But when you have a coach with a strong personality who is honest and who does his work for the good of the players and the team, it works. Because then you have both a strong personality and humility in one person. It's an unbelievable combination in a leader. Coach Heyneke is also like that at the Boks. And from that very first meeting with the players and management, it was clear that this was a man we could follow and who would lead us with the best interests of the players and the team in mind, not his own.

'Coach Brendan let anyone speak who wanted to at that first meeting. Anyone. Then he said to us: "I hear what you say, and I'll do this and this for you. But here is what I ask – that you will give your all in return. We work for each other." And right there he united everyone's goals. It's incredible what can be accomplished if you take your ego out of the picture for the sake of the guy next to you and strive after something special together with him.'

For Du Plessis, Venter's example was just as important as the values of honesty and work ethic. The good work ethic was a result of team unity, according to him, and the team unity was the result of the honesty and transparency of a coach who didn't occupy the coaching position for his own benefit: 'Where there are honesty and humility and a team focus, you work harder, you train harder, and if someone is picked in your place, you know that it's for the good of the team and that you are part of the team. So it benefits you as well. Every player's focus changes dramatically. You shift your focus and interests towards your friend next to you and towards the good of the team. If the team's goal is bigger than the coach's goal, there surely can't be a player who thinks that he is bigger than the team.

'I've played in teams where everyone has an incredible work ethic, but they don't play for each other. The fact that the Sharks went flat out chasing kicks and were quick to get up from the ground was due to honesty about where you yourself stand, and where we stand with and for each other. You must be prepared to work hard in any rugby team, but we put in more effort than usual because we cared, because we played for each other, for the coach and, above all, for the team. You didn't want to stay on the ground for two seconds longer because you wanted to get into the defensive line, otherwise your friend would struggle. All of a sudden, the focus was no longer on yourself and your own interest and happiness, but on each other's.'

From that perspective, Du Plessis understands why Venter didn't want to take the credit for the team's success, and this is also why he doesn't regard his own sacrifice of playing with a broken hand as out of the ordinary.

Dr du Plessis summarised Dr Venter's influence on the Sharks as follows: 'It's actually unfair that he takes so little credit. I don't want people to think I'm some sort of hero because I played with a broken hand, because I only did what everyone else did, and everyone else just did what the coach had asked of us. And now the coach doesn't want to take the credit. All people have this bit of selfishness inside them, and we like taking the credit for things and hearing that we have performed well. But that's absolutely not what the Sharks are about. The best coaches are those guys who manage to lift other people to another level, where they commit themselves to something bigger than themselves. This is what happened at the Sharks, and why we have such incredible memories of that season. We were part of something bigger than ourselves. That is what makes teams successful – when people play for each other because it's such a good feeling to mean something to someone else.'

This is culture, and this is precisely why Venter was the man Smit called upon to stitch up the Sharks' own metaphorical wounds as painstakingly as the doctor had literally done in Smit's case. And he did …

DR SHERYLLE CALDER

CHAPTER 7

Decision making starts with your eyes

*'The eye sees only what the mind
is prepared to comprehend.'*
– Henri Bergson

Ernie Els's speech was as relaxed and effortless as his golf swing when he was inducted into the World Golf Hall of Fame on 9 May 2011. He was 41, and the first player since Vijay Singh in 2006 to be immortalised among the greats of golf on his first nomination.

When the latest world golf rankings were announced the day before, Els was in 16th position. ESPN Golf called Els 'the ultimate global player of his generation'[29] and the young Australian player Adam Scott said in an interview with Golf.com: 'He's the guy with the greatest rhythm in the game. I really think he is one of the most talented players I've ever played with.'[30]

By that time, Els had won 62 tournaments worldwide, which included two US Opens and the 2002 British Open at Muirfield. The Big Easy had indeed made it look easy. Yet, on 9 May he gave his genes, luck and friends the credit for the times that he had lifted the trophy instead of occupying the forgotten second place.

Els's father, Neels, the eldest of seven children, had worked hard to support a big family after the death of his own father at a very young age. Els told the audience at his acceptance speech: 'I guess he couldn't quite get to the golf course and play until he met my mom, and obviously my mom's dad got him to the golf course, and within a year he was a one handicap, so that tells you about the talent that runs in the DNA.' Ernie Els was a scratch golfer by the age of 14.

On the night of his induction, Els referred to his friend Johann Rupert by name four times. The business tycoon had played a huge role in the development and preservation of the status of South African golf and golfers as among the best in the world – to the benefit of a young Ernie Els.

Els said, 'Johann gave me a really good entrance into some of his tournaments in the 90s. He's sponsored so many golf tournaments and I got to play in them, got my European Tour card, always had a dream to come and play here in the US, which I eventually did.

'And again, I got a break in winning the US Open in 1994 at Oakmont, the same week that Arnold Palmer retired from the US Open golf. That tournament could have gone any way. It could have gone to Colin Montgomerie, could have gone to Curtis Strange, who was in there, could have gone to Loren Roberts, and, for some reason, I was in the right place at the right time. I made so many putts that day and that really set me up to where I am today ... and they gave me a ten-year exemption as a 24-year-old and gave me a lifetime exemption on the European Tour and obviously in South Africa. That really set me up.

'And it just shows you the fine line it takes between it going either way. So many times you don't speak of guys who finish second, but so many of my majors were only by fine lines. I'm saying many – but the three that I won!'[31]

At the end of 2010, Els finished in the 12th spot in the world ranking and in May 2011 still ranked among the world's top players, in the 16th position. Els was positive about the future, as he told Golf.com: 'In many ways I'm now better prepared to win golf tournaments than I've ever been. I know if I play to my ability where I can play, I'm supposed to win tournaments and I can win majors.'[32]

And yet 2011 would turn out to be the first year of Els's professional career in which he failed to win a single tournament. At one point in the year, he was 68th in the world and in the final ranking of 2011 he finished 56th.

He could hardly have foreseen this on that evening in May 2011 when he was honoured along with George HW Bush, Doug Ford, Masashi 'Jumbo' Ozaki, the late Frank Chirkinian and the late Jock Hutchison as luminaries of the sporting code. The months that followed were the most difficult of his career. Els's putting was in a mess, and even though his troubles on the greens had started in 2010, he had at least won two tournaments that year on the PGA Tour.

In late 2011, the Big Easy's putting woes led to one of the golfing world's great shocks when he resorted to a long putter – known as the belly putter – in desperation. In 2004 Vijay Singh had improved his putting to such an extent with a belly putter that he went from 100th in the putting averages to the top ten in the PGA Tour's list for putting.

At that time, Els had been in the forefront of those who felt strongly that belly putters should be banned because he believed that 'nerves and the skill of putting are part of the game'.

With that as a point of departure, one might be forgiven for thinking that neither nerves of steel nor putting skills were part of Els's arsenal when he was ranked at 181 out of 186 players in the PGA Tour's category called 'strokes gained – putting' at the end of 2011. Matters were not as simple as that, however, and Els himself unwittingly identified his own biggest problem when in his speech he referred to his elder brother, Dirk.

'You know, my brother is a good player. Unfortunately for him, he had a disability in his left eye. He's got no vision in his left eye. Although he loves the game, plays the game very well, it was really frustrating for him because to play with one eye has got to be very, very difficult,' Els said.

Johann Rupert began to suspect that Ernie Els's biggest problem could be solved by and with his eyes. For this reason, he introduced him to the woman Queen Elizabeth II had referred to as the 'Eye Lady' in 2003 – Sherylle Calder. That meeting, on 18 January 2012, before the Volvo Golf Champions at Fancourt, in George, marked the beginning of the incredible next chapter of Els's life and career.

Calder had wanted to work with Els in 2003, but he admitted later that at that point he had been consistently second and third on the world ranking, and had seen no point in scientific intervention. But when his career, which he loved so much, seemed to be collapsing in 2012, Calder asked him that day for only six months of his time. Exactly six months and three days later, Els won his second British Open when he beat Adam Scott by one stroke at Royal Lytham & St Annes.

Calder regards her partnership with Els as the most prized of her career as the Eye Lady, and the finer details of his Lazarus-like comeback will be discussed in the next chapter.

But neither Els's renaissance nor any of Calder's countless other success stories would have been possible had it not been for the following: ridges on a garage door, Dr Danie Craven's love for Stellenbosch, 'something different' (to use Calder's own words) in her make-up as an international hockey player and Professor Tim Noakes's willingness to let her research that 'something different' under his vigilant eye.

DECISION MAKING STARTS WITH YOUR EYES

When British journalist Peter Bills wrote an article about Sherylle Calder in *The Independent* in 2009, he began by asking his readers to imagine the fantasy of being the most successful sportsperson in the world:

> Because you have been so good and because there were no national boundaries in this fantasy world where only talent counted, you represented the crème de la crème of world sport: the Springbok rugby team and England's rugby side, in both cases with whom you won World Cups. Then there was the South African hockey and Davis Cup tennis teams, the Australian cricket team, the New Zealand All Blacks rugby team, England's 2012 elite athletes' programme, the national cricket teams of emerging nations like Kenya, Canada and Holland, and the Prada yachting team. An Australian AFL side asked to see you, likewise Tottenham Hotspur Football Club in England, the French first-division club AS Monaco and a few of the England county cricket sides. But this is no fantasy; one person has achieved all these things. She is arguably the most successful person involved in sport anywhere in the world.[33]

Anyone who is serious about sport knows who Calder is, and when this book was in its earliest planning phase, there was no question that the project would be incomplete without her. But would she want to be involved?

On 7 May 2013, I met Calder at her office at the Sports Science Institute of South Africa in Newlands for our first appointment. I had expected a big office – one with walls boasting a multitude of degrees and tributes in expensive frames. But I soon realised that such an image would be a misrepresentation of the world-renowned Dr Calder: she is courteous, modest and grateful for the course her life has taken. She and her colleague Christi Botha shared an office of about 5 by 4 metres. There were newspaper cuttings and photographs everywhere, stuck to the walls with Prestik – traces of all the places she has visited across the globe.

There was a photo of her with Joost van der Westhuizen, Ruben Kruger and Jacques Olivier, taken when she had assisted the Blue Bulls' victorious Currie Cup team in 1998. Calder was pictured with British princes William and Harry in separate photos. A signed Ikeys (the 2011 Varsity Cup champions) rugby jersey hung against the cupboard. When I interviewed Professor Tim Noakes in December 2010, he had told me that Calder was working with the Ikeys and that she would help the University of Cape Town (UCT) team capture the student crown. He was right.

She took Demetri Catrakilis in hand that same year, and his kicking boot said it all – as it did a year later – when the Greek kicked Western Province to its first Currie Cup crown since 2001. By then Calder had been working with kickers for a long time, as evidenced by the *Rapport* article on the wall. 'Hockey lady makes Braam see' was the headline of a story Louis de Villiers wrote on 21 May 2000 about the resurgence in Braam van Straaten's game:

> At the start of last year everything was going swimmingly for Braam van Straaten, but by the end of the season he suffered a crisis of confidence and became increasingly timid in his play.
>
> Critics were of the view that his Springbok jersey would gather dust unless he managed to raise his level of play by 150 per cent. So he did just that. Van Straaten is back in the Springbok group, and he gives the lion's share of the credit for his comeback to the former South African hockey captain Sherylle Calder. 'Last year my confidence was shot. But I came to terms with the fact that my chance to go to the World Cup had come and gone. Confidence is a funny thing, isn't it. Your wife and your parents keep believing in you, and then a bit of that rubs off onto you. Then your teammates and your coach also start believing that you can do it, and before long you have completely forgotten about the crisis of confidence.
>
> 'It helped as well that I started standing a bit deeper, and Dan van Zyl's return was crucial to me. Dan and I understand each other very well and in the Super 12 the two of us, as a combination, played in a winning team more than 75 per cent of the time.
>
> 'But both of us must take our hats off to Calder. She helped several of us, but Dan and I were so impressed by the work she does with one's vision that we ended up going to her three times a week. Everything in my game improved, even my kicking. I learnt in the process to concentrate on detail; learnt to concentrate only on the ball. It has meant that I strike the ball better and keep my head low. And my golf has also improved tremendously!'

Van Straaten has since become one of the most sought-after kicking gurus in the world, and on 24 October 2013 he expressed his lasting appreciation for Calder's role in his life on Twitter after he had visited her at her office out of the blue: 'Great to see Sherylle after all the years, she single-handedly changed my life as a pro from the first day I entered her world.'

His work still rests on the same fundamental principles that Calder brought home to him. However, those fundamental principles are often not understood correctly, which may explain why Peter de Villiers didn't ask her in 2008 to stay on as part of his Springbok management team, after she had helped prepare both England (2003) and South Africa (2007) in their respective campaigns that led to World Cup glory.

'People think that we work only with the players' eyes and that we teach them to look at the ball. But that's no different from what we are already taught at school: keep your eye on the ball,' Calder said as she countered the oversimplification of her groundbreaking work.

'We help people improve their decision making, regardless of the sport in which they participate or whether they participate in sport at all. People think the eyes are everything, but we work just as hard with the brain and the coordination of the body. We help people make good decisions based on the unexpected. It's about space, it's about reaction time when you make a decision, and it boils down to the ability to gather the right information with good visual skills, to process it in the brain and then to make the correct response and decision.'

Even though she is a scientist, Calder can become quite philosophical about her work. 'Do you know what we really do?' she asked. 'We're in the business of changing people's lives. Our work is anchored in science and research, but our satisfaction comes from what we can do for others with that work.'

Between her international trips, and appointments at her Newlands office and her bigger workplace at the Stellenbosch Academy of Sport, Calder sees a multitude of clients. Nowadays she and Botha run her work as a business, rather than merely as a service that an ingenious researcher can offer the world.

For too long, her services and generosity were exploited, and some of her work was used and sold elsewhere without her knowledge – once by a rugby player with whose national team she had worked. Her work and research of many years, investment and intellectual property were brazenly taken from her.

For Calder, the most appalling aspect is not the dishonesty, but that these pirates sell and present her work elsewhere without the knowledge or understanding of the scientifc fundamentals on which her work is based:

HEYNEKE MEYER AND IAN SCHWARTZ

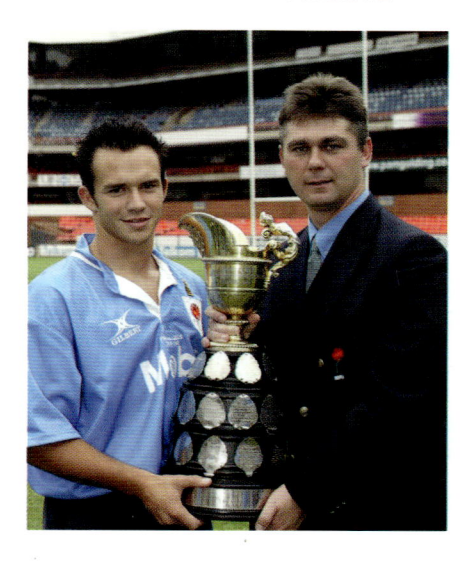

The 19-year-old Derick Hougaard scored 26 of the Blue Bulls' points when they thrashed the Golden Lions 31-7 in the 2002 Currie Cup final at Ellis Park. Hougaard, who matriculated at Boland Agricultural High School in 2001, was headed for Western Province, but Ian Schwartz and Heyneke Meyer persuaded him to become a Bull.
PHOTO: Jan Hamman, *Beeld*

Meyer and his young side celebrate their second Currie Cup win in a row, on 1 November 2003, after defeating the Sharks 40-19 in the final. The Bulls won the Currie Cup the following year as well.
PHOTO: Christiaan Kotze, Foto24

The worst day in Meyer's career as a coach: early in the morning of 7 September 2005, he was summoned to the scene where brilliant centre Ettienne Botha had died in a car accident. PHOTO: Felix Dlangamandla, *Beeld*

HEYNEKE MEYER AND IAN SCHWARTZ

Meyer is lifted shoulder high at Kings Park, Durban, on 19 May 2007 after the Bulls became the first South African team to win the Super Rugby crown. The Bulls trumped the Sharks 20-19 in the final. PHOTO: Felix Dlangamandla, *Beeld*

Meyer congratulates Bryan Habana with a kiss after the Bok winger scored the winning try in the 82nd minute of the Bulls' Super Rugby final against the Sharks. PHOTO: Christiaan Kotze, Foto24

Ian Schwartz played a huge role in the Bulls' success between 2001 and 2011 – as recruiter, contract negotiator and high-performance manager. Here he renews Fourie du Preez's contract with the Blue Bulls Company to the end of 2011. PHOTO: Craig Nieuwenhuizen, Foto24

HEYNEKE MEYER AND IAN SCHWARTZ

The Bulls' brains trust, November 2009. From left to right, Ian Schwartz, Heyneke Meyer and Frans Ludeke, South Africa's most successful Super Rugby coach. PHOTO: Cornel van Heerden, Foto24

From left to right, Johann van Graan (Springbok attack and forwards coach), Ian Schwartz (team manager) and Heyneke Meyer (head coach) singing the national anthem on 17 August 2013. South Africa beat Argentina 73-13 that day in Soweto. All three of these team-management members had previously been with the Bulls. PHOTO: Christiaan Kotze, Foto24

The 33-year-old Heyneke Meyer (on the right) with the victorious Vodacom Cup team of 2001. In the middle at the back are the young Bakkies Botha (21), François van Schouwenburg (22) and Danie Rossouw (22). Note the Blue Bulls motif in the centre of the jersey – the team's main sponsor, Mr Price, withdrew its support shortly after Meyer's appointment. PHOTO: Christiaan Kotze, Foto24

BRENDAN VENTER

Saracens has a strong South African influence and regularly has training camps in South Africa. Here Brendan Venter is talking to Springboks Schalk Brits and Neil de Kock.
PHOTO: Thys Lombard

Venter has always had an uncomfortable yet humorous relationship with the media, which is evident during this TV interview with Sky Sports.
PHOTO: Thys Lombard

Venter and his younger son, Joshua, with the Currie Cup on 26 October 2013, after the Sharks' 33-19 victory over Western Province in the Newlands final. Venter was the Durban side's director of rugby.
PHOTO: Thys Lombard

DR SHERYLLE CALDER

Sherylle Calder helps Percy Montgomery refine his place-kicking skills in June 2005. Two years later, Monty's haul of 105 points (two tries, 22 conversions and 17 penalty kicks) made him the leading points scorer in the 2007 World Cup tournament.
PHOTO: Craig Nieuwenhuizen, Foto24

Some of the Springbok management team at a training session in the Stade Jean-Bouin, Paris, about three weeks before South Africa lifted the World Cup for a second time. From left to right: Calder, Eddie Jones, Allister Coetzee, Balie Swart and Jake White. PHOTO: Christiaan Kotze, Foto24

This photograph was the author's choice. Calder worked with Serbian tennis player Ana Ivanovic on her game in Dubai in December 2012.

DR SHERYLLE CALDER

Calder meets former president Nelson Mandela shortly after the victorious Boks returned from the World Cup tournament in France in October 2007.

Sherylle Calder and Ernie Els take a breather in the run-up to the BMW Championship at Wentworth in May 2012. Two months later, Els won the British Open, his first major in a decade, for the second time, six months after he and Calder had started working together.

Calder and Els with the Claret Jug at his home in Florida, a few months after his British Open win at the Royal Lytham & St Annes Golf Club, in England.

PAUL TREU

Paul Treu and Blitzbok captain, Kyle Brown, after the team had finished the 2010/11 World Series with consecutive tournament victories in London and Edinburgh. PHOTO: Nasief Manie, Foto24

Before a match, Treu gazes over the rugby field at the Nelson Mandela Bay Stadium in Port Elizabeth with the Blitzbokke in the foreground. PHOTO: Thys Lombard

Treu, Steven Hunt and Boom Prinsloo during a training session in Stellenbosch. Treu always has his iPad with him so that he can make video recordings and notes for reviewing matters on the field. PHOTO: Thys Lombard

GARY KIRSTEN AND PADDY UPTON

Indian cricket hero Sachin Tendulkar often practised for hours on end in the nets, and during his tenure as coach, Gary Kirsten worked just as hard helping him. Here, Kirsten throws balls for Tendulkar at the Claremont Cricket Club during India's 2010/11 South African tour.
PHOTO: Nasief Manie, Foto24

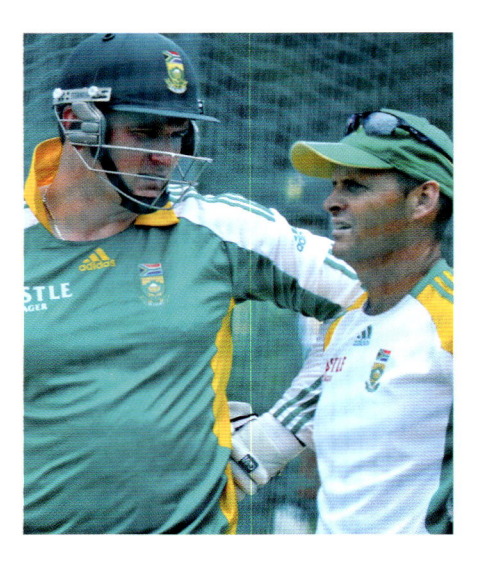

Kirsten and Graeme Smith during a net session at the Wanderers, November 2011. Kirsten had been appointed as the Proteas' coach a few months earlier, after having guided India to World Cup glory. Under Kirsten and Smith, South Africa became the number-one team in the world in all three formats of the game. PHOTO: Christiaan Kotze, Foto24

This photo, which belongs to Paddy Upton (*below, left*), was taken in Cape Town in 1996. Madiba signed the photo for Upton a year later at Newlands, but inadvertently caused a cartridge of golden ink to splatter all over it. He wiped the ink off with the sleeve of his trademark Madiba shirt before it could dry, and signed the photo with another pen. 'Thank goodness, your photo isn't ruined!' was the president's reaction. Upton regards it as one of his most treasured possessions.

DR SHERYLLE CALDER

'To give you an example, I developed a prototype for the England rugby team. I produced proposals. An IT guy then developed the information into a computer program and returned it to me so that I could make corrections. Because we were still working on that program, there were spelling errors on the prototype, my name appeared on it and the explanation for one training exercise was linked to the wrong activity. We found that same program a few years later on the computers of a certain rugby union – complete with the same spelling and program errors. But we didn't have the money to fight it. In any case, by that time, the program was obsolete and no longer relevant.'

The demand for her impact on athletes' performances did eventually enable her to start protecting her intellectual property, and this led to the development of the current version of EyeGym – the latest product to originate from her initial research after years of evolution. Nowadays it offers considerably more than some of the earlier programs.

The beginning

Calder was born and bred in Bloemfontein. She started playing hockey at the age of eight and represented South Africa in field and indoor hockey between 1982 and 1996. She played in 50 tests after 1992 and was considered one of the best players in the world.

'I knew as a student that there was something different about my game, but I could never put my finger on it. When South Africa started competing internationally again, Australian coach Ric Charlesworth regularly quizzed me about my preparation, "Tell me how you train. Tell me what you do."'

Calder didn't do anything unusual in her preparation and she attributed that 'something different' in her game to her urge to benchmark herself against the very best.

'During the isolation years, I didn't think that I would ever get that chance. That's why I went to play club hockey overseas for five seasons without anyone knowing. I went to Europe with no money, on my own. I had to wrap up my hockey stick so that no one at the airport could see that I was going to play overseas. I spent a season in Germany, two seasons in the Netherlands and then another two in England.

DECISION MAKING STARTS WITH YOUR EYES

'I worked in coffee shops and cleaned dog kennels to earn money, because the only thing I wanted to do was to prove myself at that level. Everywhere I went, coaches wanted to know how I managed to do – and how I saw – certain things. My conclusion was that my skills were natural and normal, and just the product of my own curiosity. I always wanted to try new things.

'When South Africa was readmitted to international hockey, our very first series was at home against England. By then, I had started wondering about my abilities. We beat England in that series and participated in an Olympic qualification tournament, and I was selected for an international top 11 to play against Australia. At the time I received a letter from a man who had been involved in the club I played for in England. His daughter played for Great Britain, and he himself attended international hockey tournaments all over the world. He wrote that he had watched a lot of hockey in his life, and I was the only international player he had seen who did not run on the field. He told me I had exceptional spatial awareness and that I was always in the right place at the right time. It was then that I had a light-bulb moment – there was indeed something noticeably different about my game,' Calder recounted.

The fact that she had special visual abilities was as clear as day. But, for a long time, she was unsure of where these abilities had come from – until her brother gave her a hint a few years ago: 'When I eventually started coaching hockey at Stellenbosch, I based all my training sessions on decision making. We never just ran and passed the ball, there was always decision making involved. There was always something that could influence your decisions.

'I had already acquired those skills in my childhood, although I didn't know at the time that it was happening. My brother Hilton reminded me a few years ago that I used to hit balls against our garage door for hours on end – tennis balls, squash balls, anything. The surface of the door had ridges; it was one of those doors that rolled up along the ridges. When I hit the ball incorrectly or struck one of the ridges, the ball would shoot away in any direction and I had to react to that. I believe that this is, among other things, how I developed those skills.

'The crux of this is not eye-hand-ball coordination, although it is an important skill for children to develop, but you also need to make the right decision under pressure. It is about an awareness of what is going on around you, and where and how you conduct yourself in that fluid environment.'

Doc Craven and the Stellenbosch years

Calder completed her undergraduate studies at the University of the Free State before moving to Stellenbosch to do her master's degree. There, she also embarked on her PhD, for which her research was aimed at understanding how people like herself managed to develop their skills and sporting performance to the elite level that set them apart from other athletes.

One of the great influences on her life was rugby giant Dr Danie Craven. It was thanks to his partiality for the Stellenbosch lifestyle, that Calder followed a career focusing on the role that vision plays in performance. He was also one of the few people who knew that she was playing hockey overseas – and he supported her in this.

'I did extra work in the sports office while I was in Stellenbosch,' said Calder. 'We had a tea break every morning at 10:00 and Doc would sit at a table in the Sports Bureau and tell stories. He and I had a special bond, and he also watched us play hockey at times.

'I learnt a tremendous amount from him. I used to spend many hours chatting to him in his office and I was extremely fond of Doc. He was years ahead of his time and he had unbelievable empathy for people. I received a job offer from Johannesburg at the time and consulted Doc about it. He gestured with his massive hands and asked in that characteristic deep voice why one would want to live in Johannesburg when for less money you could have a better life in Stellenbosch. It influenced my decision. I stayed and, in retrospect, my whole career took another course, which wouldn't have been the case had I moved to Johannesburg.

'I would never have started working in the vision and performance field. Another influence of his was the fact that Doc and I talked about everything: hockey, rugby, cricket. I didn't realise in those days what a lasting impact those conversations with Doc would have on my life.'

Craven's public-relations exercise promoting the beauty of Stellenbosch succeeded in keeping Calder in the student town. She coached the women's and later the men's hockey teams. With her international experience – which was inevitably unknown to the rest of South Africa at the time – and her increasing interest in visual abilities at an elite level, she started a so-called 'hockey revolution': 'We looked differently at how you hit the ball, how you position yourself, all kinds of things. I saw how the players responded to this approach and improved. My immediate conclusion was that those abilities and skills didn't have to be developed from early childhood, but that with the right intervention they could be acquired and trained. This formed the basis of my doctoral study.'

Calder's research took up much of her time, but she was not yet ready to pack away her hockey sticks. So she approached the world-famous Professor Tim Noakes of UCT about the possibility of working under his mentorship while she continued to play hockey: 'He said it would be a privilege to have me in his department. It was thanks to Tim that a profound appreciation and understanding of sound scientific research began to take root in me. Although I have coached many teams and individuals over the years, I regard myself as a scientist first and foremost.

'I stopped playing for South Africa and started doing research because I wanted to prove that what interested me worked – especially because my research was about something that no one had ever done before. And I knew what that something was because I had always had it. I hid it under a bushel, however, because I thought that everyone had those skills – until I realised that we were dealing with something that could put athletes in the forefront of elite performance. It was cutting edge.'

The science

The following is an extract from Calder's doctoral thesis, which was completed in 1999 – the start of her groundbreaking work:

> Having played international hockey for South Africa from 1982 to 1996 and having also been involved in coaching since 1988, my experience has been

at all levels of the game. However, from an early age I was never given any coaching instruction regarding vision and its possible role in the visually demanding game of hockey. The sole advice I received was the traditional admonition of most coaches to 'keep your eye on the ball'. I, however, experienced – and even more so at international level – that my visual and perceptual system was 'different' to others and I perceived that it was an important part of my performance at an elite level.[34]

With that experience as a base, Calder began researching the underinvestigated field of visual-performance skills (her own term) and this would eventually become EyeGym.

The thesis resembles a telephone directory in size and looks quite intimidating. The science behind it, however, can be described in simple terms. Calder wanted to prove with her research that the performance skills of elite international field-hockey teams and players could be improved if one were to develop a unique visual-intervention programme for a visually demanding sport.

It sounds like a mouthful, but is actually quite straightforward. There are certain skills that any hockey player should possess. These skills are the product of coordinated movement between the body, a hockey stick and a ball, which has to be manipulated on a playing field. These are hockey-specific skills – for example, being able to hit the ball.

Then there are visual skills (see Table 4). In her early research, Calder aimed to establish whether there was a significant difference between the visual skills of elite international hockey players. Her initial finding was that there was no significant difference. She then did a further investigation into differences in visual-skill levels between hockey players in different positions, because different positions make different demands on players. With the advent of artificial playing fields, a goalkeeper needed to stop hockey balls travelling at a speed of 160km/h. It would be absurd, therefore, to have a goalkeeper who stood firmly in the goal but didn't have good peripheral vision, visual ability and visual reaction time.

Calder found that at the elite level there was no significant difference in visual-skills levels between the four different positions. Consequently, no significant distinction could be made between either elite players or positions and, therefore, visual skills alone couldn't be used to enhance a team's performance or to gauge potential.

Visual skills	
Peripheral vision	Everything that is visible to the eye outside of the central focus area (i.e. side vision).
Visual reaction time	The ability to react quickly to visual information.
Visual memory	The ability to recall what you have seen before.
Saccades	Quick, simultaneous movement of both eyes in the same direction in an attempt to shift the focus quickly from one target to another.
Pursuits	The ability to follow a moving object closely with the eye without losing your focus on it.
Visual recognition	The ability to perceive an object's physical properties (such as shape, colour and texture) and attribute meaning to it.
Depth perception	The ability to perceive spatial relationships, especially distances between objects, in three dimensions.
Visual discrimination	The ability to discriminate between different objects.

Table 4: Visual skills (Sources: *SA Sports & Health Monthly*, September 2013; Wikipedia; www.thefreedictionary.com, accessed 19 October 2013)

It was important, nonetheless, to do visual-skills exercises, despite the general assumption that those skills – the hardware of the visual system – couldn't be changed. Calder believed that intensive eye exercises would strengthen the ocular muscles, like any other muscles, and that this would result in enhanced visual skills.

For the purposes of her research, she chose specific eye exercises that could enhance hockey-specific visual skills. But she found that visual-skills exercises on their own didn't have sufficient impact on players' performance.

Calder then added a supplementary and unique element to her research, namely visual-awareness training. This was a novel concept that had never been used before, with which she wanted to improve both the hardware (physical visual skills) and the software (perception and decision making) of the visual system at the same time. In the case of visual awareness, the emphasis is placed on the conscious and correct use of the eyes and the visual system. Therefore, it is a cognitive process.

DR SHERYLLE CALDER

She called the combination of visual-skills exercises and visual-awareness exercises a visual-skills-enhancement programme.

Visual-awareness exercises are defined as follows in her thesis:

> With visual-awareness exercises, the emphasis falls on the correct use of the eyes and the visual system. For the purposes of this thesis, specific training activities were devised with the aim of enhancing players' use of their visual system. For example, players were taught how to use their specific visual skills to sharpen the effectiveness of their sporting skills. Adjustments were also made to specific technical sporting skills. In some cases the skills were changed, and in others new techniques were developed. The hitting technique was improved by acquiring and using the unique visual-awareness skills. These adjustments were developed specifically for the player's visual system and position on the field. They included teaching players *how* to look while executing the various sporting skills.[35]

Calder wanted to examine what would happen if players were taught not only to keep their eyes on the ball, but also to consistently maintain awareness of how they were holding their own in an environment where they gather as much visual information as possible, interpret it and make decisions accordingly. This whole process took place on an individual basis, as opposed to all players or positions being treated alike.

To examine the impact of visual-awareness exercises, Calder divided a group of international hockey players into three test batteries. Each player was tested beforehand in 4 specific visual skills and 22 hockey skills. The same tests were repeated after the players had undergone different intervention programmes that lasted four weeks. Group one followed the full visual-skills-enhancement programme – in other words, visual-skills exercises as well as visual-awareness exercises. In the case of this group, there was a significant improvement in 12 of the 22 hockey skills. Group two did only visual-skills exercises, and showed an improvement in only 2 of the 22 skills in the post-programme tests. The third group received only conventional hockey coaching and didn't improve in any of the 22 skills. These were international hockey players for whom even the slightest improvement could ultimately mean the difference between winning and losing.

The earliest conclusion of Calder's research was that a visual-awareness programme could enhance on-field performance in a visually demanding sport such as hockey. Conventional coaching had no positive impact. In addition, she found that visual-skills exercises could only enhance performance if used in conjunction with her unique visual-awareness programme.

Calder's research was focused only on hockey, but in the 1990s she started thinking about the wider applicability of her work. It was clear that specific exercises for the enhancement of visual-performance skills could become a major role player in elite-level sport. However, this would require sport-specific analyses of the visual demands of a wide variety of sporting codes, as well as an analysis of the skill techniques in each sport that could be improved by means of visual-awareness exercises.

Accordingly, three things were important: first, an in-depth understanding of the individual with whom you work; second, an in-depth understanding of the individual's sporting code and the particular perfomance skills and visual skills it demands of him or her; and, third, a tailor-made training programme that would enable the sportsperson to become faster and better at gathering information, processing it and making the right decision on the basis of those unknowns.

Calder's work has developed considerably since her doctoral research, but these are still the fundamental principles. The initial focus was to develop athletes' skills by training their eyes and teaching them how to use their visual system.

'While skills still form the basis of what we do, the emphasis has shifted to decision making – that is where the focus lies with EyeGym,' Calder explained. 'Every individual or team with whom I have worked has added new knowledge and understanding to what we do. I have learnt something from all of them, and that is how my research and computer programs go through an evolution, you could say, and become better and more advanced and innovative. That combined knowledge is what has made us migrate over time from purely technical work to decision making.'

The EyeGym programme is, therefore, the product of more than two decades' research and experience. Calder sums up the programme by saying that it teaches people to make the right decisions under pressure: 'But you can't make the right decisions if you can't see correctly or can't process the visual information correctly. Your eyes have to be fit to see correctly. If your eyes are unfit and you don't have the necessary visual skills, you won't pick up important things. And there is no way that you can make the best decision if you don't possess as much visual information as possible to help you. One of the spin-offs of the EyeGym programme is that it improves your ability to concentrate. This is crucial when you have to process information and make decisions under pressure.'

And it is that aspect that represents Calder's greatest contribution to sport – not to get people's eyes fit, but to help them make better decisions. She said, 'It is trainable and it starts with your eyes. So many people only work on decision making based on psychology – to them it's about the state of mind. But to me, it's based on skills. When you can improve someone's skills, that in itself will have a positive influence on his or her state of mind. But success is not possible when the situation takes place the other way round – your skills – the fundamental principles – must be sound in order to follow up good decision making with good execution.'

Ernie Els was a wreck when Calder started working with him. The details of their partnership will be discussed in the next chapter. In brief, however, Calder saw at once that there was something wrong with Els's state of mind. But she first made structural changes to his putting before placing a greater emphasis on the brain and eventually on Els's mental state.

The latest mutation of Calder's research was summed up in an article in the September 2013 edition of the *SA Sports & Health Monthly* magazine and creates the context for the discussion of some of her greatest success stories in the next chapter. The article firstly refers to the fact that the visual skills of EyeGym have nothing to do with eyesight:

> People with bad eyesight can still have great visual skills, and vice versa. The EyeGym is a software program that begins by measuring 12 to 15 different abilities that may vary greatly across different sets of athletes' visual systems. Then Dr Calder designs bespoke exercises for each athlete to use in order to sharpen up the exact skills that are paramount in his or her game. Ernie Els, for example, like other golfers, hardly needs to rely on his peripheral vision in the same manner as would a rugby player, like Jean de Villiers, who needs to be on the lookout for a tackle from the side.[36]

The article then makes mention of two factors to be kept in mind when one aims for optimal performance: how the eye perceives and reacts to things, and how that information is coordinated and interpreted between the brain and the body. Calder aims to teach people how to sharpen up their visual awareness and speed up their visual response – two fundamental aspects of decision making in visually demanding sporting codes.

The *SA Sports & Health Monthly* journalist draws a neat distinction between the hardware and the software of the visual system. The hardware: 'The first element of the EyeGym programme assesses the basic performance of the eye and develops a training regimen specific to the athlete's needs.' The software: 'The second part of the EyeGym programme entails the processing and decision making that an athlete needs to make and how quickly he or she can do so based on information received from the eyes.'[37]

According to Calder, processing of visual information and decision making can be trained and improved. In conclusion, the article encapsulates the crux of her work as follows: 'Athletes training with EyeGym can, therefore, also improve their levels of concentration, judgement and ability to focus for longer periods, amongst various other important skills. By the time the athlete has worked at both the visual skills and the processing skills, the research shows conclusively that there is a measurable improvement.'[38]

Calder even established through research that cricket players had improved their on-field performance by making use of EyeGym's computer sessions alone – without the additional practical work. These consist of numerous exercises, some of which entail having to make a great number of decisions within a very short time. One is under pressure while doing the exercises, and high concentration levels are required (awareness). Because, according to the Eye Lady, decision making starts with your eyes.

CHAPTER 8

Life-changing science

'Thank you for making my eyes as quick as my feet.'
– Bryan Habana

The Claret Jug is to golf what the small terracotta urn in the Ashes series is to cricket. It's iconic. It's tradition. It's holy. Since the present Claret Jug, a replica of the original, was first awarded to the winner of the British Open in 1928, the champion has been allowed keep the trophy for a year, on condition that the holder returned it to the Royal and Ancient Golf Club of St Andrews before the next Open.

The trophy's proper name is the Golf Champion Trophy, but it got the name by which it is commonly known from what it actually is – a wine jug, like those from which red wine was poured in the 19th century. (The word 'claret' comes from the French *clairet*, a red wine made in the Bordeaux region.)

After Ernie Els had held the Claret Jug aloft on 21 July 2002 at the age of 32, the trophy travelled with him the following year to wherever he played. For Els, the possibilities and origin of the jug outweighed the ornamental value. A receptacle that can hold wine *should* hold wine ...

In an interview published in *The New York Times* on 17 July 2012, Els recalled the last time he touched the Claret Jug before he had to relinquish it: 'When I returned it, I had to give it a real cleaning because we had poured so many different drinks inside it.'[39]

At 32, Els had already won three majors, and there was little reason to believe that he couldn't eventually overtake his great hero, Gary Player. Player had won nine majors, and in 2004 the Big Easy had the chance to win all four that season, but failed to cut the knot in each case. Phil Mickelson's final round of 69 in the Masters Tournament was enough to pip Els (67) by one stroke. After three rounds of the US Open, the South African was tied for second place and Retief Goosen was in the lead. But a final round of 80 caused Els to drop to a tie for ninth. Goosen was the winner. Els lost in a play-off to Todd Hamilton in the British Open, and a three putt on the 18th cost him a place in the play-off in the PGA Championship.

His left knee was operated on in 2005 after a boating accident. The article in *The New York Times* commented as follows on that injury: 'That may have felt like a bad bruise compared to his wounded psyche, which some feared might never properly heal.'

The publication date of that article on Els can be regarded as a landmark in his career. Exactly a decade had passed since he won his third major, at Muirfield, and it was five days before he would get the chance, on 22 July 2012, to pour his own wine into the Claret Jug after one of the greatest comebacks in professional golf.

After three rounds of the 2012 British Open, Australian Adam Scott was in the lead on 199 (−11). Els was six shots behind in a tie for fifth. Scott was well on track to clinching his first major title after a birdie on the 14th in his final round. But then he bogeyed each of the last four holes, and ended up carding 75 in that round. Els had finished two groups ahead of him and carded 273 (−7) after a round of 68. Later that afternoon, it proved to be enough to beat Scott by one stroke.

Els was supposed to board a plane to Canada directly after the Open. His wife and children were in London, however, and he decided he would rather celebrate with his friends and family from the Claret Jug and fly to North America later on his own steam, 'maybe by Tuesday'. Friends such as Sherylle Calder, who by then had been working with Els for six months, also opted to miss the flight.

'Ernie's Open was by far the most incredible moment of my career,' she said. 'I remember how nervous he was on that first day of the tournament. He was worried because he was coming from two or three years when he couldn't putt. He had tried putting coaches. He'd started using a belly putter, doubted things, started doubting himself. Sometimes Ernie even failed with a putt of 2 feet. He told me that it was humiliating. And that pressure was horrible – he seriously considered packing his clubs away.

'But part of our work was to help him cope with that stress from the first tee. We talked about it. We practised putting for hours. The putting green in the practice area at Lytham and the first tee are very close to each other. We worked there calmly each day on his putting both before and after the round. I followed him to every hole. Some people think that because Ernie seems so laid back he doesn't work hard. But he does. He works until he's dripping with sweat.'

The Open was going well for Els, but Scott was firmly in the saddle. When Els sank his last ball on the 18th, Calder knew that she had five minutes to collect her belongings from her guest house so that she could be in time for the flight that would take a number of players to Canada. In 2012 she was present at 14 of Els's tournaments.

'I got my bag, loaded my stuff and was on my way back to the golf club when someone came rushing towards me half hysterically. "Ernie's looking for you! Ernie's looking for you!"

'I realised then what was happening with Adam, and Ernie realised he was possibly on the verge of winning his first major in ten years. When he saw me, he said: "Where have you been, Sherylle? And what should we do now? Help me quickly."

'I handed my passport, my bags, all my things, to a complete stranger. But I couldn't care less, because Ernie and I quickly wanted to do some putting. It was all that mattered. We kept getting information from the course, and I was firmly convinced that no one would beat him that day if there had to be a play-off. Just the way he talked, how well he putted – he was ready for anything. Ernie's life changed that day. That is what makes our work so precious.

'Isn't it nice to see how Ernie is playing now? He looks comfortable. He told me the other day that he now gets a kick out of putting, whereas for a long time he didn't even want to take his putter out of his golf bag. Now he looks forward to practising, to working hard and enjoying it. I'm absolutely convinced that most negativity in sport can be caused by *and* solved by the eyes.'

Calder's colleague Christi Botha recalled the day in George when Els first approached them for assistance after Johann Rupert had strongly advised him to explore that route. 'Ernie asked Sherylle the Wednesday after the Pro-Am of the Volvo Golf Champions to meet him at Fancourt's practice putting green,' Botha said. 'We were there to work with Retief Goosen and Robert Karlsson, and when Ernie arrived, he said: "Right, girls, what can you do for me?"'

Calder asked him to make a few putts, and her reaction stuck in his memory.

'Do you know what Sherylle said when she looked at me roll a few putts?' he asked in an interview with *Golf World* magazine in August 2012. 'I was the worst she'd ever seen. "Worst at what?" I ask. "Your brain, man!"'[40]

Calder believes that the best coaches in the world are those who are not only better than others at spotting a mistake or a problem, but who are also able to correct it – a talent with which she has been blessed.

'Sherylle observed how Ernie went about his putting and, for the time being, offered him only two suggestions,' said Botha. 'You don't want to change a lot of things about a guy's game just before a tournament. Ernie told Sherylle her suggestions were incredibly close to what he used to do at the time when he still consistently played well and won. He eventually competed against Retief and Branden Grace in the play-off, which was won by Branden. Nevertheless, after a single session with Sherylle there was already a big difference.'

Why was Calder so keen to help him? I asked. 'Because I knew I could,' she said. Their new partnership was established immediately after the Volvo championship at a ten-day 'training camp' in the US, and their focus was solely on Els's putting.

'He was extremely tense,' said Calder, 'and that has an influence on your entire game. We first wanted to get Ernie's putting right, because if we could remove that stressor from his game, he would automatically become calmer and get back into playing the kind of golf that gave him his nickname.'

Els was put on the EyeGym programme, which included, among others, five exercises based on decision making and visual awareness that he did on a laptop – a regimen he still follows today for 15 minutes before every round of golf that he plays. In addition, there were practical training sessions on the putting green.

He had no routine or consistency in the way he approached his putting. Els explained this as follows to *Golf World*: 'Week to week I would change things. One week I would be getting my hands higher only to change it back the following one. You become desperate and the next thing you're gone.'[41]

He didn't believe that the problem lay with his putting stroke, as such. In his view, it was rather a matter of not being able to think clearly. 'My mind was so cluttered with stuff that I couldn't think. I don't think there was anything wrong with my stroke, but my set-up was all gone, my eyes were moving and I wasn't calm and collected – I wasn't the Ernie Els that I know.'

While the intensity of this sporting code is completely different from that of field hockey, Calder did the same with Els as she had done in the 1990s with her hockey players – she first found a structural solution based on her scientific research.

Els described in the *Golf World* article how his putter was 'closed', his footwork wasn't right and the ball was positioned too far back when he stood over it, with the result that he viewed the ball too much from the side.

'There were quite a number of visual factors that played a role. The main thing is that we identified Ernie's specific needs and worked on that. There is no generic solution,' Calder said.

They looked at how Els set up for a putt on the green, his coordination, his stance over the ball, where he looked, how he assessed the situation and read the green. His strokes were structured accordingly, but this only represents the practical work that was done with him. His focus, his concentration and the psychological aspect of his game were also factors that gradually received attention.

Said Calder, 'I'll be able to work with Ernie for the rest of his career, because this is an ongoing thing. There are no lasting quick fixes. I wouldn't have been able to help him in 2013 if we hadn't first worked on certain things the year before. Those things are the scientific principles, and if you want to take short cuts without first getting the scientific principles across to someone, he will struggle and get stuck in a vicious cycle.'

Her early successes with Els and his British Open title were powerful testimony of Calder's work and of Els's perseverance to get his career back on track in an unusual way. To Els, the Open was a turning point in his career, but at that time his putting wasn't as consistent as it should be. Els could have won two tournaments in the PGA Tour in 2012, but his putting let him down. He was on course to win the Transitions Championship in March that year, but fell short after missing two short putts over the last three holes. A month later he threw away the Zurich Classic in New Orleans when he missed a putt of less than 2 metres that would have won him the play-off.

The Classic took place at the end of April – three weekends after Bubba Watson had outplayed Louis Oosthuizen in the contest for the green jacket at the Masters Tournament at the Augusta National Golf Club. For Els, that bungled opportunity in New Orleans would have felt like a trifle compared to his disappointment at not being invited to compete in the Masters for the first time in 18 years. It had been too long since he won a major, and in the period before the Masters he had fallen out of the top 50 world rankings. Despite many chances to earn an invitation, he failed to meet the requirements in time. Mostly because he had been let down by his putter.

The partnership between the Big Easy and the Eye Lady arguably reached its crowning moment not when Els won the British Open a few months later, but when he finished the 2013 Masters with the hottest putting of all.

Els didn't win the tournament – the victor was Adam Scott. But it was with considerable satisfaction that Els declared to the media the following week before the RBC Heritage tournament: 'I think I was number one in putting last week at Augusta.' (He was.) 'I worked with Sherylle, my putting lady. She really got the message across of what she wanted me to do. And I started feeling that.'

As far as putting is concerned, Augusta is the toughest major course in the world. The greens of golf courses that are used for majors are usually slightly faster than those used elsewhere.

US golfer Brandt Snedeker once equated putting at Augusta to putting in a bathtub, and Jason Day pointed out that even in good weather the greens get a reading of 14 on the stimpmeter. (The stimpmeter is a device used to determine the speed of a putting green. The general categories are slow [4.5–6.5], medium [6.5–8.5] and fast [8.5–10.5]. Augusta has greens with readings of between 12 and 14 on the stimpmeter.)

American daily *USA Today* tried to explain this putting puzzler at Augusta in its sports pages a week before the 2013 Masters:

> The 18 greens get their pitch and movement from the rolling terrain. Adding to the puzzlement is a SubAir system, which uses heating coils, blowers and pipes underneath every green to allow the green temperature and moisture levels to be monitored. If Masters officials determine the greens are too slow, they can pump out moisture to ensure they arrive at the beloved speed tournament officials want. And the elevation change of the course, the drop from the highest point (the back right of the green on the first hole) to the lowest point (Rae's Creek guarding the 11th, 12th and 13th holes) is 175 feet [almost 55 metres] and has a major impact on the movement of putts. So much so that a board in the caddie's hut has drawings of every single green and a large dot signaling where Rae's Creek is in relation to the green. Further, every yardage book features arrows on each of the drawings of the putting surfaces, indicating which direction the green breaks toward Rae's Creek. Yet players are still puzzled.[42]

The greens themselves are only the last, and fairly high, hurdle among a variety of factors that can make Augusta National as difficult for a player as it is beautiful. Favourable ball placement on the green is crucial. On a fast green with steep slopes and contours it is not advisable to make a putt from above the hole. That is why approach shots are almost more important than putts, and good putting figures at Augusta cannot be judged independently from good approach shots – as Jason Day summarised succinctly in the *USA Today* article: 'You try to keep yourself below the hole at all times. If you happen to do that, that's great. If not, then you're kind of screwed.'

Dean Knuth is the man who developed the United States Golf Association's (USGA) rating system for golf courses. In April 2010 he wrote an article in *Golf Digest* titled 'How Tough is Augusta National?'. Following the USGA formula for rating courses, Knuth graded each hole on the course for ten obstacle factors on a scale of 0 to 10, with 10 the most difficult.

'Green target', in other words, how difficult it is to get onto the greens and get a good ball placement, is rated as factor 8. Aspects such as the size, firmness and shape of a green in relation to the length of the approach shot are taken into account for the rating. 'Green surface' is factor 9 referring to how difficult it is to play on the greens. Slopes, contours, stimpmeter speeds and hole placement are considered in this assessment. Els would have had to overcome both these factors to be number one in putting. According to Knuth, the ninth factor is one of the most notable features of the course during the Masters.

Hole 11 (par 4) is rated $^8/_{10}$ on factor 8 and $^9/_{10}$ on factor 9. Els struggled at this hole and made a bogey in three of the four rounds – hence one stroke over par. Hole 10 (par 4) has the same ratings on the respective factors, and there Els made par three times and carded one bogey.

Hole 15 (par 5) is rated $^9/_{10}$ on the difficulty of the green surface. Els was on top form on these longer holes, and over the four rounds he was 15 under par on the par-5 holes. He was particularly impressive on the 15th where, despite the high obstacle rating, he scored two of his three eagles as well as two birdies.

Els finished the Masters tied for 13th after having let himself down in the second round in particular. Some interesting comparative statistics between him and the five top players at the 2013 Masters are noted in Table 5.

Pos.	Name	Analysis	Eagles	Birdies	Par	Bogey	2 x Bogey
1	Adam Scott*	-9 (69, 72, 69, 69; 279)	0	15	51	6	0
2	Ángel Cabrera	-9 (71, 69, 69, 70; 279)	0	19	43	10	0
3	Jason Day	-7 (70, 68, 73, 70; 281)	1	17	43	10	1
T4	Marc Leishman	-5 (66, 73, 72, 72; 283)	0	16	45	11	0
T4	Tiger Woods	-5 (70, 73, 70, 70; 283)	0	15	49	7	0**
T13	Ernie Els	-1 (71, 74, 73, 69; 287)	3	14	36	19	0

*Scott beat Cabrera in the play-off. **Woods made one triple bogey.

Table 5: Masters Tournament, Augusta National, 8–14 April 2013: Top five players and Ernie Els compared (Source: www.augusta.com, accessed 11 March 2014)

Calder believed she could help Els, and she was right. 'Ernie deserves the credit. I only helped him to get a few things right – to see better, to exercise better judgement, to be better with execution, to play better, to get better scores and to feel better.'

About his partnership with Calder, which has developed into a friendship, Els said to ESPN Golf: 'I don't think I ever doubted her and thank goodness she didn't doubt me. We were right on track from the first time we actually spent time together. And with all the wobbles that I had through the year and not winning, it obviously hurt, but I really felt this was something I could stick to. I felt if I stuck with it, things would only get better, and that's the way it turned out.'[43]

Bryan Habana, the English and annoying school coaches

In 2010 Bryan Habana was playing like a child who was desperate to please his teacher and his classmates. It was as if whenever there was a question, his hand was the first to go up. But he seldom had the right answer.

It was painful to watch him from the Newlands press box as the IRB's Player of the Year for 2007 tried so hard to be the old Habana again, but without success. Knock-ons. Failed tackles. A try drought. It was the same person, but not the same player as the one Sherylle Calder has a photo of in her office.

The photo, which was taken a few minutes before the 2007 Rugby World Cup final, shows her and Habana doing visual-awareness exercises. The Springbok winger later signed it for her and added a message: 'Thank you for making my eyes as quick as my feet.'

By 2010 that player had gone missing, and even his Stormers jersey didn't prevent the Newlands faithful from jeering him. But it's interesting to note what a long time a year can be in rugby. In Habana's faltering season, it was often wondered whether the time hadn't arrived for him to play rugby overseas on a French retirement package.

France and Japan were then still mostly regarded as retirement homes for rugby players who wanted to see out the last days of their declining careers in a financially rewarding manner. However, in the course of a season the tide turned to such an extent that these two markets now both attract and handsomely reward the cream of rugby players from across the world. While Habana does play for the French club Toulon today, it is not because he wanted to finish his career away from the cursing at Newlands, but because, at the time of writing, he was playing his best rugby to date.

There is seldom a single factor that gives rise to athletes' success, and it would be irresponsible to suggest that this is the case. Keeping in mind, therefore, that Calder's involvement in Habana's career was not the sole reason for his successes, over the years since 2007, there was a noticeable difference, however, when he wasn't working with Calder.

She was involved with the Springboks in 2007 when they won the World Cup and Habana was the best player in the world. In 2008 Calder worked in London, and had no contact with Habana in that year. It was also in 2008 that the Bulls had a poor Super Rugby season, and some of the reasons for this were discussed earlier in the book. Calder's absence from Habana's life may well have been a contributing factor. They briefly had contact in 2009, and in that year both the Springboks and Habana were once again at the top of their form. When TV broadcaster the BBC asked Habana during the series against the British and Irish Lions who had been most crucial in helping him recover his form, his reply was 'Doc Sherylle'. He described her as a 'vital cog' in helping him get back to his best.

'She's helped me put myself back on the map again and hopefully I won't stop working with her for a long time to come,' the winger said at the time. But then he stopped working with her and, from 2010, his career once again suffered a decline.

'We started working together again intensively in 2012,' Calder said. 'Bryan was named South African Rugby Player of the Year, and he gave me the credit when he received his award at the ceremony.'

Calder became slightly exasperated as she recalled the criticism Habana had endured during those difficult times: 'I hate it when commentators say that a player is overeager, because that's not what it is. His timing is out, that's all. Just look at the kind of tackles that Bryan missed. If I go in too early for a tackle and there is, say, 1.5 metres between us, I'll miss you. If I come too close, on the other hand, you're going to push me off.

That perception — depth perception — is one of the things we do with Bryan. Exactly the same visual skill is used when you go for a high ball or when the ball is in space.

'The last true intercept try we've seen for years in test rugby was when Bryan scored one against Argentina in the semifinal of the 2007 World Cup tournament. He was on his own try line and intercepted a good pass to score a try, thereby putting enormous pressure on the Argentinians. A true interception is when you intercept a good pass because you saw something, interpreted it and reacted correctly to it — not because you saw a poor pass: that is decision making, which involves a high degree of awareness. If you don't keep practising that skill, though, it becomes blunted. And that's what we saw in Bryan's case. He's an incredibly talented rugby player, but, at the elite level, why would you turn down the chance to become even just 1 per cent better? Good decision making is often that 1 per cent that differentiates a champion from a finalist.'

Calder was already involved with the All Blacks in the early 2000s when the England rugby coach, Clive Woodward, asked her to work with the England team in the run-up to the 2003 World Cup tournament and during the tournament.

She said, 'I told Clive that the team that made the best decisions in that World Cup would win the tournament. And that is exactly what happened in the final against Australia. It's small decisions that make the difference. I did a lot of work with Steve Thompson because his judgement in lineout throwing wasn't very good, on account of his depth perception that wasn't good. In those last 30 seconds of that final, so many things happened, and the players' decision making was excellent: decision making that had been made possible directly by our fundamental principles — skills.

'Steve, a guy who until fairly recently hadn't been able to judge depth, fed the lineout with a deep throw. A ruck formed, and Matt Dawson, the scrumhalf, assessed his environment in a split second, and broke through a minuscule gap right next to the ruck. It's about the ability to see space when spaces exist, and those breaks were exactly what we practised with the scrumhalves. Then, Jonny Wilkinson got the ball and put the decisive drop goal through the posts with his weaker foot. Australia had to restart, and when you look at how England jogged back after that drop goal, they seemed like a team that thought it already had the victory in the bag. There was no order, and there were open spots to which Australia could kick. Elton Flatley saw this, and kicked on a prop. And what does Trevor Woodman do? After two hours of rugby, that loosehead prop jumps almost a metre into the air like a fullback, wins the ball for his country, and England win the World Cup. If he hadn't jumped for that ball, Australia could have regained possession and, given the disorder in the England ranks, the Wallabies would probably have scored a try and won the World Cup. This is decision making – and decision making begins with what you perceive. And it can be trained.'

Calder is firmly convinced that the Springboks would have won the 2011 World Cup too if their decision making had been better, regardless of Bryce Lawrence's disgraceful refereeing: 'What cost us that quarterfinal? Not Bryce Lawrence. There were forward passes. Knock-ons on the try line. These are small things that wouldn't have happened with visual awareness – with the fundamental principles of decision making. The All Blacks were not the best team at that World Cup. South Africa was. And it was that 1 per cent that the Boks lacked that prevented them from winning back-to-back World Cups,' said the only management team member in rugby who has ever won back-to-back world titles (with England in 2003 and with South Africa in 2007).

Calder is concerned about a disregard for, or misconception about, decision making in rugby, especially when it comes to the way in which children are coached at school.

'Don't think it's easy to talk to rugby players about decision making. For them, rugby is about strength and size,' she said. 'I just shake my head when I hear coaches talking about accuracy in execution. I've worked with many backs, and for a large part of the time teams practise structured phase movements. You do this movement and that movement, and you run through it on the practice ground until you've scored a try or forced a penalty. But how often do you complete a phase movement in a match? Not often. Yet, for much of the time, we practise set movements that are seldom completed on the playing field.

'Most things in rugby happen from broken play, and then you have to look up and decide what you're going to do. Some school coaches can be the worst. They tell a player that when you have the ball and you find yourself here and this guy comes charging at you, you must give the ball to that guy. And if you don't complete that phase play, if the movement is broken up before the end, they can get cross with you. All that they are doing is depriving a player of the opportunity to develop decision-making abilities when he is confronted with an unforeseen situation.

'Nowadays rugby is broken play. A kicking pattern is broken play, because that is where the points lie. This is what we, at EyeGym, teach players – to make the right decisions based on the unforeseen. We practise it. For example, if I find myself here, how can I end up over there and score a try? Can I see space? The feedback I get most often from rugby players is that they have started seeing space, while it has never been part of their experience of the sport before. Gurthrö Steenkamp once came off the field and told me he had seen more space in that match than he had ever noticed before. People can be trained at this, and that was exactly what tipped the scales in England's favour in 2003: a prop who made the right decision.'

The horses and pearls

Shortly before South Africa won the Polocrosse World Cup in 2011, the organisers were not comfortable with the eventual champion team. However, what initially raised suspicions about possible cheating was simply the South Africans' ability to see better.

'The South African coaches came to see us,' said Calder, who was also involved with this World Cup team. 'They told me that South Africa had never managed to advance beyond the semifinal of the tournament – Australia always beat us. England was also there. The next World Cup was going to be in England and if you go there, you have to use their horses. The coach told me that they had to find something to make them better than the other teams, even if the other teams had better horses. I agreed to work with them.

'We started training on farms, I gave them the necessary software to train their eyes, and we also worked on the field in Newcastle. Eventually they went to the World Cup, and the team won their first game. That evening an official meeting was held. The officials had watched South Africa and they decided that they were playing with racquets that were bigger, and asked them to hand in their equipment for closer inspection. Polocrosse also has lineouts, where the umpire throws in the ball and you take the ball with your racquet. The South African team took balls from opponents – they intercepted them. They took balls that had never been taken before, and they ended up winning the World Cup for the simple reason that we had given the team the best skills.'

The more Calder worked in sport and the longer she observed the influence of her work, the more she started seeing the impact it had outside of sport. In 2007 she worked with Grey College's first rugby team. It was Robert Ebersohn's matric year. Grey's rugby team performed excellently and, with only a few players from other schools in the team, they beat Western Province 52-3 in the main match at the Craven Week that year in Free State garb. Even the school's Afrikaans teacher waxed lyrical about Calder's involvement.

Said Calder: 'The then principal, Johan Volsteedt, asked me after that rugby season to remain involved with them. When I returned to Grey College in 2008, the Afrikaans teacher thanked the heavens that I was there again. Apparently, the comprehension skills in class of the rugby boys who were on EyeGym had improved markedly, and this had a positive effect on their academic performance. Based on that and on research I had done in England in 2008, we developed a specific school programme which we can now tailor to the needs of the group or individual that uses it.

'I did much of my research for this when I was in London in 2008. I worked with a school and used a group of 60 children. We did cognitive tests with the children before we put them on EyeGym for six weeks. When we had cognitive tests done again after this period, the children did 72 per cent better on average than in the first test. Then we knew that this programme has a cognitive effect and that it can improve the learning ability of children.

'The child is taught to work more effectively. For learning, you need the ability to follow something with your eye. If you can get the eye to function effectively, the brain functions effectively and the learning experience can take place at a deeper level.'

This offshoot has grown spontaneously from Calder's work, and from that early curiosity about 'something different' in her own abilities, a science has grown which has far-reaching consequences in many applications.

'We currently support a six-year-old girl who comes from a disadvantaged area where she was raped. As a result, she is behind her peer group in terms of development. She started doing EyeGym, and is now gradually beginning to function on the same level as the other children, as we have accelerated her performance. This, in turn, has an effect on many other things in her life. She has regained her self-confidence.

'There is a perception that we work only with the eye and with sport stars. But this science is wide-ranging, and it enriches our lives every single day. There isn't a more satisfying and moving experience than seeing how something that you do changes and improves another person's life.'

Dr Sherylle Calder's international clients include the following: Surrey County Cricket; Pakistan cricket team; Italian Prada America's Cup yachting team; All Black Rugby; Belgian men's hockey team; Kenya/Netherlands/Canada/Namibia Cricket; Australian World Cup cricket team; England World Cup rugby team; Spanish men's hockey team; England men's hockey team; England Cricket; Southampton Football Club; Great Britain Winter Olympic athletes; Springbok rugby team; Springbok sevens team; Scotland Commonwealth athletes; South African netball team; Great Britain Commonwealth golf team; South African Davis Cup team; British Olympic group; Monaco Football Club; Wolverhampton Football Club; West Coast Eagles AFL; Tottenham Football Academy; Vancouver Canucks NHL; Williams Formula 1 team; Proteas cricket team; International Cricket Council; Lions Rugby; Suntory Rugby (Japan); Brumbies Rugby; Ernie Els; Bryan Habana; Retief Goosen; Dutch Olympic team; IRB referees; Tim Henman; and Ana Ivanovic.

PAUL TREU

CHAPTER 9

The optimal experience

'The empires of the future are the empires of the mind.'
– Winston Churchill, September 1943

There was just one thing that was puzzling about the 2011 South African Try of the Year. Sibu Sithole, the rugby player who scored it, couldn't remember how the try had happened. His lapse of memory was not the result of concussion, although the brain most certainly had a hand in it.

On 29 May 2011, Sithole scored the tournament-winning try, which led to the South African sevens team beating their Australian counterparts 36-35 in the final of the Edinburgh Sevens at Murrayfield. It was the last tournament of the IRB's 2010/11 Sevens World Series – the second tournament won by South Africa in the space of two weekends.

The Blitzbokke (the national sevens side) had won the London tournament a week before as a result of their tactical excellence, and that victory will be discussed later. From an outsider's perspective, however, it seemed unlikely that the team would match that exceptional performance immediately afterwards in Scotland: at that stage no team had won successive tournaments since 2008, when South Africa had done so in Dubai and George.

In addition, the probability of back-to-back victories was diminished by other compounding factors. A South African side beset with injuries took on Australia with only 8 of its original 12 players. Branco du Preez (knee), Neil Powell (rib) and the captain, Kyle Brown (ankle), had been injured before the final. When, on top of that, Paul Delport had to be taken off the field in a cart in the first half of the final, it seemed to be the nail in the coffin. Australia had a 28-7 lead after 11 of the 20 minutes.

The Blitzbokke, however, launched an impressive fightback. Commentator Nigel Starmer-Smith described the contest afterwards as 'the most phenomenal finale. The most remarkable turnaround I've seen in all these years of World Series sevens [since 1999]. What a game. What a finale. What a win!'

THE OPTIMAL EXPERIENCE

Steven Hunt scored two tries in a flash, the second one a mere 46 seconds before time was up. Cecil Afrika – a man who would be named as the IRB's Sevens Player of the Year a few months later – overcame his erratic kicking performance and put South Africa within striking distance of the Australians with his conversion kick, moving the score to 31–35.

In rugby sevens, the team that has scored does the restart kick. When Afrika kicked off after Hunt's second five-pointer, there were 16 seconds left. The Blitzbokke won back possession after the siren had gone. Sithole gathered the ball in the midfield from a ruck, sprinted sideways, fended off one opponent along the right touchline, ran around another and celebrated what would be the winning try by diving triumphantly, landing just within the dead-ball line. New Zealand had already won the World Series earlier that day, but the Edinburgh victory put South Africa in second place in the overall standings. They had been in fifth place after the first three tournaments of the series, but with three cups in the last five tournaments, the Blitzbokke emphatically stole the limelight. They also won the Las Vegas tournament in February and played in the final in four of the last five tournaments.

When the team landed at Cape Town International Airport shortly after the Scottish triumph, I asked Sithole about his try, but he was unable to recall the run-up to the try. He was under the impression that Afrika had given him the ball and had even thanked him for that after the match.

'The adrenalin had probably kicked in,' said Sithole in an attempt to explain the haziness of his memory. I later spoke to Steven Hunt and Frankie Horne. Although they could remember Sithole's try, all three of them had certain shared experiences of the match that were not consistent with the effect that adrenalin has on people: they said they had been calm; they couldn't hear the crowd; time stood still for them; everything that could go right for them went right.

This is not the typical experience of a team that is 31–35 behind after the siren has already gone. Nor was it adrenalin that carried the team through that fightback. It was more likely to be what Hungarian psychologist Mihaly Csikszentmihalyi has described as a 'state of flow'. This is a psychological phenomenon, which Daniel Kahneman describes as follows in his book *Thinking, Fast and Slow:* 'People who experience flow describe it as "a state of effortless concentration so deep that they lose their sense of time, of themselves, of their problems", and their descriptions of the joy of that state are so compelling that Csikszentmihalyi has called it an "optimal experience".'[44]

It is indeed an optimal experience. Adrenalin, by contrast, triggers the fight-or-flight response – a far cry from a calm experience of effortless concentration. The fight-or-flight response is a physiological one that serves a crucial and necessary purpose, but in a motivational and sports context it does not belong in the same company as a state of flow.

I concluded my match reports in *Die Burger*, *Beeld* and *Volksblad* newspapers as follows: 'What was lacking in their game at the start of the series is what caused the Boks to play in the cup finals of the last five tournaments: a belief in a new kind of sevens, where players think before acting on instinct.'[45]

I was right about the thinking team, but not quite about instinct being relegated to a lesser role. Natural instinct is an indispensable factor for the state of flow to manifest in an individual or a team. It does, however, require a deep awareness of yourself, your environment and your teammates to reach the state where practised skills and strategy are applied in the right place and at the right time thanks to a natural instinct. Therefore, what seems effortless to others and is experienced as effortless by you is in fact the reward for the hard work that preceded it.

In the case of this particular Blitzbok group, it was not primarily that hard work that they did on the practice ground and in the gym. Instead, they integrated the brain as the trump card in everything they did: how they thought, how they talked, how they understood each other and how they intended to outwit their opponents.

Their theme for the tournaments in London and Edinburgh was 'concentrate to focus'. That focus was influenced by a multitude of factors. And to achieve the 'optimal experience' to which Csikszentmihalyi refers, then Blitzbok coach Paul Treu sought the advice of an internationally acclaimed creativity specialist, Dr Kobus Neethling, at the start of the series. That meeting brought about a radical change in Treu's philosophy of and approach to coaching. There was a shift in emphasis from traditional sports coaching to whole-brain thinking – a concept that has its origins in examining how the two hemispheres of the brain function differently, which can help explain personality differences.

Before explaining how whole-brain thinking can be applied to rugby, it is useful to understand the background, which is taken from the book *Creative Rugby* by Neethling and Naas Botha (1999).[46]

Neuroscientist Roger Sperry was awarded the Nobel Prize in Physiology in 1981 for his split-brain theory. He and Michael Gazzaniga treated patients who suffered from epilepsy, and found that the corpus callosum – the band of nerve fibres that connects the left and right hemispheres of the brain – facilitated vital communication between the two hemispheres. Because some of the patients were in danger of dying from their condition, Sperry and his colleagues decided to cut the connection between the two halves of the brain. The severity of the epileptic seizures was immediately reduced to an acceptable level.

In split-brain patients, the two hemispheres of the brain could, therefore, be studied independently. The research showed that each hemisphere receives and interprets information in different ways, and is, at the same time, largely unaware of how the other hemisphere learns and processes information. Each half of the brain was shown to have its own specialist functions.

Sperry proved that the part of the brain an individual uses most has a strong influence on the person's physical and mental abilities, problem-solving abilities, personality traits and approach to people and things. The research also showed why one person may be, for example, very good at working with numbers (left brain), but at the same time uncomfortable in group situations. Another person may come up with wonderful ideas (right brain), but may be unable to structure and implement them him or herself.

According to Neethling, this phenomenon is found not only in individuals, but also collectively in groups or organisations.

Researchers such as Ned Herrmann and Bryan Kolb later extended the split-brain theory from two halves to a model of four quadrants, with each of those areas representing different thinking styles. Building on that research, Neethling found further significant differences between the quadrants besides thinking styles.

This led to the development of the Neethling Brain Instrument (NBI), which is used to measure individuals' thinking preferences and compile personal brain profiles – the tool that Heyneke Meyer first used at the SWD Eagles and later applied at the Blue Bulls, mentioned earlier.

The four quadrants in the NBI were eventually further subdivided to give an eight-dimensional view of an individual's thinking preferences. The NBI has two questionnaires from which, firstly, the four quadrants and, secondly, the eight dimensions are determined in a given individual.

The quadrants and their applicable dimensions in the NBI are:
- L1 (realist, analyst);
- L2 (stalwart/preserver, organiser);
- R2 (socialiser, empathiser); and
- R1 (strategist, 'imagineer').

From a sporting perspective, Neethling specifically adapted this instrument to apply to different sporting codes such as golf, cricket, soccer and rugby. The explanation below of the application of the four quadrants to rugby players will help one understand how coaches think based on their own brain preferences.

L1: Realist, analyst

This quadrant refers to the extent to which a player is focused on keeping his mind on the game, being attentive to the essence of each moment of the game, thinking well and logically on the field, not making mistakes, employing the existing knowledge of the coach, remembering what was coached and using all of that coaching. Players apply the skills that have been developed and acquired: ranging from the routine a player follows before he kicks, scrumming, playing a tactical role in the lineout, to a scrumhalf breaking around a scrum. The player is able to take this information from his L1 memory and apply these skills in L2, in the way that he has been coached to do.

People who tend to be dominant in this quadrant prefer focusing, thinking logically, being committed and meticulous, and thinking concretely and rationally. They prefer using specified and existing knowledge, functioning from memory, drawing logical conclusions and acting on the basis of a specific coaching methodology.

L2: Stalwart/preserver, organiser

This entails a step-by-step thinking preference. It is where coaching takes place and discipline is cultivated, such as being on time, learning certain steps and processes, and the development of fixed patterns. Although this quadrant is of particular importance, it may also be the quadrant where failure originates. By focusing on the L2 quadrant, it is possible that a player may keep executing the four or five learnt patterns regardless of the actual circumstances of a game. For example, they may persist with the same strategy even if it doesn't work. They may stick to it because the L2 quadrant dominates their style of playing rugby and their understanding of the game. In this quadrant, the preference is to follow a systematic, step-by-step approach to the task at hand. Those whose thinking preferences fall predominantly into this quadrant are dedicated, and prefer discipline, order, learnt patterns, rules, regulations and thorough planning.

R2: Socialiser, empathiser

The spontaneous group cohesion of the team is situated in the R2 quadrant. A strong R2 awareness may serve as a counterbalance to the pitfalls associated with L2, because a team is able to sense when a strategy isn't working and can regroup and try something else. There is a spontaneous flow of teamwork that is not based on predetermined steps, but on intuitive awareness of the moment and of each other. This is where team spirit is formed and where it should be sustained. R2, therefore, represents the seat of emotional intelligence and is important for reaching a higher level of maturity, being able to manage emotions and deal with conflict on the field and in crisis moments in an emotionally mature way.

According to Neethling, this quadrant is of paramount importance in a more modern rugby environment, where the emphasis on the left brain should be complemented by a stronger right-brain focus and emotional maturity. For Treu, the R2 quadrant is the glue that needs to keep the whole-brain mindset together.

R1: Strategist, imagineer

It is from this quadrant that space is created for the individualism of players. Creative play resides here, on the spur of the moment when the planned L2 strategy doesn't work. Here, players act intuitively and create new patterns that suit the circumstances. A player who has fully developed the qualities of this quadrant sees the bigger picture on the field from his 'gut feeling' and knows instinctively when to fall back, where to break and where to kick. In other words, it is about decision making. He realises spontaneously that a movement is not going to work in the specific situation and that there needs to be a quick switch to another strategy.

Acting in this quadrant enables a player to continuously orient himself spatially so that he always has the whole field in view and can, therefore, come up with surprising movements. People who are strong in this quadrant are unfazed by change and switching from one plan to another doesn't cause them anxiety. Therefore, the preferences here are for individualism, imaginativeness, the unorthodox, the unusual, innovation and intuition. In this quadrant it is also about the ability to think of more than one thing at the same time, to see the big picture (spatial perception), to experiment and to act instantaneously.

While the quadrants indicate certain preferences and skills, a preference doesn't necessarily mean that it is well developed, or that an individual may not also have well-developed personality preferences and skills in some of the other quadrants. The NBI helps one to gain an understanding of how different people learn, think and experience things differently,

THE OPTIMAL EXPERIENCE

My eight-dimensional brain profile

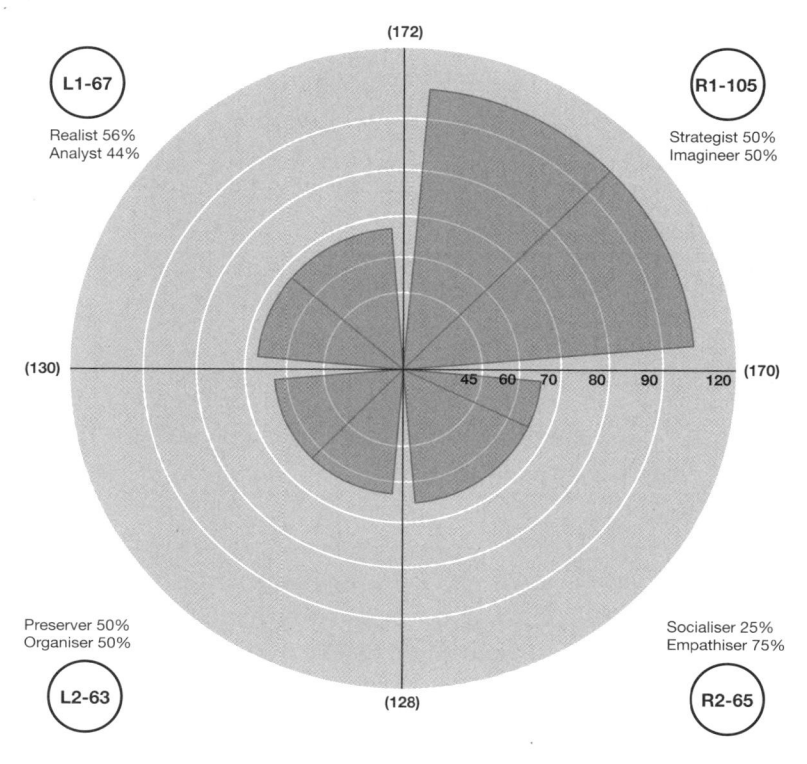

(172)

L1-67
Realist 56%
Analyst 44%

R1-105
Strategist 50%
Imagineer 50%

(130)   (170)

Preserver 50%
Organiser 50%

Socialiser 25%
Empathiser 75%

L2-63   (128)   R2-65

The above eight-dimensional results indicate the percentages of each quadrant. When you move into the L1 thinking mode, for example, 80% Realist and 20% Analyst will mean that you think realistically 80% of the time and analytically 20%.

Figure 6: Brain profile of the author

and how that very information can be used to allow individuals to fulfil their personal potential.

A brain profile that is compiled based on an individual's responses to the questionnaires of the NBI would look similar to the diagram of my own brain profile (see Figure 6), which was done during the interviewing process to serve as a frame of reference.

This profile indicates a dominant quadrant (R1), thus the strongest preference, with a further subdivision between strategic and imaginative thinking, to which equal time is devoted when I move into my dominant thinking mode. The other quadrants are all more or less equal. The aim of brain profiling is not only to identify the individual's personal preferences and strengths, but also to determine where there may be scope for development – hence the term 'whole-brain thinking'.

When interviewed, Neethling said, 'It will benefit rugby players and coaches to learn more about brain preferences and the effect they have on people's behaviour. For instance, some people think in a logical, organised and systematic way, while others are disorganised, tend to daydream and don't pay much attention to detail. Coaches would realise that it is better to help develop the brain preference of the individual under their supervision for his own sake and that of the team, rather than trying to change it. They would also understand that they can help make him a better and more creative human being by fostering in him an awareness and understanding of the brain preferences of the people with whom he lives, works and plays.'

As beneficial as it may be for a coach to understand his players' brain preferences – and even to develop ideas of suitable positions for specific brain preferences based on those insights – it is equally important that he should understand his own preferences and develop the secondary and tertiary quadrants for the sake of the team.

This was how Meyer initially used brain profiling (coincidentally, this was when he was at the SWD while Treu was still one of his players). Meyer has a strong right-brain dominance but when he started coaching the Blue Bulls, more than 60 per cent of the players had a left-brain preference. Knowing this, and given the quality of the players at his disposal, it made sense to play a structured brand of rugby, with which the Bulls achieved great success over a decade.

'The advantage of this lies in knowing in general how an individual approaches life and, more specifically, how he analyses rugby, because we want thinking people on the field,' said Neethling.

He said, 'John Smit, for example, is R2 dominant – he's very good with people and that is why he was the right captain at a specific point in South African rugby. He was able to unify and inspire people.

'A guy like Naas Botha is R1. He has a spatial brain and could spot space extremely well. That's why Naas was one of the few guys in the world who could kick the ball to places where no one was. Very few people manage to do that, and if you coach the brain together with the body, you have the perfect combination.

THE OPTIMAL EXPERIENCE

'If you're a front ranker, like Jannie and Bismarck du Plessis, it's very good to have an L1 brain. Victor Matfield, on the other hand, is double dominant in both L quadrants. So is Andries Bekker, and some of the greatest locks in the world are dominant in these quadrants. We developed an instrument for referees as well, and André Watson has mentioned how useful that knowledge was to him on the field. Martin Johnson is also dominant in the L quadrants, and when André refereed the 2003 World Cup final between England and Australia, he knew how to communicate with Johnson. He awarded a penalty against England and when Johnson wanted to know why, Watson could simply point out the facts to him: look at the man who fell over the ball and is still lying there – his feet indicate that he came in from the side. Therefore, knowledge of the quadrants teaches you to communicate in the appropriate way with specific individuals.'

Neethling said, 'Teachers mostly prefer a teaching style that is in line with their own brain dominance, but my research has shown that 72 per cent of children in a class don't understand what the teacher is doing because the teacher's preferred teaching style and the child's preferred learning style are at odds with each other. The same applies to coaching. You should bring those two things – your own preference and the players' preference – into alignment. And it's your role as mentor to guide a player in understanding how the brain works, how it can work for him and the team, what his preferences are, what makes him happy and what makes him tick. This is also what Brendan Venter did at Saracens.'

In Neethling's view, golf is a good example of the quadrant model and he used Trevor Immelman's victory in the 2008 Masters Tournament to explain his point: 'Trevor led by three strokes on the Sunday. And when you're there, it doesn't matter what your dominance is – you *have* to play from your L1 brain. You don't try to do anything funny or gimmicky. You want to focus absolutely, and right up to the 18th hole it didn't look as if anyone was going to catch up with Trevor. He just focused. But when I'm three strokes behind and I try to play from L1, my goose is cooked. In that case you need to play from R1 – like Ernie Els, Bubba Watson and many of the Spaniards do. You should try playing in an unorthodox way and risk trying a few gimmicks. You have to shift your brain based on the circumstances and what part of your brain can serve you best at that particular point. It requires an enormous amount of time and effort to understand, develop and use that whole brain.'

In this respect, Treu took the whole-brain strategy to another level, according to Neethling: 'Paul did a number of interesting things in sevens. He had the brain profiles of his players and managers done and thereby established team cohesion. He knew how to talk to both left-brain and right-brain people. He knew he was dealing with different mindsets, and that determined his communication. But what distinguished him from other coaches was that he didn't just use the brain profiles as a useful tool for communication, but rather built his entire strategy around this central concept. He developed a language, in the purest sense of the word – it

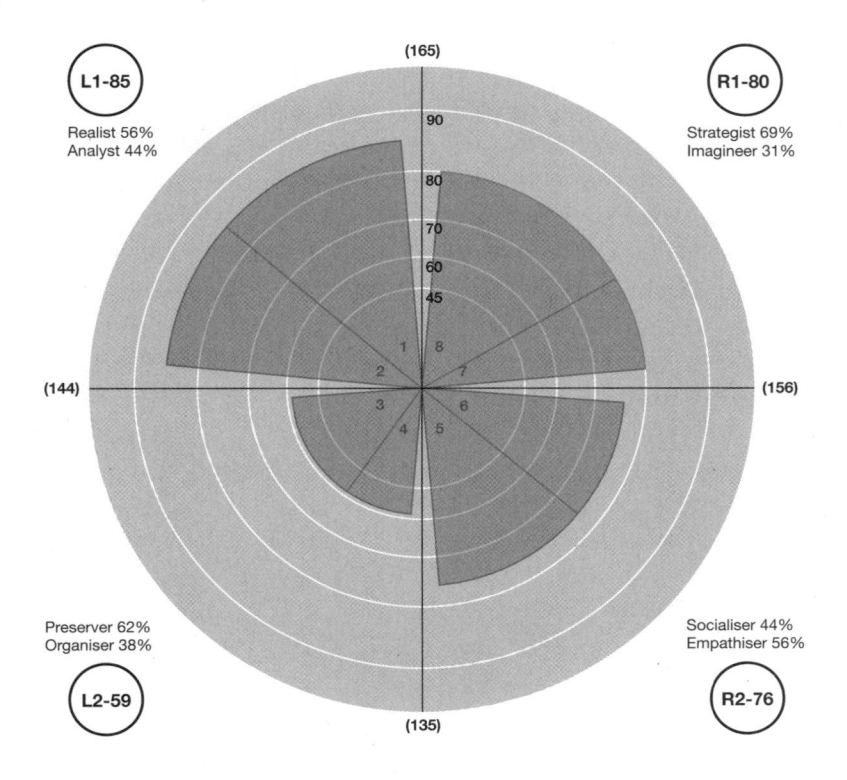

Figure 7: Kyle Brown is L1 and R1 dominant, but he also has a healthy tertiary R2 quadrant, which enables him to keep the team positive with good communication and empathy.

THE OPTIMAL EXPERIENCE

was a code that directed the team's existence, their understanding of each other and their way of thinking. He used keywords, which made the guys focus at the right time on the right things and with the most appropriate style of thinking.

'In sevens there is a massive emphasis on the upper quadrants – R1 and L1. You should be able to see space at all times and focus simultaneously. You should be able to see gaps automatically, and you have to coach your brain to see that space – it's coachable. But you should never lose focus, because poor defence is a focus problem and then guys will run past you in a sporting code that allows very little time to compensate for mistakes. L1 and R1 are, therefore, incredibly important at all times. But you also need R2 – you need inspiration. There are many setbacks in sevens and little time. So you need to be able to put setbacks behind you very quickly, and that is what Kyle Brown (see his brain profile in Figure 7) is so good at. He can instantly get guys focused and positive again.'

The L2 quadrant only really comes into play during coaching, according to Neethling. This is where you learn your skills and your tactics, and the more you repeat those processes and tactics, the quicker they become a habit that is automatically recalled in the R1 memory.

The value of the whole-brain approach completely changed Treu's perception of coaching. It made him think differently about his own, his managers', his players' *and* his opponents' thinking styles. For Treu, the whole brain provided all the answers he needed to make his team a consistently successful sevens giant in an innovative way.

CHAPTER 10

A creative revolution of the brain

'There is always a second question.'
– GT Ferreira

The Helshoogte Pass, outside Stellenbosch, has just the curves and contours for someone who loves sporty cars. Like Paul Treu. First his BMW Z4 and later the BMW 1 Series M Coupé could be spotted on that road a few times a week.

Only if he had a passenger in the car would he make the engine roar around the bends on request. Yours truly pleads guilty to the charge. But for Treu, that is a drive to be taken at one's leisure, like going to church. And his church was the Tokara wine farm.

Treu is at his most comfortable on his own, and he is most relaxed when in the company of one or two friends. Or people, often businesspeople, from whom he can learn. Starmer-Smith has described him as an intense individual. But that English commentator, too, has socialised with Treu at Tokara – the place where the joker, the philosopher and the entrepreneur all come to the fore spontaneously, and where he recharges his spirit and thoughts.

He usually chooses his table in the restaurant so that he can look through a ravine of vineyards and olive trees as far as Table Mountain in the distance. Open spaces and silences are the things that edify him. There are many silences at his table too. His iPad is always with him. His thoughts seemingly elsewhere. Sometimes he simply wants to be, without saying anything. Then, out of the blue, he will ask a question or solicit an opinion. 'What do you think of this?' 'Have you read this book?' 'Have you seen this app in the iStore?' 'What do you know about this person?' 'I wonder whether …' 'It would be interesting to see what will happen if …'

For Treu there is always something more: the next challenge, the next innovation. And it was at Tokara that the owner of the wine estate, GT Ferreira, told him: 'There is always a second question.'

'That is often the difference between winning and losing. Between short-lived success and a legacy,' reckons Treu. He doesn't drink wine, but at Ferreira's wine farm he found a wisdom, a truth, that guides his thoughts and his way of thinking.

'Everyone makes good wine nowadays. And everyone makes good wine that costs R50 a bottle. So, what makes you different? The same goes for a rugby team. There has to be that something different in your make-up that sets you apart from other teams. Too often we ask the wrong questions when we wonder why things don't work. Or we ask too few questions. There's always a second question, and because we as a team always asked yet another question, we had answers in difficult situations – both on and off the field. You aren't supposed to ever find yourself in a corner,' he said.

'Do you know what was interesting about that final in Edinburgh?' asked Treu. 'There was not a single scrum or lineout. Just penalty kicks and restarts. One of the greatest fightbacks in sevens was characterised by an absolute focus, and that is precisely what we had worked so hard at. We had answers.'

For him, that search for flow began when he took over the coaching reins of the Springbok Sevens team from Chester Williams in 2004.

'It was really tough for me, because there was absolutely nothing I could use as an example to make our rugby sevens sustainably strong. There wasn't anything like the Crusaders, who were an example of success in 15-man rugby. There was not one sevens team in the world that was different. My question to myself and the players was, what did we have to do to beat top sevens countries like Fiji and New Zealand when we didn't have a strong sevens culture ourselves?'

Treu was the first to do many things. Most teams, for example, utilised DVD recordings to analyse their matches afterwards. But Treu employed live data analyses during matches so that he could make adjustments where possible before the end of the match. He was the first sevens coach in the world to make use of central contracting – in other words, working with full-time sevens players. He was the first sevens coach who used a permanent practice facility with full-time staff, where his team could train, learn, eat and stay. At the end of 2010, Treu contracted some of the country's very best under-18 rugby players, on the assumption that they would eventually leave to play 15-man rugby, but would be able to return with sevens experience when rugby sevens makes its debut at the Olympic Games in 2016. Much of his pioneering work is now common practice across the world, and since sevens obtained Olympic status in 2009 for the 2016 Games, more and more countries have started taking sevens rugby seriously by implementing Treu's pioneering work domestically.

The biggest innovation, however, was not those tangibles, but the way in which Treu interpreted the whole-brain approach and the NBI, and tailored the models to his own purposes. It can be discussed in three categories: language, management of players and analysis of opponents.

Language

Treu's brain profile indicated a double dominance in R1 and L2, but, according to him, the preferences of a coach should become irrelevant if he wants to use the whole brain correctly: 'You should be able to function in any of the four quadrants because you have different preferences in your team. To really communicate with someone, you have to talk to him and spend time with him in the quadrant that is best for him – the area where he learns, where he understands what is said to him. To some guys, it will be detail. To another, it is emphasising his role in a greater vision. It is about effective communication.'

And according to Treu, this knowledge and understanding of players cannot be limited to team talks. 'It's a continuous dialogue with players, because he is who he is, his teammates are who they are, and sometimes a player will have to set his preferences aside for the sake of the team and function in his weaker quadrants because this is what the team needs at that point. It's about empathy for each other.'

The team created its own keywords for each quadrant: 'anchors' is L2, standing for steadfastness; 'laser' is L1, or focus; '*gees*' (meaning team spirit, morale, enthusiasm) is R2; and 'white space' is R1.

'A match demands different kinds of focus from you,' said Treu. 'Our training sessions were planned in such a way that we would, for instance, have an L1 session. So, when we were in a match and Kyle said the word "laser", the team knew immediately how to play without the need for a big discussion. "Laser" implied certain things, and we then executed those things with an L1 focus. It's about quick decision making and adjustment. When the guys had to get their minds right and remain positive — in other words, stay above the line — you just said "*gees*" and everyone knew immediately where the focus should be, and that we had to tune in to R2.

'When we wanted to open up a game but with structured play in between, the guys knew that we had to be able to shift gears between R1 and L1. We practised that — one moment we would have an R1 session, but when we said "laser", the structure in our play would change immediately and we approached things differently.

'We converted the brain profiles in the team into our everyday language, and by making it so tangible we kept that continuous dialogue going, which, in the first place, established among the players a better understanding of themselves, their teammates, the team as a whole, and their circumstances.'

Players were drilled in skills, strategy and tactics in L2 with repetition and discipline until these aspects would come naturally to them during a match. But for these things to come naturally, the team's intuition (R2) and creative abilities (R1) also had to be trained. Ultimately, the individuals had to complement each other so that the team could function as a unit in any of the quadrants.

The combined brain profile of the team that beat Australia in Scotland that day (including the injured players) is depicted in Figure 8, and it shows why it was possible for the team to function in any of the four 'gears'. In certain matches and against certain opponents, there would be a need for a stronger presence in one of the quadrants, and Treu then simply picked a team that would boost the average in the specific quadrants.

A well-developed and trained right brain is vital to the ability to play in all four quadrants. Yet it is this part of the brain that is neglected in traditional coaching, which is why players tend to be unable to make good decisions or to adapt on the playing field on instinct. The two 'L' quadrants very easily become comfort zones where processes and certainties are relied on, while the right brain creates the freedom and confidence to move outside of those comfort zones when familiar processes and strategies don't work.

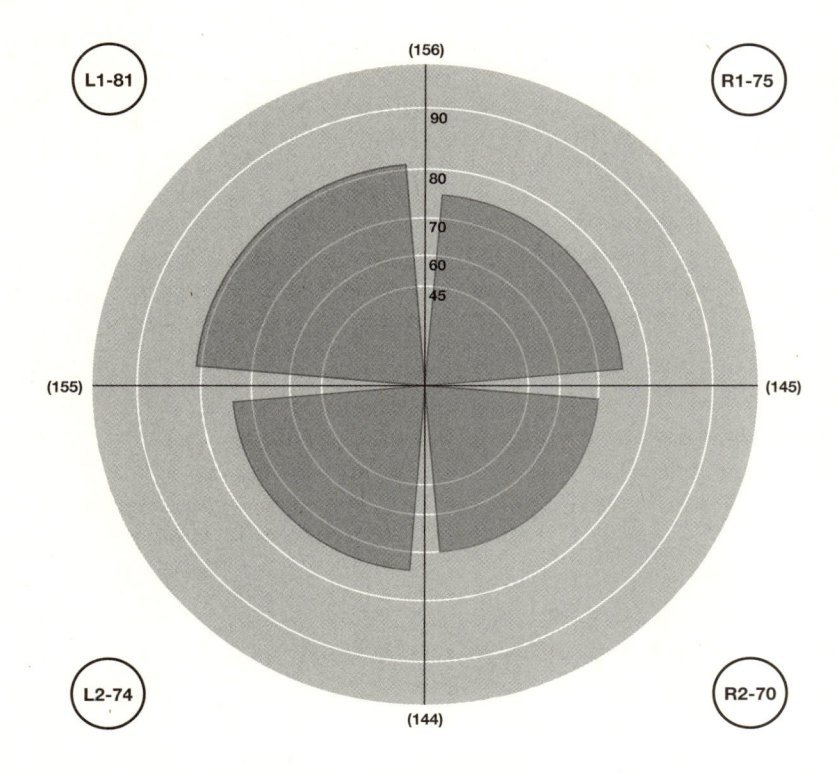

Figure 8: Combined Blitzbok brain profile, Edinburgh 2011

Each of the two R quadrants has a particularly important function in sevens rugby, but also beyond that. In Treu's view, R2 is the most underrated quadrant. 'It's the quadrant that determines your mindset, and if your mindset is right, this is the quadrant that makes you successful in a changing environment. And here the concept of "playing above the line" was the single most important factor that sustained our culture of positivity.'

The team had various '*gees* activities', such as forming a circle after every part of a training session – regardless of how gruelling it had been – and looking each other in the eye, high-fiving every man and emphasising *gees*.

'We had core concepts – *gees*, family. Those concepts were continuously emphasised in a team context. In the way we celebrated our tries, the way we formed a circle. Everything symbolised something, and we found symbols for ourselves that could be emphasised at a given moment – all aimed at staying above the line, whether it was a powerful and applicable quote, a video clip, or something on the field.'

Neethling used the term 'beyonder' in this regard – someone who breaks through boundaries and performs better than what was generally expected of him.

'Paul didn't always work with the best rugby players in South Africa,' said Neethling. 'But he made them world-class sevens players – he turned them into beyonders. And this is where the whole brain comes in, because with an unusual approach you help a human being become better and better. The question is how you can transform an 80-percenter into a 100-percenter. You do this by breaking down beliefs that cause someone to look at life from an ordinary perspective. You provide him with tools for becoming a better human being and a better player.

'That growth and awareness of what you and your team can become, can only happen when your state of mind is sound. And this is where the above-the-line principle is so important, and why Paul continuously made it part of his team's language and strategy. Because you should know what the things are that draw you down below the line and address them. Is it people? Are there too many things that demand your attention? Is there a problem at home? Because we are human beings, and there are things that frustrate us and steal our joy. You then analyse these things, you look for that poison and you try to solve the problem. And the moment you start functioning above the line, your life changes completely. You can't play rugby when you're below the line – it's a mental attitude and something that you have to manage consciously. Once you start taking control of the factors that influence your frame of mind, you develop emotional maturity, and an emotionally mature person is able to handle conflict and changing situations without being put off his stroke or feeling uncomfortable. That ability lies in the R2 quadrant,' Neethling explained.

According to Treu, the continuous development and nurturing of that quadrant is the glue that keeps the whole brain together and what enables one to focus on the right things at the right time. He never played with a player who was below the line – the team couldn't afford it.

The R2 quadrant is also the one where empathy is situated, and where one finds problem solving that focuses on the human being rather than on goals and effective processes.

Neethling cited defence as an example: 'A guy who botches tackles has an L1 deficiency — it's a focus problem. But it also has to do with commitment, and that, on the other hand, lies in L2. If I see that a guy misses many tackles, I know it's either an L1 or an L2 problem. But I'm not going to solve the problem by simply telling him to pull himself together and focus. You don't look at the behaviour and identify that as the problem. You look instead at what could possibly have led to that behaviour; you look for the root of the problem and you solve that. You can solve anything, providing you ask the right questions. You may find that a guy is overplayed. He's exhausted because of overplaying, and that influences his focus and may look like an attitude problem on the face of it. But it isn't. By asking the right questions and being genuinely interested in him as a human being, you help him get back on track and also keep him above the line with that sincerity, instead of just focusing on the task or goal from inside one of the other quadrants. This is emotional intelligence.'

R2 may not be a player's or a coach's dominant, or even secondary, quadrant, but for someone to be able to function in a team environment it is important that this quadrant is developed.

A healthy R2 quadrant unlocks the R1 quadrant — the creative quadrant that offers the unpredictability the left brain cannot give you. And here lies a significant trump card from a playing perspective — that 'white-space creativity' with which Sithole forged his path to the try line on 29 May 2011.

'The R1 people rely very strongly on intuition — they're creative guys,' explained Neethling. 'They notice space and opportunities that other people fail to see. We have the saying that you need a fresh pair of eyes. You should be able to walk down the same corridor as someone else, but see something different from what he sees. One of the most important things I learnt about the brain and creativity is that creativity can be taught and learnt — all that it requires is dedicated mentorship.'

Neethling maintains that a well-developed R1 quadrant is becoming increasingly important because elite teams seldom hold any surprises for each other: 'With today's technology, you know exactly how your opponents will play. You can analyse them. You study them before you play against them. You know the players. If Western Province have to face Free State and they watch Free State's kickoff 30 times, they have a pretty good idea of the restart pattern and where the Province players should position themselves.

A CREATIVE REVOLUTION OF THE BRAIN

'When you don't know how to position yourself, it's because you don't know what your opponent will do. Playing from the R1 quadrant is the only way of preventing people from knowing in advance how you will play. This applies in any sporting code. In netball, for example, the ball is thrown from player to player to player. It's a pattern. My technical guys study that pattern, and we know exactly what our opponents will do. But if I don't throw from player to player to player and instead throw the ball into open space, they don't know what I'm going to do because there's no pattern – that is white-space creativity. There are only open spaces, and I coach my players in anticipation abilities rather than in patterns – they run in space and they know where the ball will be. If you can start coaching *that*, you and your team move to another level. You will be totally unpredictable, but then you have to teach your players to anticipate, along with all the other essential coaching. We see this kind of play in South African rugby among the likes of Gio Aplon, Cheslin Kolbe and Willie le Roux, but if we can start coaching it, we'll become unstoppable.

'You should be able to evade coached tactics at any time. Teams like the Bulls used pattern play. They were so good that they could win trophies with it. But the moment you no longer have the kind of players who can enforce such a pattern, you need to be able to do unorthodox things based on intuition and decision making. Then you have to take risks. It is vitally important, however, that a lot of time is spent on the practice ground on activities that help develop intuitive abilities and decision making, and generate that white-space creativity.'

This was indeed what Treu did, and because each of the quadrants was emphasised continuously through language, symbols and signs, the players began to understand and embrace the whole brain as an integral part of their experience of being professional players – especially once they started beating top teams with it on a regular basis.

Management of players

Treu explained: 'We used the players' strengths to the advantage of the team. If each guy in the team knows how we want to play and how each of us thinks, it's much easier. This approach helped me tremendously with a guy like Paul Delport.

'He always threw forward passes, but it wasn't a skill problem. It was just that he saw that white space so quickly and passed the ball to someone in that space before the other guy had seen the white space. Paul is extremely strong in the R1 quadrant (see his brain profile, Figure 9), hence we knew that his creative abilities and his ability to see space could be very valuable to us.

'I had to teach him, however, that while he could see certain things, the other players were not yet able to see the white space in the way he wanted them to see it. So let's make it easier and better for them. We give

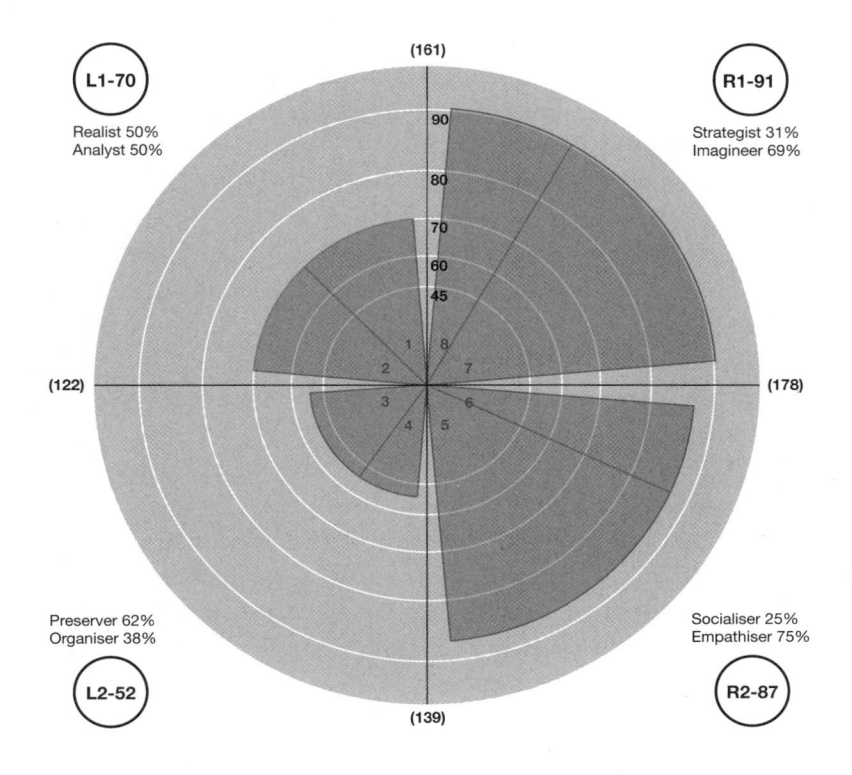

L1-70 (161) **R1-91**
Realist 50% Strategist 31%
Analyst 50% Imagineer 69%

(122) (178)

Preserver 62% Socialiser 25%
Organiser 38% Empathiser 75%

L2-52 (139) **R2-87**

Figure 9: Paul Delport is very strong in both R quadrants, but his marked right-brain preference had to be tempered with the knowledge that the spatial and intuitive abilities of the rest of the team didn't equal his own. Hence his strong suit could only be employed as a strength if he oriented himself within the team.

A CREATIVE REVOLUTION OF THE BRAIN

them one or two options on the field, but to Paul we give just one at first. Because, if he had three options, he wouldn't know what to do with them in that team – he sees things differently from the rest. But the rest of the team also understood that Paul could see things and make things happen which not everybody could do. And when we played an R1 game, with the code words "white space", we wanted Paul to be involved as much as possible. If you want to play a wide game, you want guys like Paul Delport, who can throw a skip pass at just the right moment or who can aim a cross-field kick at where there is space that nobody else has seen.

'Your ability to play in the R1 quadrant as a team depends on a guy like Paul. But he also needs to understand that, from start to finish, he has to maintain his focus and be aware of where his teammates are and what strengths they have.'

Neethling stressed to Treu and his team that the right brain could only be enjoyed if one first had respect for the left brain. Treu used that fundamental principle to gradually guide players who were recovering from injury back to the right quadrants: 'Chris Dry and I sat next to each other on the bus after the Tokyo tournament in 2013. We had won the tournament, but Chris had returned after an injury and he wasn't quite where he wanted to be or at the level he knew he could play. I told him that we should think in terms of the infinity symbol that runs through all four quadrants. There should be an uninterrupted flow between the quadrants (see Figure 10, Dry's brain profile). If that symbol is interrupted in one of the quadrants, you lose the flow that connects all four quadrants to each other.'

'When someone returns from an injury, there doesn't necessarily have to be a break in the symbol, but where you resume the flow is important. Let's say Chris returns from an injury and he immediately wants to start playing again as he did in Vegas, where he was very good. He wants to start in R1 again straight away, for example, but he's not ready yet to play in that quadrant. He tries, but he doesn't manage to get to where he should be on the field, he fails to see what he should see and his passes don't go where they should. He gets caught with the ball and it frustrates him. His injury becomes something that he struggles with anew.

'Now we simply say that we're not going to resume the flow symbol in R1, but instead in L2. In order to enjoy the right brain, you first need to have regard for the left brain – processes, the sharpening of skills and focus. The basics of the game should first be addressed in L2 and L1.

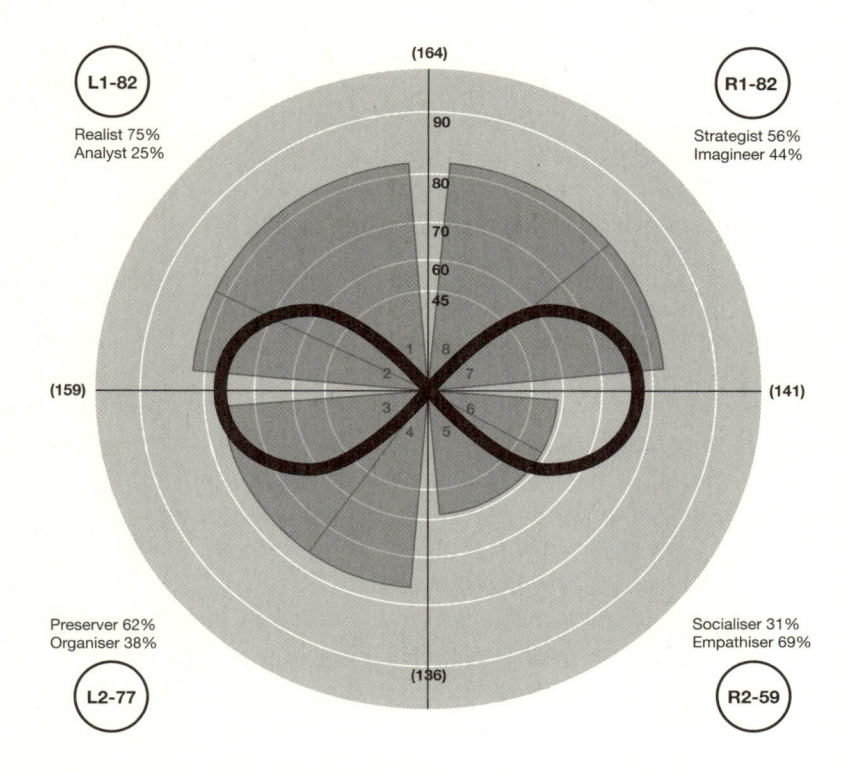

Figure 10: Chris Dry's brain profile

In other words, I'm not going to force myself to do things from R1 on the field, but rather gradually allow myself to regain that sharpness before I will once again be able to play and attempt to play the way I did in Vegas. This is how I, as coach, understand it, and I then ask Chris to see it in that way too. Hence there is no pressure on anyone to meet unreasonable and unrealistic expectations. I will help Chris to get his left brain correct, and he will know when he is ready to shift to R1 again. It's a decision that he makes for himself and for the team, and that's why honesty and self-knowledge are necessary. When he then plays in R1 and finds that it's still not working, he simply shifts back to L1, where a deeper focus on the basic aspects of L2 is required.

'The quadrants and the infinity symbol provide you with a useful framework for talking about yourself and your progress. When Cecil Afrika comes back from an injury, he knows already that he needs to be patient. As good as Cecil is, he knows that after an injury he shouldn't immediately try the kind of things on the field that he's capable of doing when he's at the top of his form. Give it time, you have the ability, and don't allow yourself to get caught up in a battle between your left and right brain. When you can make this decision, it's also a way of staying above the line. We have to keep emphasising that.'

When the Blitzbokke decided on the theme 'concentrate to focus' in London and Edinburgh, Treu also saw the infinity symbol as the golden thread that interlinked all four quadrants. When the score stood at 7-28 in the Edinburgh final with only nine minutes left and it was vital to focus, to process the magnitude of the game, to be aware of what was happening and respond to it intuitively, there was cohesion in the team and symbiosis between the four quadrants.

'This is flow, that optimal experience,' reckons Treu. 'Flow can only exist when there is an intense focus on each of those quadrants. When you get to that place where each of the quadrants simultaneously complements the next one, you spontaneously reach a heightened state of consciousness and complete absorption from which you are not easily distracted. In a sports team, that is harmony in its purest form.'

Analysis of opponents

One of Treu's most ingenious applications of brain profiling was to profile each of the national teams in the World Sevens Series, which he compiled in conjunction with Neethling and his players. Treu proceeded from the assumption that the understanding of brain preferences and the emphasis on the above-the-line concept could be used as a counter to their opponents' strengths if employed for an opposite purpose than in their own case. In other words, this process would force a team to start playing out of its comfort zone and below the line.

Neethling explained: 'We watched the other teams closely over a period of time, and after a while they give you a good indication of the kind of methodology they prefer, the kind of decisions they make. When you observe that, you get a very good idea of the quadrant from which those guys play rugby. Then you simply need to jerk them out of that quadrant, because in so doing you take them out of their comfort zone and you beat them where they are below the line.'

This was a unique touch, and it changed Treu's approach to analysis. 'In the last few years I didn't pay much attention to individual players when analysing teams,' he said. 'I was much more interested in how the team played as a whole, and in the coach's thinking. Often I didn't even know who they were talking about when people asked my opinion about a certain player. My focus was simply different. If I knew their coach's thinking pattern and how he approached the game, there were not likely to be many changes in his sides, regardless of who the players were.

'As a team, we categorised each of the other national sides according to the quadrants where we reckoned they were dominant, based on what we observed. Fiji, for example, play from R1. They look for space and don't play in a very structured way. New Zealand, however, is strong in all four quadrants, and that posed unique questions.'

These two teams in particular warrant closer inspection.

Fiji

'We knew that Fiji played from the R1 quadrant. They're able to score a try over 100 metres, and can advance the length of the pitch within one or two passes. If you want to beat Fiji, you have to force them into L2 – it's the exact opposite of how they prefer to play.'

Treu discussed this notion with Rassie Erasmus, at the time the Western Province director of coaching. Eramus, who is technically exceptionally gifted, suggested that they surprise Fiji with a driving-maul tactic. Said Treu, 'I thought Rassie's suggestion was a wonderful idea, because driving mauls had never been used in sevens before. It was the best way in which we could deny Fiji the kind of opportunities on which their play thrived and take them out of their comfort zone.

'Rassie helped coach the players in the technique of setting up lineout drives. It's funny, though. The first time we used it against Fiji, in 2011 in Hong Kong, we lost 19-24 in the quarterfinal. No one noticed it. But when we beat Fiji with it in the final of the London Sevens, the tactic was on everyone's lips. It was revolutionary, and I found it significant that, in the next season, even New Zealand employed the driving maul once or twice.

'But, as far as Fiji was concerned, we knew where they were at their most comfortable, and therefore we knew what would discomfort them. We were comfortable with playing in the left quadrants, but it wrong-footed Fiji completely.'

According to Neethling, Fiji is a team that becomes emotionally perplexed when they are forced to play below the line: 'Fiji has a clear discomfort quadrant. Once things start going wrong for them, they lose their sharpness and their grip on their emotions. And that is what you want to focus on. You want to force the side below the line by taking them to L2. That quadrant requires discipline, and the Fijians become extremely ill-disciplined when they are taken out of their comfort zone – you leave them with no other option than trying to fight back with their weak points, and no team can play from below the line.'

New Zealand

New Zealand has always been the toughest nut to crack, and claiming their 11th title overall out of 14 Sevens World Series in May 2013 speaks volumes about the side's dominance. South Africa, Fiji and Samoa won the other three series.

In the 2012/13 Series, however, the Blitzbokke played New Zealand five times and won four of those games, the last three of which were all cup finals. The results of the five contests are as follows:

- 13 October 2012 (Gold Coast, Australia): South Africa 31, New Zealand 21
- 9 December 2012 (Port Elizabeth): South Africa 5, New Zealand 12
- 10 February 2013 (Las Vegas): South Africa 40, New Zealand 21
- 31 March 2013 (Tokyo): South Africa 24, New Zealand 19
- 5 May 2013 (Glasgow): South Africa 28, New Zealand 21

The New Zealanders walk to the dressing room in a diamond formation before every game. The captain, DJ Forbes, usually walks in front and the rest of the players complete the formation by binding with the guy in front of them with an outstretched arm. As this team was a particularly close-knit unit with hardly any weaknesses, Treu was of the opinion that this very unity was the best of its strengths they should disrupt.

'To beat New Zealand, we firstly had to ensure that we ourselves were strong in all four quadrants. We had to deny them opportunities, so our lineout throws, our kickoffs, our discipline, everything, had to be 100 per cent. Especially in view of uncontrollable factors, like referees, it was crucial to have a firm grip on all the things that were within your control. And you had to believe that you could beat New Zealand. The more we beat them, the easier it became and the less they wanted to play against us.

'The crux was to break New Zealand's family bond, and you do that by frustrating them. You ask yourself before the match: in what structure on the field are they the strongest? In other words, how can you disrupt them in L2? What part of their focus can you disrupt in L1? You want to break that infinity symbol, in other words. New Zealand shouldn't be allowed the ball or space. You force them towards L2. If they find that they're not making headway, they have excellent individuals who then start doing things on their own. And that was exactly what we wanted – to break that cohesive New Zealand team down into frustrated individuals. But without the support of the other quadrants, that R1 approach of the individual players meant nothing. As soon as we did that, we had the ammunition to take them apart and score points ourselves. We would hit them so hard that by the last minute of the game the points difference was too big for them to still win the game. Our target was always to be ahead by at least eight points in the last minute, and we beat them by wide margins.

'We succeeded regularly in forcing New Zealand below the line, and I've never seen such a defeated All Black team as that sevens side we played in 2012 and 2013. They were emotionally in a very bad space. If something negative happened on the field, they would hang their heads. These are things you don't find in a New Zealand rugby team. They were at their wits' end. They ran out of answers to all the questions we put to them on the attack and the defence. In each quadrant there was something with which we forced them out of a comfort zone, and that's why I firmly believe that the R2 quadrant is the one where a team's success or undoing is brought about. It's about your emotional intelligence.'

In conclusion

The Blitzbokke inevitably also had bad days and poor matches, but they rallied again after a poor 2011/12 season and won the most tournaments of all the following season. That stranglehold on New Zealand in particular meant a great deal to Treu and his team, as the Kiwis had regularly scored big victories against them in the 2011/12 season. He described some of those defeats as humiliating – especially the times when the New Zealanders laughed at South Africa as they walked off the field. In 2012/13 the team compensated amply for those dark days with an average score of 26-19 against the Kiwis.

Treu and his troops were always too resourceful to experience long droughts. For him, there was always a second question and the next innovation. On a few occasions even some of the smaller rugby nations were victorious against South Africa with strategies and tactics that Treu had introduced to the game. Rugby sevens increasingly became a more competitive sporting code because there was a coach who believed that 'clever and adaptable' could trump shortcomings such as 'too small and too slow' against the giants of sevens. As a student of the game, Treu often went in search of answers to his questions beyond the game itself. From businesspeople, from experts such as Dr Sherylle Calder, Rassie Erasmus, Dr Ross Tucker and Dr Kobus Neethling – and also from other sporting codes, such as American football, Aussie rules, rugby league and touch rugby.

When Treu was appointed as Kenya's new head coach in November 2013, Neil Powell succeeded him at the Blitzbokke. Powell, Vuyo Zangqa, Marius Schoeman, Renfred Dazel and MJ Mentz are among the players who won tournaments and a World Series under Treu, and eventually started coaching themselves. For Gio Aplon, rugby sevens was the second life he needed after a difficult period in the 15-man code. And for players such as Paul Jordaan, William Small-Smith, Justin Geduld, Seabelo Senatla and Cheslin Kolbe, it provided the platform where the world first took note of them.

The Blitzbokke's motto is 'Pioneers of Greatness'. It is a motto and a way of life to which Treu has remained true, and he is also regarded worldwide as a pioneer.

In 2013 Nigel Melville, the chief executive of USA Rugby, asked Treu where the next innovation in rugby sevens would come from.

'I told Nigel it won't be a clever strategy, technology or a scientific invention. The next innovation lies in the brain, because if you can think differently, you can do differently. Being able to fend off an opponent, winning 100 per cent of your lineouts and hooking 100 per cent of your scrums no longer make you special. You expect that someone should be able to do that. It's not exceptional. It's your job.

'That something different, the aspect that will distinguish the best teams from each other in the future, is creativity. There is a revolution of the brain out there. A revolution of the brain.'

**GARY KIRSTEN
AND PADDY UPTON**

CHAPTER 11

How can we help you?

'The value you can create from the human mind is enormous.'
– Michael Jordaan

Although he tried not to show it, the waiter knew exactly whose table he was serving – everyone in India knows who Gary Kirsten is. In a country of 1.2 billion people, most of whom follow cricket and worship its stars with a religious devotion, it is something of a feat to refrain from gasping in amazement when you find yourself in the presence of one of the sport's greats.

'The word "hero" doesn't even come close – Gary is a demigod in India,' said Michael Jordaan, who, at the time of our interview, was still chief executive of the First National Bank (FNB). Kirsten is the brand ambassador of FirstRand India and when you walk into their head office in Mumbai, a photograph of his face graces one of the walls – the coach who not only helped India become the number-one Test team in the world, but also guided them to the status of one-day champions with their 2011 Cricket World Cup win.

Kirsten stepped down after the World Cup tournament and later took up the coaching reins at the Proteas with his close friend Paddy Upton. But his three years in India have had such a huge impact on the country's cricket, its cricket stars and the general public that he still returns regularly. It was during one of those visits that Jordaan and he met at a hotel.

'I ordered a beer, and Gary a cappuccino,' Jordaan related. 'The waiter didn't want to create the impression that the moment was too big for him, so he pretended not to notice who his customer was. But when the cappuccino arrived, they had written the initials "GK" in the foam using that delicate barista art form. I found it very amusing. Gary is a bit embarrassed about things like that, but India has an unbelievable love for him.'

Kirsten and he were supposed to meet for only half an hour, but the conversation lasted so long that afterwards Jordaan had to rush to avoid missing his flight. 'There were so many parallels in the way we thought about leadership, and the central theme was people,' Jordaan recalled.

I had already embarked on my research on Kirsten and Upton when Theo Vorster's interview with Jordaan for *Sakegesprek* was broadcast. The fundamental similarities between Jordaan's and Kirsten's leadership philosophy were illuminated during that conversation. Unaware that they occasionally had a braai together or that Kirsten was involved in FirstRand India, I met Jordaan at his office in Johannesburg with the aim of gaining a better understanding of his leadership philosophy, and consequently Kirsten's as well.

It was a somewhat intimidating experience to meet the man who had acquired the reputation of being South Africa's first celebrity CEO. With more than 40 000 Twitter followers, to many people he is more than a businessman who only expresses and asserts himself in rands and cents. People like him. Perhaps a clue to this lies in his lack of a big ego – the first thing that struck me when walking into his office. His floor was an enormous open-plan room, with only carved dark-wood partitions separating the chief executive from the other employees. Jordaan was dressed in a white button-up shirt, jeans and comfortable shoes, and his laid-back hairstyle suggested a need to visit the barber. The sixth floor of First Place in the Bank City complex – the hub of banking in Africa – housed a bunch of happy people and a CEO who poured the coffee himself and inquired about my milk-and-sugar preferences.

FNB was named the world's most innovative bank at the BAI-Finacle Global Banking Innovation Awards in Washington, in October 2012. India won the Cricket World Cup tournament in 2011, and by the time I met Jordaan, the Proteas had already accomplished the feat of being the number-one team in the world in all three formats of the game simultaneously. Kirsten had been at the helm of both national teams. There was a common factor in these three exceptional achievements – FNB's, India's and South Africa's – that led to that success. And it was not innovation, because that, too, was just a by-product of a culture in which people are empowered to make their own decisions and carry them out.

Both in sports teams and the business world, culture is often seen as a nice-to-have rather than a must-have feature. This is probably because it is an element some leaders find hard to quantify if they are driven exclusively by results. Jordaan described this as follows: 'We [FNB] have a culture that is anchored in what we call "care and growth". In sport, for example, I can use the score to evaluate you and in business, the sales figures. This is the traditional model. If a salesperson doesn't perform well, you can punish him through his sales commission. On the other hand, you can say, "I'm using your work output as a way of measuring you because my real purpose as a leader is to make you better." In that case, the scoreboard becomes only one way of evaluating whether I am succeeding in helping you grow. So you turn the concept on its head. Most businesses use their employees to make more profit. However, turning that around, you should say that my job as leader is not, in the first place, to make the profit grow, but to make people grow, because then the profit will look after itself.'

This is an approach that will be discussed in more detail in a later chapter on Kirsten and Upton. They didn't see themselves as coaches, but rather as people who could help players become, firstly, better people, secondly, better cricket players and, consequently, more successful on-field performers.

This approach can even be quantified and, in Jordaan's view, FNB's innovation award is a good example. 'We were incredibly chuffed about that. We were up against 150 banks from 30 countries, and who would have thought that a bank here in darkest Africa is the most innovative in the world? Although there were good individual innovations, the award recognised the culture of innovation we had created.

'We started our innovation programme in 2004 and offered a reward of R1 million to anyone who came up with the best idea and implemented it. That is crucial – it's not only about the idea, but also about its implementation. It has happened before that a teller in a branch has had one of these ideas. In the ivory tower we don't always know what the best solution may be for a branch, but someone there will definitely know. For example, a particular form may be redundant or a process may take too long. When someone comes up with an idea that is good enough, it goes through the innovation programme until it gets to me.

'We implemented a total of 1 500 such ideas in 2012, and their net present value is in excess of R5 billion. The R1-million top prize sounds like a lot, but the value you can create from the human mind is enormous.

'It's a cultural thing, and that cultural thing has to do with empowerment. And that culture of innovation comes from the wisdom of the whole system, and not just one guy who sits somewhere and thinks up plans and instructions. The ideas that emerge from such a culture accumulate, and this is what ultimately gives you your competitive advantage – not just a single innovation,' Jordaan explained.

Some of the bank's well-known innovations are eBucks, eWallet, dotFNB branches, fuel benefits and FNB's applications for smartphones.

For such a culture, you need the right people and the right leader. In Jordaan's view, the only way to get the best people is to create an environment where these people can flourish, instead of one where they are merely the pawns of an autocratic leader who determines their every move.

Jordaan explained, 'Most people like to work in an environment where they have the autonomy to do things. The same goes for sportspeople and that is what Gary and Paddy did. The business and sporting worlds are still dominated by an old leadership philosophy where the thinking is done on behalf of employees or players. Rigid rules apply, and inventiveness is almost discouraged.

'But if your hypothesis is that the best people prefer to be empowered, you have to change your style. It doesn't mean at all that you stand back and just watch things happen. What it does mean is that you as a leader will go to someone and ask: "How can I help you become more successful? What are the things I can do that would make you more successful?" In this case, you lead by serving others.

'It sounds simple, but the implications of such an approach are enormous – it takes you to another level of competition. This is what Gary did in India. He had to coach a guy like Sachin Tendulkar. The previous coach [Greg Chappell] left precisely because he came across as too domineering and autocratic. When Gary took over, he told the team, "I don't have a specific vision for you. What is your vision, and how can I help you achieve that vision?" That was how he won the guys' hearts – he was truly there for them and not for himself.

'For example, he would ask Sachin what he would like to do, and he might reply that he's struggling a bit with a particular shot. Gary's reaction would then have been to help him with that, regardless of what it demanded of him as coach – he was there for the players. With this management style you listen and ask, more than you do and say things yourself, and thereby gain a real understanding of what your team needs.

From the group, you also get answers to questions when you yourself may not necessarily have the answers. The leader's role changes from that of a traditional autocrat to one of helping people improve.'

This individual approach ultimately has an impact on how the team performs. This approach also results in less micromanagement of people, because people are led as opposed to managed – and there is a fundamental difference.

'In my executive team, the guy who is in charge of risk knows more about risk than I will. And the marketing specialist is better at marketing. This applies to all of them,' said Jordaan. 'The wonderful thing about leadership in an environment where you are surrounded by people who are better than you is that your job is to get the best out of that group. In the first place you should have the self-confidence to appoint these people, and then you should empower them.

'I've always said that my function is not to make the right decision; the functional experts should make the right decision. My purpose is merely to ensure that the best decision is generated from the system. For me, it would be fantastic if an outsider, with no idea of who has what portfolio, were to walk into a room where we were having an intense debate and at the end still not know who actually holds the risk, financial or marketing portfolios. All that matters is that there was an intense discussion and that the best decision won in the end.

'The best idea should win and I, as leader of the group, am merely the facilitator of the ideas. Of course, I have my own ideas too, but you shouldn't have an ego that makes you cling to your own preferences – you should facilitate. And you should be comfortable with the fact that your ideas won't always be the best. When you decide together as a group that something should happen, you should allow those people the freedom to carry it out. The same goes for sport. To ask the team, "Right, how are we going to beat these guys? What's the plan?" is better, because everyone has their say. When you've made a decision together, the team is much stronger than it would have been if one guy simply came in and presented his plan.'

FNB had a few conditions on which that freedom could be exercised in a meaningful way, as did Kirsten and Upton. The cricketers' conditions will be discussed later; FNB had only two requirements for those who wished to submit a plan.

Jordaan expanded on this: 'In the first place, you shouldn't make a fool of yourself. In other words, think it over carefully because you have to be able to defend and substantiate your plan. Secondly, you are not here to go on a solo flight. Wanting to do something that is risky is absolutely commendable, provided that you are certain about it first. A pilot doesn't just get into a plane and take off. He first logs in to the flight plan for his destination and looks at a number of things to check feasibility. When he flies, although he does so on his own, it is not a solo flight because there are people who know where he is headed. When he doesn't arrive, they know where to look for him. So, there are a few basic rules of the game: don't make a fool of yourself, and don't do something if you can't draw the necessary wisdom from a larger group of people. In other words, maturity is important and the leader should also treat the people around him like adults.'

Jordaan believes that the crux of the matter is that there are few ideas that cannot be improved upon and it makes sense, therefore, to consult the team and have a culture where a conversation is conducted within a group instead of inside a dominating leader's head.

'I have a saying that "no one is smarter than everyone" – so, tap the wisdom of the group. The interesting thing about empowerment is that it's a paradox: the more power you give away, the more power you receive in return. If people are given more power, they can achieve more and, in the process you, as a leader, do better because the environment does better.'

To all appearances, both Jordaan and Kirsten were novices when they were appointed as chief executive of FNB and head coach of India, respectively. After playing in his last Test on 30 March 2004, Kirsten started a cricket academy. He was asked to consider the Indian team's head-coach position at the end of 2007, and when he took up the coaching reins at the beginning of 2008, he was only 40. Similarly, Jordaan was appointed in his CEO role at the youthful age of 36, and the first thing both of these leaders did within their respective team environments was to establish a new culture based on empowerment and individual autonomy.

Jordaan said, 'If someone had asked me at the time how on earth I became chief executive at 36, I wouldn't have known what to say. In the beginning you actually pretend a little bit that you're in control, but inside you feel panicky. It takes time, and the hardest thing to get used to is that you are not always right or don't have the best ideas. You become a leader of leaders, and that requires a shift of emphasis in the way you make things happen.

'But, once again, you have a paradox – if you do less, more happens. If you do less because you give other people the freedom to do more, this causes more things to happen. When you question every guy and concern yourself with details, there is less creativity, less buy-in, less empowerment – and, as a result, less happens.'

According to Jordaan, culture was the biggest thing he (although he uses the word 'we') had to change when he was appointed as chief executive.

'Rand Merchant Bank acquired FNB, which was a merger, but in practice a takeover. And when the merchant bankers arrived here, they realised that they couldn't really add value because the work that they do doesn't have much bearing on how you manage a branch or invest in systems.

'So we said we could raise the level of the internal intellectual conversation by ensuring that we appoint smart people. At that stage there were, for example, only four chartered accountants in the entire bank, and today there are probably 200 CAs and actuaries. The principle of empowerment is central in this elevated intellectual conversation. The conversation depends on the people and the situation. In financial services, which is largely about the mind and attracting the best people, it is a long-term plan to have this empowerment model in the environment – probably also in international cricket, where the team is together for up to eight months of the year.'

Establishing such a culture is not child's play, even though the end result should be to ensure that adults are as happy and excited as children when they come to work. The RMB takeover and the cultural shift were already in process when Jordaan arrived there – he just had to manage the 'cultural revolution', as it was called.

'We spoke to 50 executives at a time in the course of two days about how we saw things and what empowerment meant. These things were already happening when I arrived and I only had to drive them. The key thing at a time like that is your own behaviour. When everyone came to work in suits, I wore jeans. Today our offices are open plan and they are still beautiful, but they used to be closed-off offices. There was a parking space reserved for the CEO, but I said, let's change that and after that the guy who arrived first in the morning got the best parking. These are small things that are sometimes to your own detriment — like a parking space — or to your advantage — such as not having to wear a tie every day. The underlying principle is how you behave towards people.

'Your own behaviour as leader is what counts most of all when you want to change a culture. You can write down all these things on a board or send it to people via email, and say that our new thing is empowerment, but you yourself should act in the appropriate way.'

Kirsten's story will be discussed in the next chapters. In brief, however, one of the decisive factors in his success in India was that he was always fitter than any of the players, so that he could live up to his promise to help them at all times and without limits in so far as he was able to. This meant that he was often found throwing down a thousand balls per day for Sachin Tendulkar in the nets because that was what Tendulkar felt he needed.

Jordaan and Kirsten also talked about empowerment that day in Mumbai — about the notion that the score would take care of itself if the coach took care of the players.

'Every individual wants to win,' said Jordaan. 'Sometimes we forget that. It's a natural thing in every human being and if we businesspeople can succeed in cultivating that innate need to win and do well, then we've done our jobs.'

In his view, the 'secret of life' is very simple: it is about people and about surrounding yourself with people who are better than you. He commented: 'You shouldn't actually assess a leader on his own merits. You know a leader by the people with whom he surrounds himself. And the best leaders surround themselves with people who are better than they are. That's my philosophy of life.'

It may seem extreme when a leader evaluates himself in this way, but another attribute of good leaders is the absence of a big ego. Gary Kirsten had both these attributes, and the person who is inextricably part of his story as a player and a coach is his close friend, comrade and business partner, Paddy Upton.

CHAPTER 12

Old school vs new school

*'Knowing others is intelligence;
knowing yourself is true wisdom.
Mastering others is strength,
mastering yourself is true power.'*

– Lao Tzu

Gary Kirsten and Paddy Upton are business partners, but their relationship is more like a tenth-wicket partnership on the fifth day of a gruelling Test – that part of a match where, as Kirsten has said, it is not your skill but your character that is being tested. In this partnership, Kirsten is the anchor. But his skill as a batsman will amount to nothing without an Upton at the other end who blocks when he has to, takes singles whenever he can and ensures between overs that his batting partner remains focused and positive.

It is not possible to understand Kirsten as a player in his last season and later as a coach without including Upton in the sum total of his success. The two have been friends since their schooldays. Upton attended Wynberg Boys' High School in Cape Town, while Kirsten matriculated at the nearby Rondebosch Boys' High. Upton was a student at Stellenbosch and Kirsten at the University of Cape Town when their paths kept crossing in the Western Province cricket team. Kirsten started playing for South Africa in 1993; Upton was Bob Woolmer and Hansie Cronje's full-time fitness guru at the Proteas from 1994 to 1998. Between 1999 and 2004, there were events in Upton's life that ultimately had an influence on the way in which Kirsten ended his last season as an international cricketer. It was also as a result of these years that the duo later began coaching together. First, Upton worked with Kirsten as assistant coach and mental-conditioning coach with the Indian national team, and subsequently in the same capacity as performance director with the Proteas, a position Upton still holds today. At the time of writing, both of them are coaching teams in the Indian Premier League – Upton the Rajasthan Royals, and Kirsten the Delhi Daredevils.

But it is in his role as mental-conditioning coach that Upton has had the greatest influence on cricket. This role is much more than that of a psychologist. He is a confidant who works with players' fears, their perceptions and their skill deficiencies, and he looks for solutions to what are ostensibly technical sport problems in places that are not traditionally associated with the ability to perform. A useful metaphor for describing Upton's role at the Indian cricket team and the Proteas is provided by the way in which American Scott Summit manufactures artificial limbs. Summit's aim was not only to help find a biomechanical solution to such disabilities, but to do it in a way that took the complexity of human beings into account.

Summit is an industrial designer who has done design work for Apple and various other Silicon Valley companies. As a child of the 1970s, he was entranced by the TV series *The Six Million Dollar Man*, about a man with bionic implants. This sparked Summit's admiration for people who have to walk by means of prosthetic legs.

On 26 October 2011, Summit said in a lecture at Stanford University:

> The thing I was always reminded of is don't stare [at people with prosthetic limbs]. You can't stare at these people. You'll make them uncomfortable. That is the worst possible response you could have. How do you make somebody more uncomfortable than saying don't stare, because it will make them uncomfortable. That struck me as strange. So because of this one challenge we have a wall of separation. We have to disconnect from this one group of people because we can't engage them, we can't connect with them.

Summit found it strange that this was a prohibited topic and that there was such a stigma attached to the loss of a limb, while a similar reaction didn't exist in the case of most other disabilities – such as having to wear glasses because of weak eyesight, for instance. He pointed out that there are as many people today who wear glasses without the corrective function as there are ones who need to wear them in order to see better. The crucial difference, according to him, is that designers became involved and turned a functional, yet strange, object into a fashion accessory. This eliminated the stigma, and hence people without eye problems starting wearing glasses that helped accentuate their personality. Glasses became a medium of self-expression.

The same approach was not followed in the field of prosthetics, however, and, in Summit's view, the biggest problem was the entrenched idea that an object's form should be determined by its function – thus 'form follows function', as the American architect Louis Sullivan put it in 1896 in his article 'The tall building artistically considered'.

Challenging this notion, Summit described it as 'kind of a bastardisation of what was once said more than a hundred years ago by Louis Sullivan. And it has come to mean form follows mechanical function and we've now come to accept that this is a mantra passed down by Sullivan that gives us free rein of creating something that is clunky and mechanical instead of something that really has form and beauty to it. When you talk about form follows function in the amputee world, it stops at about this point – form follows mechanical function. Get somebody walking.

'But it overlooks the complexity of humans. We are a little more nuanced than that. The body isn't just something that keeps the head from falling to the ground. It is something we adorn, we wrap, we cover with jewelry, we tattoo. It is so much more nuanced than something like a mechanical solution can allow. So when you think of a prosthetic in that aspect, and the idea of a function and what does a function offer, it is much, much broader.'

Since prosthetic limbs are mechanically such complex devices, it has until recently been easier to manufacture a generic product through mass production. The problem with mass production, however, is that it is in essence generic and impersonal.

'The nature of mass production is one size fits all – it is inherently impersonal, it's inherently mechanical. There is nothing individualised about it,' said Summit in the lecture.

But this flies in the face of what the human body is – it is customised, unique and emotive, and it gives expression to who and what a person is. That is why Summit does not consider a generic 30-mm titanium pipe an adequate replacement for a real limb. The body represents more than just mobility – the function to which generic prosthetics attempt to offer a solution.

The prosthetics industry changed radically when three-dimensional printing turned the manufacturing process on its head. When this laser technology was still in its infancy a few years ago, one could print low-quality objects that wouldn't last long. But the moment it became possible to print more solid and durable objects, there were enormous implications for, among others, the manufacturing of prosthetic limbs, and it was no longer necessary to do things in the old way.

With 3-D technology, all the parts of an artificial leg can be printed simultaneously – like a ball-and-socket joint in the foot – at a fraction of what it would have cost traditionally to manufacture each part separately and then assemble them. According to Summit, an artificial knee that would have cost $20 000 to manufacture in 2001 could suddenly be printed at virtually no cost, with only the initial investment in the technology as well as the service that would carry a cost.

Summit's initial aim was to start a prosthetics revolution in developing countries by providing more affordable artificial limbs to landmine victims, among others. He would have been able to make these at $4 000 per prosthetic limb, but the Red Cross wanted him to try to get the manufacturing costs down to $200. This did not prove to be possible.

His focus then shifted to the United States market, and with his company Bespoke Innovations, which he founded, he started using the new technology to meet the mechanical and at the same time the more deep-seated needs of amputees. The complexity and individuality that were not financially viable considerations in the era of mass production could now be incorporated in prosthetics at a fraction of the cost and with even better mechanical performance than in the past. With 3-D printing it became possible to imitate the biomechanical features of a real limb by integrating the parts during the manufacturing process as finely as was possible in the case of a non-human object. Summit photographed people and transferred the symmetry of the remaining leg to the design of the artificial one by means of a computer – the first step in giving a unique touch to every prosthetic limb.

'What I came up with was that if you're going to do that, you're going to have to create something that was really created by the person, for the person and of them that is as unique as their fingerprint. It has to be as fluidlined as possible, it has to be sensual and sculptural. It has to present their personality as well as their physicality if you're really going to do something that is part of that person,' Summit said.

His hope was that more beautifully crafted and individualised prosthetics would change society's perceptions about amputees, and at the same time change the way the amputee perceived his or her own body. He wanted to change the stigma, and to him it would be a significant advance if he could change perceptions about these disabilities, if he could change the conversation by turning something that previously had only a practical function into an impressive extension of an individual's personality.

'It has to give somebody their symmetry back, but not in a way that is mimicking or emulating human. That takes us into this area we call the uncanny valley – something that is uncomfortably human, but not human. So the idea is to create something beautiful, that suggests the person, that is unique, but doesn't try to be something that it is not,' Summit explained.

For example, they printed prosthetic limbs that had different components, such as a chrome-plated or a leather-coated part, that could be unhooked and replaced with another piece of hardware. There was a fashion element involved. Some of the prostheses were enhanced with patterns and designs. In some of the more interesting designs they incorporated tattoos that had appeared on the amputated leg. In the case of a client who had tribal tattoos on his calf, these patterns were used in the design of the new leg. And, said Summit, whereas the tattoos previously only decorated the leg, they now formed the entire structure of the leg.

Therefore, they didn't try to conceal the loss of a limb, but rather turned that loss into something that was perceived in a different way by the person concerned and by others than had traditionally been the case with such disabilities.

'We have three rules that we live by: we are not trying to emulate human, we can never be human. It's wrong, it's not allowed. Secondly, we can never violate the person's physicality. We use that scan and we don't alter it. We don't change them in any way – that is like photoshop magazine covers and that's just wrong. And, third, we don't do any gimmicks – bottle openers, LED lighting, pistol holsters, knife holsters, you know. That's not what a leg is about. It is about the body.

'Our whole goal is really to embody that person and to change their perception of how they feel about being an amputee, about their condition. About the way they [experience] every day. If we can get them psyched to wear shorts and put that on and change the way people perceive them, then that's the victory we've set out to achieve. It means we've nailed it,' Summit stated.

A passionate advocate for this new kind of thinking about prosthetics is double amputee Aimee Mullins, a Paralympic record-breaking athlete, model and actress, who has made designer legs glamorous. In an article on Summit's work in the *Los Angeles Times* of 4 April 2012, she is quoted as saying with reference to their collaboration: 'A prosthetic limb doesn't represent the need to replace loss anymore. It can stand as a symbol that the wearer has the power to create whatever it is that they want to create in that space.'[47]

The essence of what Summit has done with prosthetics and for amputees brings us to the core of what Paddy Upton does on a mental level with and for players.

He helps them to understand their own shortcomings and personal problems, to change their perceptions about these 'disabilities', to emphasise their strengths and personalities, and to acknowledge fears and the inevitability of failure and disappointment as a normal part of life. His premise is that cricketers are able to perform better if coaching includes a significant component that is focused on the human being instead of just on the cricketer and the technical requirements of the sport. Upton and Kirsten, just like Summit, see the human individual as a more nuanced being than one that can simply be improved by means of a generic solution. To them, there is an 'I' in 'team'.

'We understand that things outside the team environment have a big influence on the players,' Upton remarked in the course of our conversation. 'We try to create an environment where the players feel free to talk openly about such matters. For that, individual relationships and trust are essential. Gary and I cooperate extremely closely in this regard, because we really want to do all that is within our capacity to enable a player to be as successful and happy as possible – both as a person and as a cricketer. The two are inseparably linked.'

At times, illness and family or relationship problems would play a role, and then Upton would be on hand to listen and to assist where he could. Such open-hearted interaction is not likely to occur during visits and sessions that are arranged by appointment – it should happen continuously by building sincere relationships with players. For that reason, Kirsten insisted in 2008 that Upton, like himself, be appointed on a two-year contract at the Indian team.

While this approach may sound too philosophical to some people, it has a very practical application on a daily basis – as the following example from the South African Test team demonstrates. Ego, which will be discussed in more detail later, mostly has a negative influence on elite athletes unless it is controlled. Ego is a strong driver of success and hard work on the training field, but it renders a player vulnerable once he steps onto the playing field. Besides, it is not an attribute that is associated with a willingness to learn. Upton explained the reasoning behind their approach as follows: 'In the South African team we put a premium on an authentic and genuine perception of ourselves and of each other. We regularly emphasised humility and sincerity. In such an environment you are discouraged from having a big ego. During the 2012 Test series against England, for example, we walked onto the field one morning and the players formed a circle. When Graeme asked them how they felt, AB said that he was really nervous about the day's play. To us, as coaches, this was wonderful, because here was someone who acknowledged in front of the whole team that he was jittery. There was a sincerity, and if someone is not nervous before a big day's cricket, he's not focused.

'But AB's nerves were on edge and the moment he acknowledged it, a number of his teammates acknowledged that they, too, were nervous. By acknowledging that you're nervous, the nervousness actually decreases. And if the whole team acknowledges it together, you stand in this little circle full of nerves and they feel it together. The nervousness decreases. And it's okay to feel like that – we accept it, and we take both that and positive thinking along with us onto the field. If you had simply said: "Come on, guys, let's grab the bull by the horns and thrash them," you merely increase the nervousness because there isn't an environment in which you can acknowledge that you are in fact just human.

'That wasn't how we went about things. We would talk things over after a match and because the players had been nervous, we would talk openly about that. I would ask the players, for instance, how many times you get yourself out, and how many times you were out because of a good delivery by the bowler. The standard answer is that batsmen get themselves out between 80 and 90 per cent of the time.

'Then the follow-up question is: "What happens at that moment when you get yourself out?" And 90 to 100 per cent of the time, the players would say it was an error in thinking – the pressure got to me, I was nervous, I had decided beforehand what shot I was going to play, I acted outside of my game plan, I was too aggressive, my shot wasn't well thought through, I was scared of failure, and the like. These are all errors in thinking. And no one said that they had a problem with their technique.

'As an example, when a guy has a fear of the short ball, what we see on the video is that he bats quite nicely and then the ball is pitched up and he doesn't get a good stride in. His hands go at the ball a bit and then he nicks it and he gets out. And then he sits with a coach. And the conversations we have with guys are: "What do you do about this?" You look at the video analysis and you see you didn't get into a nice, strong front-foot position, your head isn't over the ball and your hands have gone on. Then they go into the nets and they have throw-downs. And from throw-down number 1, they get it 100 per cent right. That is what everyone in cricket does these days – they fix their technical errors in the net. They assess them on a video and they fix them in a net.

'I would then tell the players that, in their own opinion, they lose their wickets 80 to 90 per cent of the time through their own doing, and that 90 to 100 per cent of those times can be attributed to errors in thinking. The question is then how you fix that error, what you learn from it, and what conversation you should actually be having with the coach. I would then ask them: "Who in this team has ever gone out because of the following mental errors: fear, fear of failure, fear of the short ball, premeditation, nerves, overconfidence?" And everyone's hand would go up. But do any of them ever sit down and talk about these things to their teammates, a coach or whoever? Not one hand would go up.

'It then becomes obvious what kind of conversations we should have, because if they make the sum, they never talk about 75 to 80 per cent of their errors. And there's a simple reason for that – a traditional coaching mentality where instructions are dished out and a hierarchical coach who punishes you when you make a mistake. If you had to tell that coach that you folded under pressure, he won't pick you again. Coaches want guys who are supposedly mentally tough. But I'm pretty sure that out of the 150 top international cricketers there are perhaps five players who are mentally tough. And actually it's not even that – it's simply the ability to manage the processes in your mind. There are uncertainties, vulnerabilities and cracks inside every single human being. But given the way most coaches work with their players, they are discouraged from talking about those cracks.'

Under Upton and Kirsten, honest conversations were conducted in a team context to prevent just that. The players would refer to parts of a match and, say, acknowledge that at a specific point they struggled to cope with pressure, or that they were worried, became panicky and then perhaps tried to hit a six.

But, according to Upton, one of the clearest signs that a player is folding under pressure is precisely when he tries to hit a six at the wrong moment.

'If you don't know what to do in one-day or T20 cricket, you try to hit a six. I'm panicking, I don't know what to do, so let me try hitting a six, because even if I go out, I'll be excused because I played with abandon and would have been a hero if it had been a six. That is a classic example of a cop-out, and you'll never have the right kind of conversations if there isn't a culture that is built on genuine relationships and trust. In such a culture the guys become stronger as people and as players because they get to know themselves better – warts and all.

'That was how we worked and how we knew what was going on. As a result, South Africa now has cricket players who talk about these things, about their uncertainties, their mistakes and their errors in thinking. And this is how it should be. Once one player talks about it, there are always more who join the conversation. Gary, too, talked about his uncertainties and about the times when he did things wrong. In that way, the players saw that this guy was normal. He was also prepared to say, "I don't know." This creates an environment where people can learn, and it allows everyone to take part in the conversation. An environment and a culture like that make it possible for the guys to grow – as people and as cricketers.'

The absence of judgement and criticism, and the presence of a culture in which frank conversations are conducted are strong characteristics of Kirsten and Upton's leadership philosophy. Michael Jordaan sees his role as leader as someone who should facilitate growth, learning and ideas, and this is exactly what these two coaches do as well. And Upton's role in their work is to dig deeper on an individual basis and find ways that take the complexity of the human being into account.

Kirsten regards relationships, trust and gaining personal mastery of oneself as central to the way in which he coaches. Just like the Indian and the South African players, he, too, experienced the influence of deeper self-examination and self-knowledge in his playing days when Upton worked with him in 2004. But before we get to that discussion, and seeing that Upton's role has as yet only been summarised briefly, it makes sense to look more closely at Upton's life between 1999 and 2004.

OLD SCHOOL VS NEW SCHOOL

As Upton explained to website Cricinfo shortly before his Indian appointment: 'I have gone outside of sports into business, philosophy, theology, spirituality and taken the best of all of them and seen how this works in sports ...'[48]

The life of a Stellenbosch sports-science student is an exceptionally pleasant one – I can attest to that. So can Upton, who likes to joke that in his student years at Coetzenburg he was always the first to take on the Eerste River in a tube when the river was in spate. He and his classmate Mike Horn – now globally renowned as one of the greatest modern-day adventurers – were not among the most diligent when it came to class attendance. But life was good, and for a few years afterwards that would continue to be the case on the face of it.

After qualifying as a biokineticist at the then University of Port Elizabeth, Upton obtained his master's degree in sports science at the University of Cape Town. At the end of 1993, he decided to pack away his cricket bat and embark on a new chapter in his life. Bob Woolmer, the then South African cricket coach, was ahead of his time as far as scientific innovation was concerned. Woolmer was one of the first coaches to use computer analysis, in consultation with Professor Tim Noakes. They did away with some of the antiquated coaching methods recommended in the MCC's 'bible of cricket coaching' and, with Hansie Cronje as captain, the one-day team had by far the best one-day international (ODI) success rate in the world. Another of Woolmer's firsts was to appoint a full-time fitness coach who would accompany the team everywhere on their travels. Paddy Upton was that man, and besides his responsibilities in respect of the team's conditioning, Woolmer involved him in every aspect of their technical and strategic planning. Upton was 25 when he started working for Woolmer and he would occupy that job for four years, from 1994 to 1998. Said Upton, 'I was in my twenties, and I had the most unbelievable time. I travelled all over the world with guys who were the same age as me, I saw places, stayed in luxury hotels, I was treated like a king everywhere, and I was paid extremely well. It was certainly the dream life every man in his twenties would have wished for.'

To Upton, however, that life was not the Utopia it appeared to be to his friends. He had no idea what was the matter with him, but only knew that there was an 'emptiness' inside him. He didn't know why. It didn't make sense.

'I started noticing it in the players around me as well. Life was wonderful. They were delightful people to spend one's time with. They made runs, took wickets and made money. They were famous, girls flocked to them, and they partied everywhere. Every conceivable thing one could desire was there. But, at a deeper level, something was missing. I wasn't really happy, and neither were some of the players. That was my experience at the time, but I couldn't put my finger on what was wrong,' Upton said.

He began to wonder whether the problem didn't perhaps lie with cricket, and left the sport to work as Western Province's fitness coach in the 1999 Vodacom Cup rugby competition. But when his experience there turned out to be the same, he decided to leave the sports industry – the field to which he had devoted his life as a player, as a student with three degrees and as a member of management.

'This was where my journey started. I realised that what I had been experiencing was an emptiness at a spiritual level. I found that so strange in the South African cricket team: Bob was innovative; the players did well. But, as a team, we didn't perform to our full potential. Something was lacking. I wanted to find out what that something was.'

Upton then worked with Cape Town's street children for two years and experienced life in its most raw form. Although he lived in the lap of luxury, he found frightening similarities between the life of a cricketer and that of a street child. Both were survivors in a merciless world. Only the strongest made it. Only the most hardened individuals survived. As a street child, you needed skills to survive and to defend your environment. There were hierarchies, teamwork. It was tough. But that was what it was.

During this time, a friend told him about a master's degree course in executive coaching at Middlesex University.

'There I was exposed to some of the most innovative companies in the world, and from those companies I learnt for the first time how you can get the best out of people. The best leadership philosophies and the best companies worldwide have the ability to get something special out of people.

'In leadership approaches in the business world, there had been a clear shift in emphasis towards true people management. Leadership had moved away from the old-school style where leaders knew more about the game or the industry than anyone else, and told others what to do and what processes to follow. In the case of the emerging leadership style, leaders sought to help people become what they can be. Hence they facilitated growth by serving others' needs. That model gets the best out of people.

'It is an art, however, because you need a totally different skill set to master the art of managing people. You need to have a fairly high level of mastery and peace in every aspect of your life to make that model work. And if you can pull it off, it undoubtedly surpasses the old model. Today it makes even more sense than at the time I did my research, because young people who enter the business or the sports worlds are really not interested in being told what to do. What they look for instead is someone who can help them grow so that they can be the best they can be.'

Drawing on those new insights into how truly successful companies manage their people, Upton did his master's thesis on the coaching methods employed by South African provincial and national cricket coaches between 1991 and 2004.[49] His hypothesis was that those methods were ineffective because the coaches created an overstructured and excessively performance-based environment.

He worked with 21 senior provincial cricketers (averaging 257 caps per player), 8 of whom were also national players (averaging 100 international caps per player), who provided information on their personal experiences of being coached. In the 14 years since South Africa's re-entry into international sport, the Proteas had had 6 coaches, the Springboks 10 and Bafana Bafana 12. Upton wanted to establish why these coaches failed, but his approach was from a player's perspective. So he analysed whether the coach managed the players in the best conceivable way and, when compared with the business environment, whether the coach did the right things to get the best out of individuals.

The thesis is comprehensive and interesting, but this discussion will be limited to the main points. Upton identified a number of coaching methods and asked the players to indicate their preferences, which he then compared with the coaches' own preferred methods. The section that follows deals with statistically significant differences between players' wishes and coaches' methods. Upton also found with his research that the approaches preferred by the players corresponded strongly with the international best practices in companies that were at the leading edge of their industries.

Instruction vs collaboration

Instruction-based coaching is characterised by an authoritarian, dogmatic and dictatorial approach where the coach's word is law. The collaborative style may range from a strongly democratic to a laissez-faire, hands-off approach. Kirsten's style has at times been described as laissez-faire, but this is an oversimplification of his leadership style.

According to Upton's research, coaches had a preference of 53:47 per cent for instruction-based coaching, whereas the players preferred a collaborative style in the ratio of 57:43 per cent.

There was an interesting distinction between provincial and national players. The provincial players preferred to have more collaboration than instruction, while the national players preferred a greater balance between the two. This could be because Eric Simons had been sacked as the Proteas coach shortly before. Simons had a laissez-faire style, but some players saw this as a weakness and someone like Lance Klusener – who had flourished under Woolmer and Cronje – was left out of the team because, in Simons's view, he had a bad influence on young players. Hence a slightly more structured approach was advisable to restore the balance, and when Ray Jennings was appointed after Simons, this was exactly what the Proteas got.

All the players, both provincial and national, were, however, upset about coaches who had a rigid or dictatorial style. In those environments, the players were apparently frustrated, unhappy and unmotivated. Over time a kind of apathy had set in among some of the players because they were openly criticised or punished when they didn't do things the coach's way. If players spoke up about this, their discipline was questioned.

In his study, Upton refers to Sir John Whitmore, the author of *Coaching for Performance*. According to Whitmore, the appeal of the instructional style from a coach's viewpoint is that it makes for quick decision making. It makes the coaches feel as if they are in control. But Whitmore points out that the converse – or the power paradox, as Michael Jordaan refers to it – is actually applicable here: the more power coaches appropriate to themselves, the less power they have in reality.

External focus vs internal focus

An internal focus addresses more abstract things such as feelings, mental attitude, thoughts and team spirit, hence the 'art of cricket'. An external focus is more on tangible and measurable aspects, such as skills, fitness, strategy and management structures – hence the 'science of cricket'. Both these categories are vitally important at the elite level, but coaches tend to have a greater external focus. The respective aspects of these categories are summed up in the matrix shown in Figure 11.

	INTERNAL Intangible/subjective/art/moral values/ transformational leadership	EXTERNAL Tangible/objective/science/technology/ transactional leadership
INDIVIDUAL	Mind, spirit, emotions, feelings, thoughts, convictions, values, needs, intentions, mental condition **Art**	Body, performance, behaviour, physical attributes, technique, physical skills, deeds, actions **Science**
TEAM	Team values, team culture, team spirit, what is best for all **Moral standards**	Laws of the game, competition rules, match strategy, tactics, management structures **Science**

Figure 11: Matrix of internal and external focus

In this case, too, the preferences of the coaches and the players were reversed. The coaches indicated a 58 per cent preference for the external approach, whereas players had a 58 per cent preference for the internal focus. The implications were that coaches had a more scientific and mechanical approach to coaching and therefore a greater focus on how the players trained, played and prepared.

While these aspects were also considered important, the players preferred an approach that was later used by Kirsten, where individual players reflect on, analyse and try to understand their own game, techniques, body, mind and feelings. Also, there was an environment in which all the players determined the team values, the team culture and the team spirit. This suggestion came directly from Upton's research, and was formulated as follows in his thesis: 'In order to have "thinking players" who can make in-the-moment/on-the-field decisions, and adjust their game plans, players would need to have been actively involved in the reflection, analysis and planning, and not have it simply imposed on them by the coach.'

PERFORMANCE FOCUS VS PERSONAL FOCUS

The third and last model Upton examined can be seen as the most fundamental of all. It relates to the distinction Jordaan made in the previous chapter between someone who uses the scoreboard to evaluate a player and someone who uses a scoreboard to evaluate himself in terms of the extent to which he has succeeded in helping a player grow and develop.

A performance focus and a personal focus represent two completely opposite approaches to leadership. This was also where Upton found the biggest discrepancy between coaches' preferences and players' needs. While the players indicated a 52 per cent preference for a more personal approach (a focus on who the player is as an individual), the coaches had a 67 per cent preference for a performance-based environment (a focus on what a player does – for example, his results, skills and fitness).

According to Kirsten, it is that personal focus, in all its facets, that tips the scales when it comes to the crunch in big Tests. Through a personal focus, a player gains a better understanding of himself as an individual and as a player, and the emotional maturity that is cultivated in the process ultimately leads to what is called mental toughness – the ability to manage your emotions and your focus.

Kirsten batted for more than 14 hours when he recorded his highest score of 275 in December 1999, against England. It is still the second-longest Test innings in history, and surpassed only by the 1958 innings of Pakistan's Hanif Mohammad, which lasted more than 16 hours.

That innings is noteworthy for several reasons besides the impressive score. At that stage, Kirsten was out of form with the bat and, by his own account, he was on holiday with his family in Kenton and hoped that he wouldn't be called up for the Durban Test. He was selected, however, and failed to score any runs in the first innings. That evening at the team hotel, he told his wife that he would be playing in his last Test the next day. His confidence was a thing of the past. But the personal focus is wide-ranging, and precisely because it involves more than what takes place in the team environment, the influence of this focus is not only limited to coaches. To Kirsten, that focus also includes a spiritual aspect, and in his case praying with his wife brought about a calm and peaceful frame of mind in which he went out to bat the next day. He played shots that he had never played before and struck the ball in a way he hadn't done for months. He saved the Test for South Africa and revitalised his career in the process.

Years ago Tim Noakes was part of a research group that sought to establish what exactly were the factors that had contributed to the mental strength of the toughest of the English cricketers of the 1980s and 1990s. They came up with a hierarchy of factors ranked from the least to the most important: environmental influences, a strong character, a hardened attitude, and, right at the top, tough thinking. And *that* is an aspect that is developed by means of a continuous and individualised personal focus.

Armed with this research, of which I have discussed only a fraction, Upton approached Cricket South Africa in 2004 and said that cricket coaching at the top level locally was ten years behind best practice in the business world and still rooted in old behavioural models. There was a fundamentally better way to lead people, Upton believed and he was convinced that South Africa would be far ahead of the rest of the cricket world if he could apply that thinking here.

To him, better people management, not science, was the next great differentiator in sport, and in a way he said this at his own expense, referring to the glory years under Woolmer. Said Upton: 'Those innovations were all external, visible and scientific. The world saw them, copied them and then innovated even further. Science has contributed immensely to sporting codes such as rugby and cricket over the past 15 years. Because we understand things much better nowadays, we have been able to fine-tune those sports and take them to another level. Video analysis, fitness analysis, diets, rehabilitation, medical care, food supplements – all these things have helped tremendously. But while they remain vital, they are no longer differentiators between teams and players. We live in an era of information and technology. It's very easy to copy science. I sit in conferences where people discuss how they will improve supplements from 90 per cent to 95 per cent effectiveness. Then you need to ask yourself where the next big thing in sport will come from, and actually those advances have been there for a long time in the business world. The ideas Gary and I play around with regularly are that the things that used to work for our coaches no longer yield dividends at the highest level today. And that brings us back to the human being and how you can create an environment in which he comes into his own.'

Between 1999 and 2004, therefore, Upton's views on sport changed from a purely scientific approach to a more holistic view of the human being. In 2011 the former South African fitness coach returned to the national team as their performance director and mental-conditioning coach, a role he had fulfilled at the Indian team until shortly before.

By 2004 Upton and Kirsten's paths had been running along the same lines for many years, but in the 2003/04 cricket season they converged to such an extent that it would determine their future in the years that followed. It was Kirsten's last season – five years after he had thought in Durban that his Test career was at its end. At that stage, Cricket South Africa was not overly interested in what Upton had proposed, hence he worked in executive coaching. But sport was still closest to Upton's heart, and the first player with whom he started working was Jacques Kallis.

By that time, it was more than a year since the colossus of South African cricket had last scored a century. Although Upton never spoke in depth about his sessions with players, we do know that Kallis's run drought coincided with the death of his father and a relationship that didn't work out.

'Jacques and I are friends,' said Upton, 'and we just started talking and working through these things together. By his own account, our conversations restored a clarity in his thinking that had been missing for a long time. He got himself out as a result of mental errors: when there are things on and off the field that trouble you, the runs tend to dry up because of the way in which people conduct themselves in difficult times. When they have to play, they think only of that run drought and they become trapped in a cycle. All Jacques needed was to take a step back so that he could gain perspective and clarity about himself and his life. When you come back after that, you have a new way of thinking and a new perspective on the future that is accompanied by peace of mind.'

When Kallis scored five consecutive centuries shortly after his conversations and sessions with Upton, he gave a great deal of the credit to the influence the mental coach had had on him. In an interview with the *Weekend Argus* of 7 February 2004, he stated that, as far as off-the-field matters were concerned, they had looked closely at the things that are important deep inside one, and he had tried to incorporate some of those things in his everyday life. 'I learnt more about myself,' Kallis said, 'and I have been able to make better choices as a result.'

The exact nature of these things has stayed between Upton and Kallis. But Kallis's reaction sums up Upton's approach to people – to be a happy player, that player also needs to be happy in other spheres of his life.

Upton's next 'client' was Ashwell Prince, followed by his childhood friend Gary Kirsten. Upton wrote on Cricinfo that Gary had said during their first conversation:

> I'm searching for the authentic Gary Kirsten – someone who is accepting of his shortcomings and is confident in the knowledge of who he is. One who is willing to have a positive influence and add value to society in my own unique way. I want to make a difference to people's lives and give them similar opportunities that I have had. My perception of success is not about how much money I can earn in the next ten years but rather what impact I made on people I came into contact with.[50]

It is now ten years later, and Kirsten has indeed changed people's lives irrevocably. One of the things he and Upton talked about was his fear of the short ball. While this may seem like a small thing in the greater whole, it can be likened to innovations – the more they accumulate, the greater the impact. Besides the personal development and mastery that was taking place in Kirsten's life outside cricket, it was also a liberating experience to him when he finally admitted his fear of the short ball and was therefore able to recognise the effect that fear has on him. While he never felt comfortable about those deliveries, having been honest about his fear made it easier for him to play them. This is similar to what Scott Summit did – while he couldn't give someone his leg back, he could help the person to change his perception and experience of himself by acknowledging his unique inner nature and incorporating it in the prosthetic solution.

In his last season as a player, Kirsten scored five of his 21 Test centuries, which included two against England in a series where he scored 462 runs at an average of 66. His swansong became his very best season. After his retirement, he and Upton became business partners and started consulting company Performance Zone together with businessman Dale Williams in 2006. Their motto is 'performance through awareness'. That awareness of himself, his environment and the people around him was the 'something' Upton had been looking for in his 20s. It later had a fundamental influence on Kirsten's life.

When Ravi Shastri contacted Kirsten at the end of 2007 about the Indian head-coach position, there was therefore no doubt in Kirsten's mind that Paddy Upton was just the man to help him help a group of people become the best cricket team in the world.

CHAPTER 13

The influence paradox

'In Indian cricket, it is seldom that someone is sought after even when he is quitting. Kirsten is that rare commodity.'

– Amit Gupta

Gary Kirsten was 26 years old when he played in his first cricket Test for South Africa in 1993. In those days, children were still dependent on the *YOU* magazine centrefold and a set of trading cards if they wanted pictures of and statistics about their sporting heroes. Even when he started playing Test cricket, Kirsten was an unlikely poster boy, and a trading card about his older brother, Peter, was more highly prized than one about him.

Peter Kirsten, who is 12 years older than Gary, has been one of the greats of South African cricket since the mid-1970s. To the eye of a connoisseur, Gary didn't appear to be equally blessed with natural cricketing talent. As a child who grew up on cricket at Newlands, he could never have foreseen that he would become the first South African cricketer to play in 100 Tests. Yet in 1994 Peter had predicted that momentous day in Gary's life for reasons other than talent alone.

Journalist Neil Manthorp, Gary's biographer, explained this in 2007 on Cricinfo:

> Kirsten grew up in the shadow of his older brother Peter, who was an established star for both Western Province and Derbyshire while Gary was still in his early teenage years. Gary lacked his brother's flair, but as Peter admitted way back in 1994 after scoring his only Test century at the end of his isolation-shortened career: 'Look out for my boet – he has more heart than anyone I've seen,' and, tapping the side of his head, 'he has it here, too.'[51]

The fact that Gary Kirsten eventually got the nickname 'Professor' is a big feather in the cap of a man who compensated for his supposed lack of natural talent with an exceptional work ethic and a view of cricket as a field of study rather than just a sport. The reality, however, is that

Kirsten was a highly gifted cricketer who misjudged his own merit early in his career.

It is often the case with many other players that there was that one person or mentor in their lives who provided the spark that ultimately made their career blast off. For Gary, that mentor was his coach at Western Province, Duncan Fletcher.

'Duncan had believed in Gary before Gary believed in himself. This was one of the biggest influences in his career,' reckoned Paddy Upton, not only in the way it influenced his career as a player, but later also in the way Kirsten as a coach wanted to make a difference in people's lives.

Both the experience of what a mentor means to a young player and what Kirsten learnt about himself in 2003 and 2004 were key to the kind of coach he developed into – the kind the Indian cricket team needed between 2008 and 2011 to help lead them out of a very dark place.

More than 20 contenders applied for the Indian head-coach position at the end of 2007. India had played in the final of the 2003 Cricket World Cup tournament, but suffered an embarrassing first-round exit in 2007 under their Australian coach, Greg Chappell. When Chappell departed after their World Cup debacle, Ravi Shastri, Chandu Borde and Lalchand Rajput each acted temporarily as coach for short stints.

Finding a new full-time coach was not the Indian cricket bosses' biggest headache, however – the team and the players were broken. Chappell had an excellent cricket mind, but his autocratic leadership style had sowed fear, uncertainty, discord and mistrust among the players. Moreover, he never really came across as a coach who had the players' best interests at heart. His voice was too prominent in the media and his own profile grew while the team was falling apart. Chappell had speculated publicly why India's favourite son, Sachin Tendulkar, was still playing cricket instead of considering retirement. Promising young cricketers such as Yuvraj Singh, Virender Sehwag, Harbhajan Singh and Zaheer Khan started playing poorly under Chappell and were eventually dropped from the team.

In 2005 and 2006 the friction between Chappell and the Indian captain, Sourav Ganguly, resulted in Ganguly being removed as captain and later losing his place in the team. Indian broadcaster IBN reported in November 2013 on Ganguly's gratitude for the support he had received from Tendulkar at the time: 'When I developed a distance with Chappell, Sachin stood by me. When I was dropped, I thought it was a fight between Chappell and Ganguly. When I returned to the Indian team after months, I found it was Chappell versus everyone. There was a battle of nerves between Sachin and Chappell.'[52]

Kirsten was not among the group of more than 20 coaches who applied for the job of cleaning up that mess, and when Shastri approached him at the end of 2007 to discuss the possibility, he was initially not keen on the idea. In fact, it became public knowledge at the time that Kirsten had not enjoyed his time in India during the Proteas' 1996 tour – despite scoring a century in both innings of the second Test.

When Kirsten eventually agreed to accept the challenge and brought along Upton, as well as Eric Simons as bowling coach, the Indian cricketing public doubted whether a third foreign coach in succession was the way to go. New Zealander John Wright had been Chappell's predecessor and although the team had been successful under his leadership, it started losing form after reaching the 2003 World Cup final. In addition, Kirsten lacked a proven track record as a coach.

But three years later, it would become clear that this was precisely the clean slate the country and its players had needed at the time. By 2007 Upton, Kirsten and Dale Williams were, as business partners, already well versed in what Upton called 'the art of man management'. And that business background, as well as Upton's and Kirsten's personal life experiences, ultimately determined their approach and success.

'Individual relationships are of paramount importance in the work that Gary and I do,' said Upton. 'Without sincere relationships with players, you're unable to influence anyone to think differently, consider different ideas or do different things. You can order people to do things, but that requires a hierarchical relationship, which we didn't want. However, trust has to exist before you are able to influence people. The most important thing we had to do right at the start was to build relationships before we could even think of planning fancy strategies – relationships come first.'

While their initial two-year term in India started officially only on 1 March 2008, Kirsten joined the team from December 2007 on their tour to Australia so that he could get to know the players better. He observed how the team functioned and asked players about their families, their past and the things that were important to them. He went with them in order to listen and gain an understanding of their needs, and that was also what Kirsten did for the greater part of his first year at the helm – he sought to understand the Indian way of doing things.

A number of exciting young players were knocking at the door of Indian Test cricket, and for them Kirsten could be the mentor that Fletcher had been to him. There was also a strong group of senior players: people whom Upton described as 'extraordinary cricket minds' – Tendulkar, Rahul Dravid, Ganguly, Anil Kumble, MS Dhoni and VVS Laxman. In an autocratic environment, the knowledge and insight of players of this calibre go to waste because the coach is the one who determines the course and the discourse.

At that stage, Kumble was still the captain and, true to the old way of doing things, at their first official meeting in 2008, he asked Kirsten on behalf of the team to give them direction. Tendulkar also remarked that there were too many individuals in the team who played for themselves and not for India. It was evident that substantial dust clouds still hovered where the team had imploded under Chappell.

At the request of the players, Kirsten then set out in broad outline a vision and strategy for the future, with which everyone seemed to be happy. But when he and Upton talked to each other during a break, they both realised that the players hadn't really bought into that plan for the future. They had agreed to it, but without enthusiasm. Kirsten then spoke to the players again and, within the first two hours of his first session with the team, drew a line through the strategy he had presented as the way forward moments before.

He told them, 'Guys, you are the number-four team in the world in one-day cricket, second in Test cricket and you have a win ratio of 50 per cent. In other words, there are a whole lot of things going for you. Tell us what things you enjoy in the team, what can be improved in your opinion and what things are already working at about 60 per cent and better.'

In the fairly wide-ranging discussions that followed, the players talked about matters such as training sessions, kit, management, travelling and tours, match strategies and logistical arrangements. Upton then drew up a basic action plan based on those discussions, which Kirsten presented to the players: 'Earlier we proposed a strategy to you, but we no longer think that it's relevant. It was based on our thinking. But this is what you have given us. How do you feel about this?'

Immediately the reaction was more spontaneous. And in that strategy the players committed themselves to a greater vision: firstly, India wanted to become the number-one Test team in the world and, secondly, the players set their sights on the 2011 World Cup crown. That plan formed the basis for the course the players followed over the next three years.

'In the subsequent months and years, many new ideas and additions to the original plan occurred spontaneously, rather than at meetings or in a formal environment,' Upton recounted. 'For the most part, this happened during conversations with individuals. For instance, we would be talking and then we would involve Laxman and Tendulkar in the conversation, and ask their opinions. Then Rahul Dravid would join the discussion and after a while we would say: "This is now really an interesting idea that we should mention to the team."

'Once the whole group was together, Gary would say that Lax had been thinking about very interesting things, whereupon Lax would address the group. The players would then have a discussion and come up with additional ideas until we had something concrete that could be implemented. Even though Gary might already have thought of those things two weeks earlier, we would ask questions and encourage a conversation to test the ideas among individuals, until they had been thrashed out by the whole group. In this way, it was never difficult to get the players to buy into something new and different, because they had in effect already done so. Gary obviously also had his own ideas, but he introduced them into the group. No one was too attached to their own ideas, because it wasn't about your idea but about what was best for the environment. If we gave the idea to the team, the team would let us know whether it would work or not.

'It was just another way of going about things, and our intent – that we were there to help the players – was central to it. And if they had ideas about their game and cricket as a whole, we encouraged them to share those thoughts so that the team could decide together about the best way forward.'

The underlying assumption of such a leadership style is that the players are intelligent people who should be allowed to discuss matters and reflect on them, and determine the best course of action for themselves, instead of being told. The role of leaders in this kind of decision making is that of facilitation, which is one of the characteristics that distinguish the 'new school' of leadership, as Upton calls it, from the old school.

Kirsten's leadership style is by no means based only on facilitating conversations and ideas. Nonetheless, this is an effective method of guiding players towards thinking for themselves and, consequently, becoming comfortable with the idea of taking responsibility for themselves. It would have been absurd not to make use of the thinking of the senior players in the Indian team – not only because of the value that can potentially be created from the human mind (to use Jordaan's terminology), but also because players become frustrated when their human dignity and potential contributions are stifled and overlooked. This had been the case under Chappell. Kirsten and Upton, however, regarded the likes of Tendulkar, Dravid and Dhoni as the brains trust of the team, and never told them what they may or may not do, but instead asked them what they wanted to achieve and how, in their view, the team and players could get there.

In this way, the players were responsible for the team's vision and strategy, while Kirsten helped facilitate its formulation. The players were also personally responsible for preparing themselves for matches within the parameters of the team's strategy. Once again, Kirsten was not there to tell the players what to do, but to lead them by helping them to understand themselves better and prepare for their games.

Here, too, their approach was influenced by Upton's background in executive coaching. He has referred to the various kinds of specialised resources that business executives make use of to assist them with performance, such as mentors, instructors, facilitators and coaches. In cricket, however, there are only coaches. Upton explains the distinction between instruction and facilitation by saying that an instructor is actually a technical expert who understands, for example, the biomechanical detail of batting strokes, bowling actions and fielding techniques, and helps players exclusively with these areas. On the other hand, facilitation involves the skills used to help others in the way that has already been discussed.

A significant distinction between old- and new-school sports coaching lies precisely in different interpretations of the term 'coaching'.

THE INFLUENCE PARADOX

In old-school coaching, the concept is similar to the role of an instructor – telling a person how something works and how it should be done. However, the new style of coaching, based on how executive coaching is done in the business world, is what Kirsten used to complement his role as facilitator. This method works only if sincere relationships, trust and in-depth knowledge exist between a coach and his players.

Upton has explained that this kind of coaching is 'a complex process whereby the coach asks more than tells and encourages players to find their own best answers, while skilfully creating a fertile adult-learning environment. Players are encouraged to learn for themselves – using a mixture of their own ideas, unique techniques, strengths, learning styles and behavioural preferences, in combination with information from other people. The coach understands that the best answers are most likely to emerge from within the performer. He becomes the player's learning partner.'

A practical example of this is that 75 per cent of Kirsten's training sessions in the course of a season were optional. According to the old model, the coach makes the decisions about training sessions: what would be done, who would do what, who would practise in the nets for how long, who would bowl for how long, whether a fielding session for everybody would follow, what exercises would be done afterwards, and at what time the bus would leave. This sounds fairly normal, but only because it has become accepted as such. The reason Kirsten didn't follow this model is that a coach would then assume responsibility for the players' preparation and thereby limit their creativity and learning opportunities.

Upton expanded on this: 'We would say to a player, "Our opponents are sitting in the room next to us, using impressive technology to analyse your game in the finest detail – how they will bowl to you and how they will bat against you. So, what are you going to do to stay one step ahead of them? Now you start thinking of the things your opponent may be thinking about. What is the state of your game at present? You should start understanding yourself. You should orient yourself in terms of the pitch on which you will play. You should understand the batsmen and the bowlers against whom you will play. You should understand your role in the team, and then ask yourself whether you are 100 per cent ready to play against those opponents." We always ask whether a player has studied the whole book for the exam, and if he is not 100 per cent ready, he should know what things he would like to work on.

'In this way, the player himself determined what he still needed to work on, and so his understanding of his own game was much deeper than it would be if a coach had analysed him and told him what he needed to attend to. We trusted him with that responsibility because we treat a grown man like an adult, and then people tend to act like adults.'

When a player arrived at a training session, therefore, Kirsten's question would be: 'What can I help you with? Why are you here?' For instance, if a player had been hitting the ball too square with his cover drive, he would say that the opposition would probably set a square field to him. So he would know that he wanted to work on hitting the ball straighter. He should also know how he wanted to practise this. Did he want a bowling machine, someone bowling at him or throw-downs in the nets? In other words, he had to decide for himself how he wanted to work on what skill. Kirsten's role was then to give his input, ask questions, test how the player thought and felt, and give him feedback. This meant that the coach did not withdraw and let the player carry on alone. There was continuous dialogue and interaction between them, so that the training session was a learning experience for that player after he had already done a lot of preparation. The player decided when he was happy with the skill, and then he could go home. The assumption was that the player left the training session in his own time with an in-depth understanding of his game in the context of the team's plan. He knew that he was well prepared and that the coach was there to help him.

Kirsten's teams always have one training session the day before a Test, but there are seldom more than five or six players present. The players try to be 100 per cent prepared the day before a Test, but if there still happens to be something they want to work on, Kirsten, Upton and the other coaches and specialists are available to help them. The player is, therefore, fully responsible for his own preparation. Players who are not disciplined will work themselves out of that team.

A group of senior players whose contribution and influence are appropriately valued also helps to sustain this model. In the Indian team,

THE INFLUENCE PARADOX

Tendulkar was the kingpin among the seniors in this respect. Upton has written about him:

> He paid more attention to and invested more time into practising his batting than any other player. He never once cut a corner in his preparation for a game, making sure he attended to every detail. After nearly two decades in the international game he had earned the right to stay at the hotel and rest while some of his teammates attended our trademark 'optional' practices. Yet he never did. Not a week went by where any player, youngsters included, hit more balls in practice.[53]

In his tribute to Tendulkar, Upton refers to an incident during a net practice when a young Ishant Sharma kicked the ball in frustration after a poorly executed delivery. Tendulkar picked up the ball and returned it to Sharma, telling him in his calm way, 'It is because of this ball that you have what you have got in life. Without this ball you have nothing. Treat it with the respect it is due.'

This was the attitude that Tendulkar endorsed with deeds, and he often felt the need to hit a thousand balls in succession in the nets – Kirsten would throw him those thousands of balls. They spoke the same cricket language, and it inspired and motivated the people around them. Upton related that Kirsten's socks were often dripping wet, but if the player asked him whether he wanted to rest, his response was always the same, 'No, I'm here for you and we'll be finished when you feel prepared.'

The Indian team's work ethic and level of preparation in training sessions were fairly poor when Kirsten and his staff started working with them, but in time they metamorphosed. Upton attributed the shift to Kirsten's example: 'Gary's preparation was impeccable, and when he expected people to prepare themselves well, he demanded the same from himself. Gary does what Gary says, and there wasn't a single person in that team who worked harder than him or who was fitter than the two of us. In so doing, he established the culture that later came to characterise the Indian team.

'I listened to a conversation between him and Rahul Dravid one day. Gary asked him what had changed now that the players were such good preparers. Rahul's reply was, "It's because you work so hard." The players followed Gary, and because he worked so hard, it was very difficult for anyone to loaf.

'The advantage of this kind of leadership is that you have players who step over the boundary rope knowing that they have prepared as well as possible: they took the responsibility and worked in close cooperation, consultation and negotiation with the coach on what they believed needed rounding off. On the part of the coach, this is by no means a model whereby he can sit on his hands. You dirty your hands precisely so that the players can grow, learn and think for themselves.

'It shows how vital relationships are. With this approach, the players realise that the coach is there for them and that he truly wants the best for them. Working so closely with the players, you can clearly see when something is not right. And then we don't tell them to pull up their socks, but simply remark that we've noticed something different about them. We leave it at that and if the player wants to talk about it, we are there to listen. Whether he has girlfriend problems, trouble with something outside of cricket or doesn't feel well, our players know that they can feel free to talk to us about anything and they won't be judged.'

Creativity, risk and decision making

The advantage of these kinds of relationships is that the players are able to play with a positive attitude, fulfil their potential and mostly make the right decisions without fearing a tongue-lashing. Kirsten didn't want players who played with the attitude of avoiding mistakes. In his view, such a mindset has an inhibiting effect on people's creativity, their ability to make decisions under pressure and their ability to experience self-fulfilment. With Kirsten at the helm, a player could bat with the knowledge that the coach and the team supported him in making his own decisions and that that wouldn't change even if he made mistakes.

Nevertheless, like Jordaan at FNB, who asked his people to avoid making fools of themselves or embarking on solo flights, Kirsten had four parameters within which the players could exercise that freedom.

'We want players to be creative and take chances and risks,' Upton said. 'But under the guidance of a few fundamental principles. First, it has to be one of your strengths. If you're not good at playing the reverse sweep, then don't do it in the game, work on it at practice. Second, we need to have seen that you were working on that particular thing in the lead-up to the game. If you haven't been working on, for example, hitting the ball over the top, it is not that we don't want to see you do it, but if you are going to play a certain way, it needs to be a strength. Third, it should be part of your game plan and, fourth, it needs to fit into the team's game plan. If you've been practising the whole week to hit the ball for a six, and the situation in the game doesn't warrant you to hit the ball for a six, well, don't be hitting the ball for a six. Gary never told players that they were not allowed to do something. He wanted them to think for themselves and make decisions. What he would say was, "Guys, you work out your game plan. You work out how you are going to play in a certain situation."'

In essence, this is about empowerment, although Upton preferred to talk about influence rather than power. It may be a semantic detail, but to Upton the term 'empowerment' implies that there is still someone in a hierarchy who can decide how much power he or she gives to or withholds from others. Also implicit is the possibility of disempowering someone and this was not the kind of environment they wanted to create.

Upton stated, 'We created an environment where people could learn and grow, and in an environment like that the players acquire influence. They take the responsibility upon themselves, and by asserting their influence in a team context, they empower themselves – in contrast to an environment where power is granted to them. The environment gives it to them and it's about the team and the culture, and not about what Gary and I, or Gary and the senior players, decided the culture would be.

'The environment drives everything and we don't manage the people, because once you start managing people, they become a project: this is how you must behave, this what you must do, this is what you must eat, this is how you must train, this is the pattern within which you must play and this is the reward for good deeds, but these are the consequences if you do something wrong.

'A human being is much more than a project. You manage processes, machinery, factories, but you don't manage people. People are not there to be managed, but to be allowed to be the best they can be. It may sound touchy-feely, but it's a philosophy that has worked for us.'

For that environment to work and for players to fulfil their potential in a culture that encourages relationships, confidence, risk-taking, learning and growth, it is key that your coach underscores his words and his wishes for you with deeds.

'You don't change an environment by listing a set of values and writing them down on a white board,' said Upton. 'Those things will just remain values on a white board. It's about what you say, what you do, how you talk to players and how you react to both success and failure. It's about how you react to ill-disciplined people, people who think differently and people whose opinions differ from yours. The behaviour of a leader is what creates the environment and then the players start learning, growing and developing.'

In that respect, Kirsten's reaction during and after games was crucial. Unlike the seating arrangements in rugby, a cricket coach sits among the players during a match. They watch him like hawks, interpret any reaction he displays and form impressions about his thinking. A coach's behaviour can make or break a team. If India or South Africa, say, needed five runs to win a one-day game and there were still 15 overs left, there would be no reason to take a risk. But if a player then does take a risk, plays the wrong shot and goes out, the coach has to watch his reaction. If Kirsten threw his hands into the air in such a situation and expressed his dissatisfaction, team members would interpret his reaction as a negative judgement on the player's decision and behaviour. The team members wouldn't want Kirsten to react like that if they made an error, and consequently they would not take risks for fear of disappointing the coach. While Kirsten has a calm personality by nature, it has always been very hard to gauge his thoughts, in both good and bad times, when he sits with the players – for this very reason. The same applies when the team is under pressure and a defeat seems to be in the offing. Kirsten always appears calm, even when he is not.

In Upton's view, 'there's no value in chastising a player. We don't ever want a situation where a player feels that he has disappointed his coach. We weren't there for people to disappoint us; we were there for them. And the moment you chastise someone and employ that hierarchical punishment model, you create a fear of failure. The interaction between a player and a coach is the single biggest thing that causes a fear of failure.

'The players will make errors every now and again, but that's okay because humans make mistakes and we allow people to be human.

THE INFLUENCE PARADOX

'Acceptance of failure enables people to learn and be successful. Leaders should allow mistakes. I've often watched how coaches act when their players commit errors, and then I wonder whether those coaches also encourage players to take chances and fulfil themselves. Actions speak louder than words and where you have a coach who reacts negatively to mistakes, I can promise you that his team has a fear of failure and will never play to its full potential,' Upton said.

How a coach reacts after a game is as important as his behaviour during a game. For this reason, Kirsten never talks to the team directly after a victory or a defeat. If the team is defeated by a better team, he doesn't talk after the match; if the team throws away a game it should have won, he doesn't talk after the match. Regardless of which of these results are applicable after a match, Kirsten's attitude is always the same, because people cannot learn well in a situation that is governed by emotion.

This is not to say that he doesn't have the urge to say something after a match. However, he would then turn to Upton to test his thoughts and unload his feelings. A coach who didn't have his players' best interests at heart would chastise them immediately after a game, but in so doing would only satisfy his own emotional needs and wouldn't foster an environment that is conducive to learning and growth. Instead, it is Kirsten's desire that the players should derive value from what he says and, therefore, his message has to be effective and incisive.

He and Upton discuss what Kirsten believes the players should hear. The first criterion is whether that message will be valuable to the players. If so, the message needs to be conveyed at the best possible time in the best possible way and in the most appropriate language. These variables may differ from individual to individual and also from team to team.

Upton explained, 'It requires a high level of self-awareness on the part of a coach to take himself out of the picture and think from the perspective of a player. In reality, however, it's very easy if you genuinely have the players' interests at heart. In that case, you don't need to think too much about what you will say or how you will say it. It's about the place from where you talk to the players. This is the art of coaching that Gary understands very, very well.'

This can be illustrated by means of two examples, the first from the South African camp and the second from India. Indian players simply didn't listen to a coach who was harsh with them, whereas the South African sports culture means that players are more receptive to a coach who berates them.

On 20 November 2011, Neil Manthorp described Kirsten's reaction during Australia's visit to South Africa as follows on SuperSport.com:

> If there's one thing that Kirsten knows about South Africans, it's that a good old-fashioned bollocking can work wonders. And that's what he dished out on Thursday evening after the team had thrown away a golden opportunity to bat Australia out of the series by throwing their wickets away and sliding to a miserable 266 all out. He still did not raise his voice, but the words were sharp, incisive – and honest.
>
> At dinner on Thursday evening with older brother Peter, Gary used the word 'arrogant' to describe the approach of the middle order. The tourists were a bowler down, spinner Nathan Lyon was under pressure and the pitch was playing as well as any has ever done on the first day. It required determined application to wear the bowlers down, not reckless spanking of boundaries.
>
> Kirsten was back to his calm, imperturbable best by Friday morning and even a woeful bowling display in the morning session did not cause him to lose his cool. He allowed Allan Donald to talk about the technical stuff and then reminded the players that they had a chance to become the first post-isolation team to beat Australia on home soil. And that the chance was slipping away very fast. The results were there for all to see. [Dale] Steyn led the fightback with a phenomenal spell of swing bowling, even though he was short of top pace, and the batting of Hashim Amla and AB de Villiers contained all the resilience and determination that was lacking first time around.[54]

Manthorp concluded by referring to Kirsten and Upton's partnership: 'Paddy Upton's learning in executive coaching has combined with Kirsten's playing experience to produce a management team that can bring out the best in a player with nothing much more than a sideways glance.'

This also explains why Kirsten and company didn't have a single disciplinary incident with the South African team. There were no rules, no curfews that stipulated when players had to be back at their hotel, no rigid dos and don'ts in terms of what they could eat and no disciplinary system to manage the players' behaviour. The players knew what was expected of them and if anyone showed signs of repeatedly behaving in a questionable manner, his teammates usually got him back on the right track.

'When you treat people like children and lay down rules for them, they're going to act like children,' said Upton. 'But we treated the players like adults in an environment that was relaxed, where players had influence and the freedom to fulfil themselves. There was still very strong and clear leadership, but it was leadership through service and example rather than leadership based on instructions and control. And that's why we probably actually had more influence and control over the team than coaches who primarily strove for those things.'

It took a while to establish that culture at the Indian team, but when the players learnt to trust Kirsten and Upton, and believe in what they were doing, it was easier to handle difficult situations. Kirsten's behaviour and his knack of conveying the right message at the right time were crucial. Upton recounted an incident with the Indian team: 'I'm not going to mention the player's name, but during our time in India there was a senior player who behaved unreasonably at times and posed a real threat to the team environment. He behaved negatively towards other players, which disrupted those players and the culture.

'One day, we were playing soccer during a training session. That (unnamed) senior player erupted and gave a junior player a vicious tongue-lashing. We used an Australian consultant at the time, and he walked over to Gary and told him that he had to take that senior player aside and tell him that his behaviour was unacceptable. But Gary just told him to let it go. Five minutes later, the guy came to talk to Gary again and he just couldn't understand why he was not addressing the matter. He asked me later whether Gary was scared of conflict. He again told Gary that he understood the culture we were trying to establish, but that that player's conduct undermined it completely. But again Gary told him that they should leave it alone.

'In the same way that any adult knows when he has made a mistake, that senior player realised later in the training session that he had been wrong. If Gary had gone to that player while he was spitting fire, it would have been like water off a duck's back. In addition, the player would have thought the situation was resolved and a thing of the past, and that there was no need for him to give it any further thought.

'Later that afternoon, the senior player was helping one of the other young players in the nets. Gary walked up to him and told him that he was an enormously influential guy in the team, and that it meant a tremendous amount to a young player when he helped in the training sessions by, for example, throwing balls at him in the nets. Gary just wanted to let him know that he had taken note of what he was doing for that player, and that he really appreciated it.

'We knew the players with whom we worked, and we're definitely not saying that you should only react to the positive things and ignore the negative things – not at all. But we knew who we were dealing with. And later, in the bus, that senior player sat down next to Gary and admitted that he had erred earlier that afternoon and that his actions were not in keeping with the culture the team had established for itself. He apologised to Gary, the captain and the young player – with tears in his eyes. Gary thanked him and the whole team was stronger afterwards. Growth had taken place.'

The essence of what Upton and Kirsten wanted to do for the players was to lead them to a place called 'personal mastery' – a place where the big ego disappears. Upton described this concept as follows in a Cricinfo article:

> Personal mastery is many things. It is a journey towards living successfully as an all-round human being, a tapping into your full potential. It is a commitment to learning about yourself, your mind and emotions in all situations. It is a strengthening of character and deepening of personal values. It is an increased awareness of self, others and the world around; living from the inside out, not the outside in. Personal mastery is a shift in attitude that drives a shift in behaviour.[55]

The key to personal mastery is gaining awareness of both yourself and others, because that influences personal interaction and the quality of the relationships people have with one another. The senior Indian player described above lacked a healthy awareness of how he conducted himself, how he behaved towards others and how it made them feel – until an environment was created where, with subtle guidance from Kirsten, he got himself to the position where he realised he was wrong. The absence of that awareness often indicates the presence of an inflated ego. In a country like India, where players are treated like gods, it's very easy to lose touch with reality and be seduced into believing that thanks to your cricketing talent, you are also morally superior. This image of being a special person is created and upheld by fans and the media.

'But a big ego is often just a mask for uncertainties that a player is trying to conceal,' said Upton. 'He is uncomfortable with those vulnerabilities, with those human fallibilities inside him, and that causes him to conduct himself in a certain way to cover up those things. He is boastful, he tries to impress people, he walks over others – things like that.

'"Personal mastery" is not a term we use, but it is what we strive for in our culture. A part of it is to acknowledge your own vulnerabilities and to work on overcoming them. You acknowledge to yourself that there are parts of your personality you don't like when they emerge under pressure. You acknowledge that you make mistakes and that there are things you don't know. An inner peace develops when you start acknowledging those faults – those human fallibilities – inside you. Once you have accepted them, you can start working on them. And whether it is the way you behave towards your teammates or a fear of failure, you know what to work on and you accept that it's normal not to be perfect – welcome to the human race!

'If you can offer a superstar that relief by saying to him that he can enjoy the attention of fans and the media without having to try to live up to those larger-than-life expectations, you create in him a sense of being comfortable with who he really is. It is only when the player starts identifying with his authentic self that growth can occur – whether as a player or as someone's husband, father or friend. These are the kinds of conversations we have with players and the kind of environment we encourage. And we only say to players what they already know, because we ask more questions and listen more than we tell them things. No one knows you better than you do, and sometimes you just need a bit of help in allowing that understanding to emerge from within you.'

Owing to a similar experience in his own playing career, Kirsten had a profound understanding of this aspect of cricketers. His understanding of their inner nature, the relationships he had forged with players and the leadership approach he followed made it much easier to manage thorny situations, such as omitting a player from the team. Eighteen months after he had become India's head coach, Kirsten was confronted with the prospect of dropping Rahul Dravid. In this situation, he put himself in the player's shoes by tapping into his own experience as a player when he had scored those 275 runs in 1999.

By November 2009 it had been almost a year since Dravid had scored a century and there was enormous media pressure on Kirsten to omit him from the squad for the home series against Sri Lanka. It had been a long time since he had made a significant contribution, and the selectors wanted to see what the young Virat Kohli could achieve in the Test team. However, omitting a player of Dravid's stature would have been considered sacrilege in India and so the selectors ducked the decision by including Dravid in the bigger group of 15 players.

This left Kirsten and his captain, Mahendra Singh Dhoni, with the option of either picking him for the 11-man squad or leaving him out. While Dravid's experience counted in his favour, his recent run drought was a problem. Dhoni did not want to make the decision either, and Kirsten found himself facing this challenge on his own. He turned to Upton for advice.

'It was an awkward conversation,' Upton recalled. 'I told Gary that if he left Dravid out, he would have people stoning his house in Cape Town. Omitting him would have unpleasant consequences, but within a minute of our conversation, it was clear what should happen.'

Kirsten went to Dravid's room about 20 minutes before the team meeting. To any player, a knock on the door so close to a meeting means only one thing – he is being dropped. Dravid, a true gentleman, understood the difficult situation that Kirsten was in and stated that he would support his coach, regardless of what he decided. He even offered to carry the water onto the pitch to the best of his ability, if that were to be his function.

But Kirsten took him by surprise and said to Dravid that he was the one who had to make the decisions.

'I'm faced with a dilemma,' Kirsten said. 'And I've now come to ask you whether you want to play or not. You are able to make that decision, because you are the only person who would truly know whether you are ready to play.'

By shifting the responsibility to the player, Kirsten hit Dravid for a six – he had expected to be dropped. There was no doubt in Dravid's mind that he wanted to play, and he silenced critics by scoring 177 runs in the first innings of the first Test, and 144 in the second Test. India won the three-Test series 2-0, and that Lazarus-like resurgence in Dravid's game laid the foundation for it – as had been the case with Kirsten in 1999 when he denied a tough England side a virtually assured victory in Durban.

By means of their leadership style, Kirsten and Upton put the responsibility for performing well in the players' hands to such an extent that they couldn't blame coaches when they experienced difficulties, and neither did they want to do so. When Greg Chappell had dropped Yuvraj Singh from the team, for example, the player was angry because he was struggling in an environment where the coach told him what to do. If the coach's recommendation doesn't work, it's very easy to shift the blame to him. But not in Kirsten's model, because it is the player who determines how well prepared he is and whether he wants to make use of the management team's help.

Although no one was aware of Singh's lung cancer at that stage, he was dropped from the Test team six months before the 2011 World Cup tournament. This was a blow to him, even though he retained his place in the one-day team, but he had also let himself down as far as his preparation was concerned. Upton reckoned that he may have been somewhat caught up in his celebrity status as an Indian cricketing star.

At that time, Upton and Singh had several individual sessions together and spoke in depth about the reasons for his poor form. Singh would end up earning the Player of the Tournament award at the 2011 World Cup, and that was testament to the hard work he had put in during the preceding months. Kirsten and Upton merely helped him gain perspective – accepting responsibility for himself and the team was something he did on his own.

Dhoni, too, displayed exceptional leadership skills in the World Cup final. Sri Lanka had batted first and made 274 runs. When India's third wicket fell on 114 runs, Dhoni, who had been out of form with the bat throughout the tournament, took the responsibility upon himself as captain and went in to bat earlier than he was supposed to. He and Singh were still at the crease when the match ended, and when Dhoni hit the winning runs in the 49th over, he left the field on an unbeaten 91 and was named Player of the Match.

With that triumph, the Indian team achieved the goals they had identified that morning in March 2008. They were the ODI world champions and the number-one-ranked side in the world in Test cricket. The World Cup final was Kirsten's last match with the team. In his article 'Gary on, Coach', Amit Gupta of the *Mumbai Mirror* wrote on 3 April 2011: 'In Indian cricket, it is seldom that someone is sought after even when he is quitting. Kirsten is that rare commodity.'

The leadership style that had benefited India also proved very effective when Kirsten and Upton started working with the Proteas. In August 2012 South Africa became the number-one-ranked team in all three formats of the game: T20 cricket, one-day cricket and Test cricket. Upton has high praise for the role that Graeme Smith's leadership played in these achievements. Smith has a strong personality and, according to Upton, neither he nor Kirsten 'suffers fools'. Like Kirsten, Smith is genuinely interested in the well-being of the people around him and, therefore, is able to lead effectively with his strong personality and ability to get the best out of players.

As he proved with the Indian team, it is Kirsten's example that enables the leaders around him to come into their own. He inspires people to become better human beings and better players. He is one of only a handful of people who have made the transition from player to coach with such great effect, and his capacity to empathise with other people has played a massive role.

He is a servant leader. He is a strong leader. He influences people.

Upton encapsulated his comrade's leadership style: 'When you influence people, you also give them influence. That influence spreads, and it gives you even more influence. As someone who influences others, you can, therefore, increase your influence by giving it away. And the day you decide to move on to something new, that influence stays behind. It doesn't leave with you.

'This is what Gary does – his focus is on people, and he helps them become happier, better and more rounded human beings by giving them influence. The impact of that kind of leadership is lasting and far-reaching.'

NOTES

1. Michael Mauboussin, *The Success Equation: Untangling Skill and Luck in Business, Sports, and Investing*, Harvard Business Review Press, 2012: 34.
2. Ibid.: 70.
3. Ibid.: 44.
4. Ibid.: 45.
5. '*Sege is al wat nodig is*', *Beeld*, 5 May 2007.
6. '*Bulls, Sharks in semi-riller?*' *Beeld*, 5 May 2007.
7. See http://www.sportscoachingbrain.com (accessed 14 March 2014).
8. Ibid.
9. Ibid.
10. Victor Matfield with De Jongh Borchardt, *Victor: My Journey*, Cape Town: Zebra Press, 2011: 169.
11. Pieter Jordaan, *Rapport*, 16 June 2013.
12. Anita Elberse and Thomas Dye, 'Sir Alex Ferguson: Managing Manchester United.' Harvard Business School Case 513-051, September 2012: 5.
13. Ibid.: 1.
14. Ibid.: 13.
15. Anita Elberse with Sir Alex Ferguson, 'Ferguson's Formula'. *Harvard Business Review*, October 2013: 4.
16. Ibid.
17. Ibid.
18. Ibid.: 4–5.
19. Ibid.: 5–6.
20. Ibid.: 8.
21. Ibid.: 7.
22. Ibid.: 9.
23. See http://gcc.glendale.edu/fire/Documents/Tidbits/Winners.pdf (accessed 10 March 2014).
24. Elberse with Sir Alex Ferguson, 'Ferguson's Formula': 9.
25. Ibid.: 10.
26. Ibid.: 11.
27. See http://www.espnscrum.com/heineken-cup-2010-11/rugby/story/130994.html (accessed 10 March 2014).

NOTES

28 *Mirror*, 16 December 2010.
29 See http://m.espn.go.com/golf/story?storyId=6515974&src=deskt op&wjb (accessed 19 October 2013).
30 See http://www.youtube.com/watch?v=cCVpoPON3mI (accessed 19 October 2013).
31 See www.ernieels.com (accessed 19 October 2013).
32 See http://www.youtube.com/watch?v=cCVpoPON3mI (accessed 19 October 2013).
33 Peter Bills, 'When in South Africa we were isolated', *The Independent*, 3 January 2009.
34 Sherylle Luzanne Calder, *Enhanced skill performance of field hockey players following a programme of visual awareness training*, thesis presented for the degree of doctor of philosophy, the Medical Research Council and the University of Cape Town, December 1999.
35 Ibid.
36 Charl du Plessis, 'Eye push-ups', *SA Sports & Health Monthly*, September 2013.
37 Ibid.
38 Ibid.
39 Adam Schupak, *The New York Times*, 17 July 2012.
40 Peter Masters, 'Ernie's secret weapon', *Golf World*, August 2012.
41 Ibid.
42 Steve DiMeglio, 'Putting at Augusta National daunting task', *USA Today*, 6 April 2013.
43 Bob Harig, 'For Ernie Els, the eyes have it', http://espn.go.com/golf/pgachampionship12/story/_/id/8235971/for-ernie-els-eyes-it (accessed 11 October 2013).
44 Daniel Kahneman, *Thinking, Fast and Slow*. New York: Farrar, Straus and Giroux, 2011: 40.
45 Marco Botha, '*Bok-blitse doen dit weer!*', *Beeld*, *Die Burger* and *Volksblad*, 30 May 2011.
46 Naas Botha and Kobus Neethling, *Creative Rugby*, Carpe Diem, 1999.
47 Lee Romney, 'Prosthetics get the personal touch', *Los Angeles Times*, 4 April 2012.
48 See http://www.espncricinfo.com/india/content/story/340783.html (accessed 7 February 2013).

NOTES

49 P.A.H. Upton, *Exploring the hypothesis that an instruction-based/external/performance focus prevails in the coaching of elite South African cricketers, with an analysis of why this might limit players personally and professionally, should it exist*, master's dissertation, Middlesex University, 2004.
50 See http://www.espncricinfo.com/magazine/content/story/583853.html (accessed 25 January 2013).
51 See http://www.espncricinfo.com/magazine/content/story/323842.html (accessed 17 January 2013).
52 See http://ibnlive.in.com/news/cricketnext/sachin-tendulkar-stood-by-me-during-the-greg-chappell-controversy-sourav-ganguly/432465-78.html (accessed 7 November 2013).
53 See http://paddyupton.com/newsletter/arise-sachin-tendulkar-the-cricketer-and-the-man/ (accessed 16 April 2013).
54 See https://www.supersport.com/cricket/blogs/neil-manthorp/Kirstens_new_approach (accessed 17 January 2013).
55 See http://www.espncricinfo.com/magazine/content/story/583853.html (accessed 25 January 2013).

ACKNOWLEDGEMENTS

In my second year at university, I modified a photo of four solemn old men around a boardroom table by pasting my own face and those of Elvis Presley, Nelson Mandela and Muhammad Ali onto their bodies. The image was complemented by these words: 'Sustainable success is not achievable by running a one-man show, but by surrounding oneself with great people.'

I had that picture right next to my computer while I was writing this book. And when it comes to thanking people for their involvement in or influence on *Coach*, I'm struck once again by the truth of those words – it was an enormous team effort.

I would like to express my gratitude, firstly, to Theo Vorster, Paul Treu and my publisher, Ingeborg Pelser of Jonathan Ball, who helped me flesh out the rudimentary idea until we arrived at the end product. Also to my mother, Mandi, who at times read through the chapters, making corrections and suggestions, late at night or in the early hours of the morning when my own light was burning low. And a thank you to my father, Willem, for allowing me to bounce my ideas off him.

Thank you to Riëtte Botma, who not only edited the original Afrikaans version and managed the project, but also bought into the content. I didn't experience a single bad day during the pondering, writing and editing process.

The same goes for Linde Dietrich, who had the massive task of translating *Coach* from the original Afrikaans version. Besides that, she also guided me in terms of content suggestions, adding touches that I believe will add to your reading experience.

Mark Ronan edited this book, and one sentence of thanks doesn't do any justice to the tremendous effort and thought that went into, and impact he had on, *Coach*. Thanks, Mark.

Thank you to Russ for the beautiful cover, and especially to Thys Lombard, Christiaan Kotze and Christi Botha for taking and/or tracking down photographs for the cover and the photo pages. Enormous effort was put into this, and you have added value.

The following people assisted me regularly with insights and modifications regarding the content or interviews: Barend van Graan, Kobus Neethling, Ian Schwartz, Frans Ludeke, Derick Hougaard, Marizel Swanepoel, Stan du Plessis, Tim du Plessis, De Wet Strauss and Stephen

ACKNOWLEDGEMENTS

Nell. I also owe a big debt of gratitude to Adriaan Basson and Gert van der Westhuizen, both from *Beeld*, who granted me the time to finalise the manuscript when the deadline loomed.

A lack of space, alas, makes it impossible to single out everyone's contributions. But the following people either had an influence on decisions that led to the book or made direct contributions: Wayne Goldsmith of Sports Coaching Brain, Ryan de Kock, Neil de Kock, Saartjie Olivier, Jannie du Plessis, Jacolize de Villiers, Ton Vosloo, Jaco Grobbelaar, Paul Delport, Chris Dry, Kyle Brown, Louis van Gass, Herbert Pretorius, Altus Momberg, Rudolph Lake, Charl McLeod, Nick Mallett and Vlok Cilliers.

A big thank you is also due to the people who allowed me to tell their stories or to supplement other people's stories with their own: Heyneke Meyer, Frans Ludeke, Ian Schwartz, Brendan Venter, Paul Treu, Kobus Neethling, Sherylle Calder, Michael Jordaan, Paddy Upton and Gary Kirsten. You inspire me.

And, finally, thank you to my wife, Maritza, who for more than a year of our first two years of married life saw very little of me because of the writing process. Honey, I'm home!